# GOALIES
## GUARDIANS OF THE NET

Project Coordinator: Rachel Fontaine
Production Coordinator: Martine Lavoie
Photos: Denis Brodeur, with the cooperation of Claude Brodeur and
  Denis Brodeur Jr.
Illustrations: Carleton McDiarmid
Design and Computer Graphics: Dominic Pagé
Image Processing: Mélanie Sabourin
Translation: Brenda O'Brien
Cover: Patrick Roy with the Avalanche (Photo: Bruce Bennett)

**Prepublication catalogue data (Canada)**

Brodeur, Denis
  Goalies
  ISBN 1-55013-745-X

  1. Hockey goalkeepers - Pictorial works.    2. Hockey goalkeepers -
Biography.    3. Hockey - Goalkeeping.    I. Daignault, Daniel, 1958- .
II. Title.

GV848.5.A1D45 1996        796.962'092'2        C96-930467

This book was produced using an Éditions de l'Homme laser imaging
system which includes:

- a Scitex Smart™ 720 digitalizer and a Scitex Rightouch™ colour
  retouching station;

- Kodak products;

- Apple Inc. computers;

- a Compumation Inc. photo management and printing system and
  Color Central© software;

- an RIP 50 PL2 image processor combined with the latest Lino
  Dot© and Lino Pipeline© and Linotype-Hell© technology.

EXCLUSIVE DISTRIBUTORS:

- For Canada and the United States:
  **LES MESSAGERIES ADP°**
  955, rue Amherst, Montréal H2L 3K4
  Tel.: (514) 523-1182
  Fax: (514) 939-0406
  ° Subsidiary of Sogides ltée

- For Belgium and Luxembourg:
  **PRESSES DE BELGIQUE S.A.**
  Boulevard de l'Europe 117
  B-1301 Wavre
  Tel.: (10) 41-59-66
  (10) 41-78-50
  Fax: (10) 41-20-24

- For Switzerland:
  **TRANSAT S.A.**
  Route des Jeunes, 4 Ter
  P.O. Box 125
  1211 Geneva 26
  Tel.: (41-22) 342-77-40
  Fax: (41-22) 343-46-46

- For France and other countries:
  **INTER FORUM**
  Immeuble Paryseine, 3 Allée de la Seine, 94854 Ivry Cedex
  Tel.: (1) 49-59-11-89/91
  Fax: (1) 49-59-11-96
  Orders: Tel.: (16) 38-32-71-00
  Fax: (16) 38-32-71-28

First published in Quebec in 1995 by Les Éditions de l'Homme,
a division of the Sogides group.

Key Porter Books
70 The Esplanade
Toronto, Ontario
Canada M5E 1R2

Printed and bound in Canada

96 97 98 99 5 4 3 2 1

# GOALIES

## GUARDIANS
## OF THE NET

### Denis Brodeur
#### Text by Daniel Daignault

**MORE THAN 150 GOALIES FEATURED**
**MORE THAN 500 PHOTOGRAPHS**

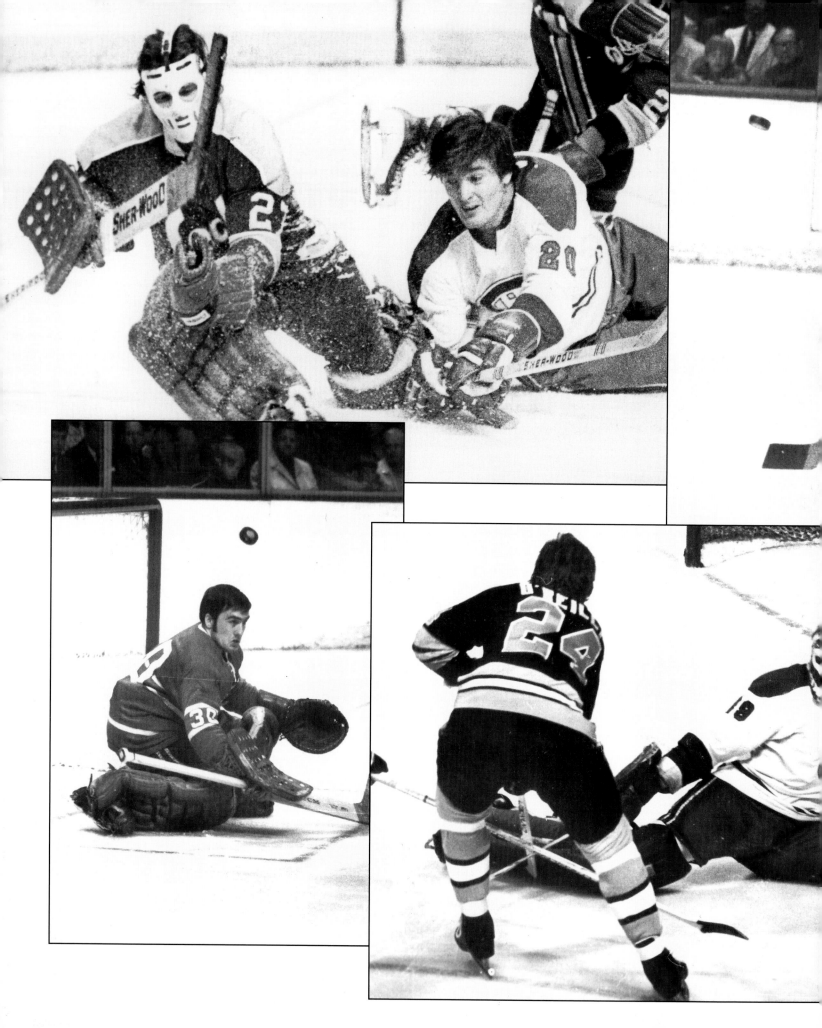

## Warning

The personal record for each goaltender includes only National Hockey League statistics even if it occasionally indicates that the goaltender played with World Hockey Association teams. In the authors' opinions, fans are interested mainly in NHL statistics. The use of NHL data makes it easier to compare the performance of professional goaltenders from various times in hockey history. The WHA was in existence for just seven years—from 1972 to 1979. Personal records for players who are still active include statistics for the 1995-1996 season.

# Spotlight on Goaltenders

This book has long been a dream of mine. Finally, after more than 30 years as a sports photographer, it has become a reality.

Unlike most of my fellow photographers, who prefer to sweep back and forth across the rink during a hockey game, my lens has always been aimed at the goaltender's crease. In fact, 99 percent of my photos show goaltenders in their nets. Anyone who knows that I was an amateur goalie will understand my interest.

This book is certainly the first to contain so many shots of goaltenders and profiles of some 150 professional goalies. If you have as much pleasure looking through it and reading it as Daniel and I have had preparing it, our mission will have been accomplished.

DENIS BRODEUR

Goalies, *Guardians of the Net* is the third in a series devoted to hockey photos taken by Denis Brodeur. The first, *30 Years of Hockey Photos,* was so enthusiastically received by the public in 1993 that in 1994, Denis and I selected a new series of photos for publication in *Hockey's Greats.* With a second bestseller on our hands, a third book was only natural.

This time, Denis—a former goalie himself—couldn't resist the temptation to use his best shots of goaltenders. Meanwhile, I delved into the history of professional hockey to find the most spectacular exploits of these hockey "backbenchers," who are often, and unfairly, eclipsed by the more flamboyant offense players.

Denis's shots remind us of the amazing performance of hockey's "human ramparts," the men who, time and time again, spelled the difference between victory and defeat, between the Stanley Cup and elimination.

DANIEL DAIGNAULT

# Goalies From Another Era

In 1917, the first major world conflict had been raging for three years already and the United States was heading into war side by side with the Allies. On February 23rd, revolution broke out in Russia: the Bolsheviks seized power. In Hollywood, the top silent movie stars were Mary Pickford, Douglas Fairbanks and Charlie Chaplin. Thomas Woodrow Wilson was President of the United States, Progressive Conservative Robert Borden was in charge of Canada's destiny, and Sir Lomer Gouin was Premier of Quebec for the twelfth consecutive year.

In baseball, the Chicago White Sox were crowned champions after beating the New York Giants in the World Series. On November 22nd, a new professional sports league—the National Hockey League (NHL)—was officially founded. Less than one month later, on December 19th, the first games were held.

Four teams took part in the first season: the Montreal Canadiens, the Wanderers, the Ottawa Senators and the Toronto Arenas. Goaltenders were delighted when the League adopted a regulation that allowed them to throw themselves down onto the ice. Previously, they had had to remain standing at all times; since 1914, the National Hockey Association—the organization that governed professional hockey before the creation of the NHL—had even levied a $2 fine on fallen goalies!

**G**eorges Vézina, a native of Chicoutimi, Quebec, was one of hockey's first big stars. In 1917-1918, he dominated other goalies with an average of 3.82. A member of the Montreal Canadiens since 1910, his greatest moments came in his last complete season, 1924-1925, when he maintained an average of 1.87 and managed five shutouts in 30 games.

Vézina won the Stanley Cup twice and recorded a career aver-

Georges Vézina

age of 3.28 in regular play and 2.78 in the playoffs. In 1925-1926, he played only one game; he died of tuberculosis on March 24, 1926 at the age of 39.

The Canadiens introduced a trophy in his honour and asked the League to award it every year. In 1927, the first Vézina Trophy was given to George Hainsworth. In 1945, Chuck Gardiner of the Chicago Black Hawks and Georges Vézina were the first goaltenders to be inducted into the Hall of Fame.

**Clint Benedict**, another hockey legend, played with Ottawa and the Montreal Maroons over the course of a 13-year career which began in the 1917-1918 season. His name was engraved on the Stanley Cup four times (three times with Ottawa and once with Montreal) and he still holds a few National League records.

Most notably, he managed three consecutive shutouts during the 1926 playoffs, a record tied in 1945 by Frank McCool of Toronto. He also holds the record for the most playoff shutouts during a career (15) and the record for the most shutouts (4) during the playoffs in a single season.

Benedict was the first goaltender to wear a mask, which was made of leather. However, he wore it only once,

Clint Benedict

in 1930 during a game against Chicago.

**John Roach** was another star of the 20s and 30s. His career lasted 14 seasons, shared between Toronto, the New York Rangers and the Detroit Red Wings. He began playing in 1921-1922 and maintained a career average of 2.46. In 34 playoff games, he recorded a remarkable average of 1.88. He won the Stanley

John Roach

Cup only once, in his first year with Toronto.

**Alex Connell**, whose 12-year playing career began in 1924, holds a fabulous record: six consecutive shutouts, an exploit he achieved with Ottawa in 1927-1928. In addition to Ottawa he played with Detroit, the New York Americans and the Montreal Maroons.

Twice (1925-1926 and 1927-1928), he recorded 15 shutouts in one season. He recorded 81 alto-

Alex Connell

gether and maintained a 1.91 career average. He won the Stanley Cup twice, in 1927 with Ottawa and in 1935 with the Maroons.

Connell was the first goaltender in history to be beaten by a penalty shot. It was during the 1934-1935 season and the scorer was Ralph "Scotty" Bowman, a defenseman with the Detroit Red Wings.

**Roy Worters** played 12 seasons in the National League. In 1929, he was the first goaltender to win the Hart Trophy, which is awarded to the player who is most valuable to his team. Nicknamed "Shrimp" because of his small size—he was 5'2" and weighed 135 lbs—Worters was playing for the New York Americans at the time.

In 38 games, he managed 13 shutouts and maintained a 1.21 average. Worters came to the NHL in the 1925-1926 season and played successively for Pittsburgh, Montreal and New York. During his career, he maintained an average of 2.27. He won the Vézina Trophy in 1931.

**Lorne Chabot** skated on NHL ice for the first time in 1926-1927, with the New York Rangers. He would also play with Toronto, Montreal, Chicago, the Maroons and the New York Americans. In 11 years he won the Stanley Cup twice (in 1928 with New York and in 1932 with Toronto). He managed 73 shutouts and maintained an average of 2.04 in 411 games. He won the Vézina Trophy in 1935 with Chicago

Roy Worters

thanks to an average of 1.83 in 48 games.

**George Hainsworth** was one of many goaltenders to shine in the Canadiens uniform. He began his career in 1926-1927 and in his first three seasons, during which he played all of his team's 44 games, he recorded fabulous averages of 1.52, 1.09 and 0.98. Over 11 years, he maintained an average of 1.91, and 1.93 in his 52 playoff games.

In 1927 he became the first player to win the Vézina Trophy, an honour bestowed on him the following two seasons as well. He won the Stanley Cup twice with Montreal, in 1930 and 1931. At the end of his career he also played three seasons with Toronto.

Hainsworth holds the record for the most shutouts in one season: 22

Lorne Chabot

in 1928-1929. He ranks second in NHL history, behind Terry Sawchuk, for the most career shutouts, with 94 compared to Sawchuk's 103.

**Cecil Tiny Thompson** was a star goalie of the 1930s. He won the Vézina Trophy in 1930, 1933 and 1936 while playing with the Boston Bruins. He began his career in 1928-1929 and was traded to the Detroit Red Wings during the 1938-1939 season. During his first year of play he recorded an average of 1.18 in 44 games, including 12 shutouts, and the Bruins won the Stanley Cup for the first time in the team's history. At the

Cecil Tiny Thompson

end of his career, late in the 1939-1940 season, Thompson had an average of 2.08 in 553 regular-season games and 1.88 in 44 playoff games.

**Wilf Cude** began playing professionally in 1930-1931 and spent 10 seasons in the National League. He played with four teams—Philadelphia, Boston, Chicago and Detroit—before joining the ranks of the Canadiens during the 1933-1934 season. He experienced his best season in 1933-1934 when, with Detroit and Montreal, he maintained an average of 1.47 in 30 games, the best in the League at the time. He ended his career with a record of 2.73 in 282 games.

**Chuck Gardiner** played seven seasons in the NHL, all of them in a Chicago Black Hawks uniform. He began playing in 1927-1928 and maintained an average under 2.00 four times (1.93 in 1928-1929, 1.77 in

1930-1931, 1.92 in 1931-1932 and 1.73 in 1933-1934). Winner of the Vézina Trophy in 1932 and 1934, he ended his career with an overall average of 2.02 in 316 games.

In 1934, after suffering from a serious chronic infection for several years, Gardiner was ill and exhausted and a source of worry for his teammates. But he insisted on taking part in the playoffs and led the Black Hawks to their first Stanley Cup victory over the Detroit Red Wings. Two months later, at the age of 29, he died as the result of a brain hemorrhage.

**Mike Karakas** took over from Gardiner in Chicago for the 1935-1936 season. His average of 1.92 in 48 games earned him the Calder

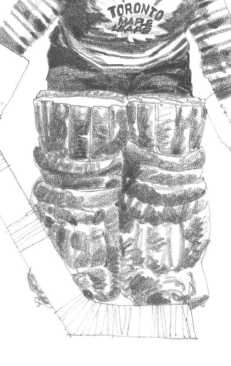

George Hainsworth

Wilf Cude

Trophy, awarded to the rookie of the year. It was the first time a goaltender was selected for the honour.

Karakas played eight seasons, all with the Black Hawks except for a few games with the Canadiens during the 1939-1940 season. In 336 games, he maintained an average of 2.92 and won the Stanley Cup once, with Chicago in 1938.

Whenever the topic turns to hockey legends, the name **Turk Broda** is bound to come up. The goalie played all 14 seasons of his career, which began in 1936-1937, with the Toronto Maple

Leafs. He won the Vézina Trophy twice, in 1941 and 1948, and had his name engraved on the Stanley Cup five times

Turk Broda

(1942, 1947, 1948, 1949, 1951). In all, Broda played 629 regular-season games and maintained an average of 2.53; he managed 62 shutouts. He did even better in the playoffs, with an average of 1.98 in 101 games.

When he joined the Boston Bruins in the 1938-1939 season as a replacement for Tiny Thompson, who had been injured and then traded to the Detroit Red Wings, **Frank Brimsek** was impressive indeed. During his first eight games he managed six shutouts, earning the nickname "Mr. Zero." He even beat Thompson's old record when he shut out the opposing team during a game that lasted 231 minutes and 54 seconds.

The 23-year-old rookie dominated the League with 33

wins in 43 games, 10 shutouts and an average of 1.58. He was the first goaltender to win the Calder Trophy and the Vézina Trophy in the same year, a feat that was only repeated 31 years later by Tony Esposito.

Mr. Zero played nine seasons with Boston and won the Stanley Cup twice, in his first season in 1939 and again in 1941. He also won the Vézina Trophy a second time, in 1942. He played his last season in the NHL with the Chicago Black Hawks, in 1949-1950.

Twenty-one years after Roy Worters, in 1950, **Chuck Rayner** became the second goaltender to win the Hart Trophy. On the basis of his average of 2.62 in 69 games, including six shutouts, he was chosen as the most valuable player.

Mike Karakas

Frank Brimsek

Chuck Rayner

He began his career during the 1940-1941 season with the New York Americans and joined the New York Rangers for 1945-1946. He played in the National League for 10 years, maintaining an average of 3.05.

**"Sugar Jim" Henry** started out with the New York Rangers in 1941-1942 as a replacement for veteran Dave Kerr, who had decided to retire. That season Henry played 48 games, leading the League with 29 wins. However, he was forced to leave the team at the end of the season to serve in the military. After his return in 1945-1946 he played 11 games, and only two the following season.

When Chuck Rayner suffered a facial injury in 1947-1948, the Rangers called Henry to the rescue. He continued his career in Chicago (1948-1949), and was traded to the Detroit Red Wings before the 1950-1951 season. However, he played only one game in Detroit since a sensational rookie, one Terry Sawchuk, had just appeared on the scene. Finally, Henry was traded to the Boston Bruins in 1951-1952, where he remained for his last four seasons in the NHL. During his nine-year career he maintained an average of 2.89 in 404 games.

A legendary photo taken by Roger St-Jean of Montreal's *La Presse* newspaper, shows an awed Jim Henry shaking hands with Maurice Richard. The two met during the playoffs, on April 8, 1952 at the Forum in Montreal; it was the seventh game in the semifinals between Montreal and Boston. With a gash over one eyebrow and feeling groggy after a powerful check from Léo Labine, Richard had scored the winning goal with only four minutes remaining in regular play. Exhausted and visibly shaken, he had skated the entire length of the rink, dodging five Bruins players, to score on Henry. Journalists who witnessed the goal are unanimous in describing it as one of the most spectacular in history.

**Bill Durnan** was another exceptional goaltender from the "old days." At the age of 27, early in the 1943-1944 season he took over from Paul Bibeault in the Canadiens net and was an instant success. He could boast the most wins in the League—38 in 50 games—and the best average, 2.18. He helped the Canadiens win the fourth Stanley

"Sugar Jim" Henry

Cup in their history, their first since 1931.

He won the Vézina Trophy that season and was selected for the same honour again in 1945, 1946, 1947, 1949 and 1950. He was the first goaltender to win the Vézina four consecutive times, a record that Jacques Plante would break in the late 1950s. Turk Broda put an end to Durnan's streak in 1948 by winning the trophy for the second time in his career, with an average of 2.38 in 60 games.

The 1948-1949 season was Durnan's best. He maintained an average of 2.10 and managed 10 shutouts in 60 games. His career average was 2.36 in 383 games and he won the Stanley Cup twice (1944 and 1945).

Finding it hard to deal with pressure, the ambidextrous goalie ended his career in 1950, after winning the Vézina Trophy for the sixth time in seven years. Gerry McNeil succeeded him as the Canadiens' goaltender.

While Bill Durnan was the focus of attention with the Habs, a 26-year-old rookie named **Frank McCool** was turning heads with the Toronto Maple Leafs. In 1944 the Leafs lost Turk Broda, who had gone to do his military service, and turned to McCool for help. He maintained an average of 3.22 in 50 games during the 1944-1945 season and managed four shutouts.

During the playoffs he tied the record set by Clint Benedict of the Maroons, managing three consecutive shutouts in the finals against Detroit and leading his team to the fifth Stanley Cup

victory in its history. In 13 games, he maintained an average of 2.23. He was the first Leafs goaltender to win the Calder Trophy.

McCool played only 22 games in his second season, recording an average of 3.68. When Broda came back from the service, McCool soon faded from the spotlight and was never again to play in the National League.

The last goalie in this historical overview is **Al Rollins**, who played with Toronto, Chicago and New York during a career that spanned nine seasons. Rollins played only two games with the Leafs in 1949-1950, but the following season played in 40 games, maintaining a top league average of 1.77 and managing five shutouts. The Leafs defeated the Canadiens to win the Stanley Cup and Rollins won the Vézina Trophy. During the season Rollins had shared goaltending duties with veteran Turk Broda.

After the 1951-1952 season he was traded to the Chicago Black Hawks in exchange for goaltender Harry Lumley. He stayed with the Hawks for five years and in 1954 became the first goalie in history to win the Hart Trophy, even though the Black Hawks had only 12 wins to their credit in 70 games. Despite his average of 3.23 in 66 games, the worst in the League, Rollins had done extremely well in the Hawks net. He ended his career in 1959-1960 after playing his last eight games with the New York Rangers.

Bill Durnan

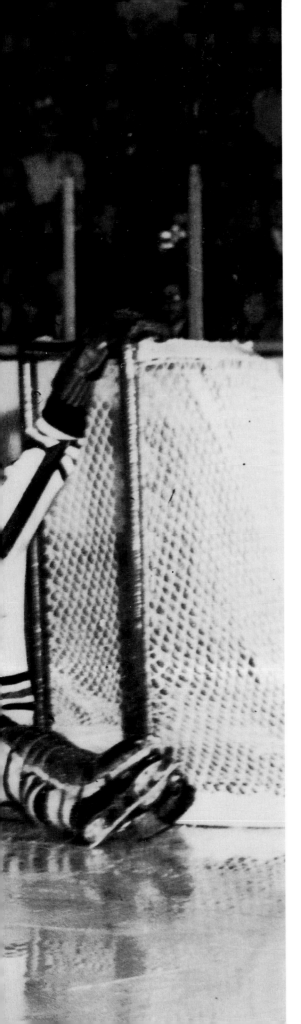

# The 5 0 s

Terry Sawchuk, Glenn Hall, Lorne Worsley and Jacques Plante were the goaltending stars of the 50s. At the time, National League teams played 70 games a season and could count on only one goalie.

In 1950, Bill Durnan of the Canadiens won the Vézina Trophy for the sixth and last time in his career and Jack Gélineau of the Boston Bruins was awarded the Calder Trophy. In the meantime, another rookie, Terry Sawchuk, was off to a sensational start with the Detroit Red Wings.

In 1952, Jacques Plante with the Montreal Canadiens, Glenn Hall with the Detroit Red Wings and Lorne Worsley with the New York Rangers had just arrived on the scene. Worsley won the Calder Trophy.

Plante was the uncontested star of the decade's second half, gaining attention for his bold innovations—notably, his mask and his tendency to leave the net, but more importantly, for helping the Canadiens win five consecutive Stanley Cups from 1956 to 1960 and by winning the Vézina Trophy five times in a row.

At a game played at the Forum between the Canadiens and the Chicago Black Hawks, star goalie Glenn Hall does the splits to stop a shot by Jean Béliveau.

# JOHNNY BOWER

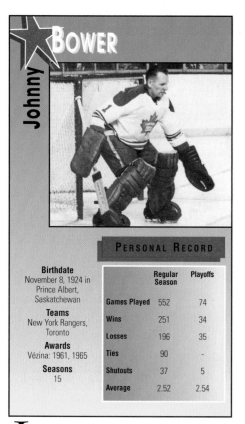

Johnny Bower

BOWER

### PERSONAL RECORD

**Birthdate**
November 8, 1924 in
Prince Albert,
Saskatchewan

**Teams**
New York Rangers,
Toronto

**Awards**
Vézina: 1961, 1965

**Seasons**
15

| | Regular Season | Playoffs |
|---|---|---|
| Games Played | 552 | 74 |
| Wins | 251 | 34 |
| Losses | 196 | 35 |
| Ties | 90 | - |
| Shutouts | 37 | 5 |
| Average | 2.52 | 2.54 |

Johnny Bower was a veteran of the minor leagues when he was called up to the NHL, at age 28, to take over from Lorne Worsley in the New York Rangers' net in the 1953-1954 season. After playing a whole season and maintaining an average of 2.60 in 70 games, he returned to the minors and played only seven games with the Rangers over the next four seasons. It was the general manager of the Toronto Maple Leafs, George "Punch" Imlach, who decided to give him the chance to make his mark in

the National League, in 1958-1959, after seeing him excel time and time again in the minors. Toronto had experienced a disastrous season in 1957-1958, winning only 21 of its 79 games and finishing last. The Maple Leafs had been eliminated from the playoffs for a second consecutive season and Imlach had been hired to bring them out of the mire. He succeeded admirably and Bower, his right-hand man, delivered the goods. He led the Leafs into the Stanley Cup finals in the next two seasons, and was one of the driving forces behind his team's four Stanley Cup wins in the early 60s.

Leftwinger Frank Mahovlich got to know Bower very well in his 10 seasons with the Maple Leafs. "Johnny was a good guy,

fairly quiet, and dedicated body and soul to his job as a goaltender. Like a lot of others, he didn't wear a mask and even with 10 stitches in his face, he came back to his net as if nothing had happened. He had to be seriously injured to give up his place. He was a great goaltender and we were all happy to play with him. We knew we could really count on him."

"He was relatively old when he came to the National League," adds Henri Richard, "and most players were surprised to see that he could get the job done. He liked to challenge his opponents."

In 1960-1961 Bower led the League in wins, with 33, and maintained the best average, with 2.50. His exploits earned him a

Johnny Bower holds off Canadiens player Peter Mahovlich as Jim Dorey watches. Bower decided to wear a mask only late in his career.

During his career, Johnny Bower managed 37 shutouts, ranking 22nd for career shutouts in the National League.

spot on the first All Star team, a one-time occurrence in his career.

His career highlights include his performance during the 1967 playoffs, when he joined forces with Terry Sawchuk to eliminate first the Chicago Black Hawks and then the Canadiens. He was especially brilliant during the third game of the finals against the Canadiens, stopping 60 shots; Toronto went on to win 3-2 in the second period of overtime play. The Leafs won the Stanley Cup for the thirteenth time in the team's history at the end of a six-game series.

Johnny Bower was 45 when he ended his career. His name appears twice on the Vézina Trophy.

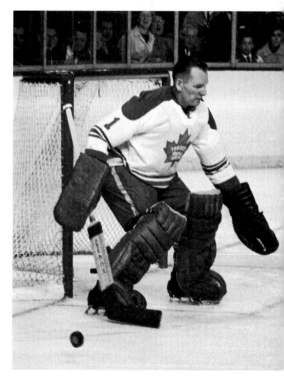

During the 1967-1968 season, Lorne Worsley led the League with a 1.98 average. Aged 43 at the time, Bower finished second with an average of 2.25 in 43 games.

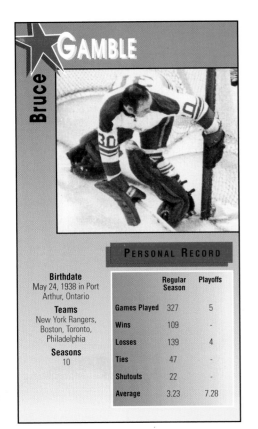

# BRUCE GAMBLE

Bruce Gamble started his National League career by playing two games with the New York Rangers, then joining the Boston Bruins for a two-year stay. His best years as a professional hockey player were with Toronto.

Gamble came to the Leafs during the 1965-1966 season. His best season was in 1967-1968 when, at the age of 29, he maintained an average of 2.31 in 41 games. He shared the goaltending spot with Johnny Bower, the Maple Leafs' other star goalie.

Gamble lived the most exciting moments of his career in January 1968, on Maple Leafs ice, at the 21st All Star game. He was teamed up with Al Smith in the net and the Maple Leafs won 4-3 over a team composed of the League's top players. That season Bower and Gamble finished second behind Lorne Worsley and Rogatien Vachon of the Canadiens in the vote for the Vézina Trophy winners.

Bruce Gamble ended his career in 1972, after slightly more than one season with the Philadelphia Flyers.

**PERSONAL RECORD**

**Birthdate**
May 24, 1938 in Port Arthur, Ontario

**Teams**
New York Rangers, Boston, Toronto, Philadelphia

**Seasons**
10

|  | Regular Season | Playoffs |
|---|---|---|
| Games Played | 327 | 5 |
| Wins | 109 | - |
| Losses | 139 | 4 |
| Ties | 47 | - |
| Shutouts | 22 | - |
| Average | 3.23 | 7.28 |

# HARRY LUMLEY

Harry Lumley played 16 years in the National League and was one of the best goaltenders of his time. He was only 17 years old when he joined the Detroit Red Wings during the 1943-1944 season.

In 1949-1950 Lumley experienced his best season with Detroit, with seven shutouts and an average of 2.35. The Wings won the Stanley Cup, the first and only such victory in Lumley's career.

However, Lumley's days with the Wings were already numbered. Before the season started, Jack Adams made the biggest trade in the League's history, a transaction involving nine players. Pete Babando, Al Dewsbury, Don Morrison, Jack Stewart and Lumley left for Chicago, in exchange for Bob Goldham, Metro Prystai, Gaye Stewart and goalie Jim Henry.

Two years later Lumley was traded to the Toronto Maple Leafs, where he enjoyed his finest seasons.

In 1953-1954, he managed 13 shutouts, heading the League and setting a team record that still stands. He maintained the best conference and career average of 1.86. His exploits earned him his one and only Vézina Trophy.

Lumley was traded to the Boston Bruins before the start of the 1957-1958 season and played there for three years before hanging up his skates.

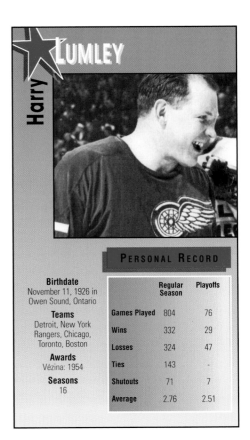

**PERSONAL RECORD**

**Birthdate**
November 11, 1926 in Owen Sound, Ontario

**Teams**
Detroit, New York Rangers, Chicago, Toronto, Boston

**Awards**
Vézina: 1954

**Seasons**
16

|  | Regular Season | Playoffs |
|---|---|---|
| Games Played | 804 | 76 |
| Wins | 332 | 29 |
| Losses | 324 | 47 |
| Ties | 143 | - |
| Shutouts | 71 | 7 |
| Average | 2.76 | 2.51 |

# GLENN HALL

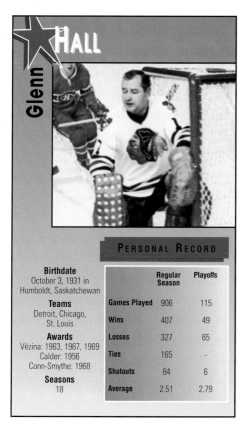

Glenn HALL

### PERSONAL RECORD

**Birthdate**
October 3, 1931 in
Humboldt, Saskatchewan

**Teams**
Detroit, Chicago,
St. Louis

**Awards**
Vézina: 1963, 1967, 1969
Calder: 1956
Conn-Smythe: 1968

**Seasons**
18

| | Regular Season | Playoffs |
|---|---|---|
| Games Played | 906 | 115 |
| Wins | 407 | 49 |
| Losses | 327 | 65 |
| Ties | 165 | - |
| Shutouts | 84 | 6 |
| Average | 2.51 | 2.79 |

"Glenn Hall was tall and wide, and he was one of the first to use the butterfly style," recalled Henri Richard. "Players who didn't shoot high into the net had a hard time getting the puck past him."

With Terry Sawchuk back in Detroit in exchange for Johnny Bucyk, the Red Wings management decided to shed Glenn Hall. He was traded to the Chicago Black Hawks along with Ted Lindsay, a 13-season veteran. A nervous player who regularly felt queasy before games, Hall was the key to his team's Stanley Cup victory in the 1960-1961 season.

His consistently good performance and his exploits earned him the nickname "Mr. Goalie." He ranks third among League goaltenders for total number of shutouts, with 84.

Selected to play on All Star teams seven times, Hall finished his career with the St. Louis Blues, a team he played with for four seasons before retiring. At age 37—along with Jacques Plante, who was 40—he won the Vézina Trophy for the third time in his career.

Today Glenn Hall is part of the Hockey Hall of Fame (inducted in 1975) and ranks fourth among NHL goaltenders for the number of wins, with a total of 407 in 906 games.

Of all the teams in the National Hockey League, the Chicago Black Hawks is the only one to retire two sweaters worn by goaltenders who excelled while wearing the red, black and white uniform: Tony Esposito and Glenn Hall.

A native of Saskatchewan, Glenn Hall began his NHL career in 1952-1953, playing six games with the Detroit Red Wings. In 1955-1956 he became the team's No. 1 goalie following a trade that sent Terry Sawchuk to the Boston Bruins. He maintained an excellent average of 2.11, managing 12 shutouts and winning the Calder Trophy for rookie of the year. After winning the Stanley Cup the two previous seasons, the Wings lost against the Canadiens in a five-game series.

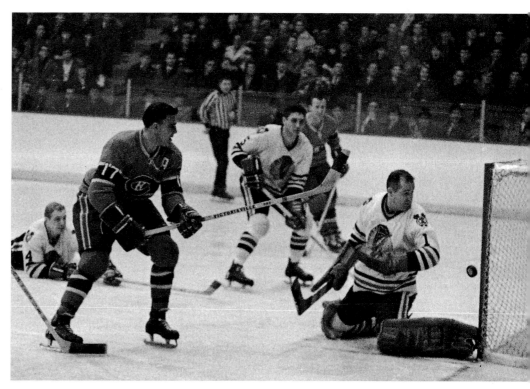

Glenn Hall stops a shot from Canadiens player Jean-Guy Talbot during a game at the Forum in Montreal. Hall was known for his bad nerves and throughout his career, suffered stomach aches before each game.

# GERRY MCNEIL

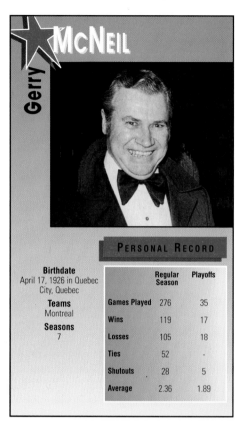

Gerry **McNEIL**

## PERSONAL RECORD

**Birthdate**
April 17, 1926 in Quebec
City, Quebec

**Teams**
Montreal

**Seasons**
7

|  | Regular Season | Playoffs |
|---|---|---|
| Games Played | 276 | 35 |
| Wins | 119 | 17 |
| Losses | 105 | 18 |
| Ties | 52 | - |
| Shutouts | 28 | 5 |
| Average | 2.36 | 1.89 |

Born in Quebec City in 1926, Gerry McNeil played only seven seasons in the National League, all in the Montreal Canadiens uniform. He got his chance to play with the Habs under coach Dick Irvin when Bill Durnan surprised everyone by announcing his retirement after just seven seasons. McNeil was the Canadiens' No. 1 goalie from 1950-1951 to 1953-1954 and had his best season in 1952-1953, managing 10 shutouts and maintaining an average of 2.12 in 66 games.

During the playoffs he played eight games, finishing with two shutouts and a 2.00 average. The Canadiens won in the last round of a five-game series against the Boston Bruins, allowing McNeil and rookie

Jacques Plante to celebrate their first Stanley Cup together.

After Bill Durnan, it was McNeil's turn to give in to pressure; he decided to hang up his skates at the end of the 1953-1954 season. Just as Durnan's retirement had given McNeil a chance to prove himself, McNeil's departure opened the door for Jacques Plante who, at age 25, became the team's lead goalie.

When Plante was injured during the 1956-1957 season, McNeil agreed to take to the ice once again for nine games, the last ones he would play in the National League.

McNeil had his name engraved on the Stanley Cup three times. He also took part in three annual All Star games, in 1951, 1952 and 1953.

Gerry McNeil and Jacques Plante, shown at the Forum during an Old Timers game in Montreal. McNeil played his last games in the National League in 1956-1957, when Plante had been the Canadiens lead goalie for the past two seasons. Both goaltenders wore Number 1 with the Canadiens during their careers; McNeil also wore the Number 12 jersey in 1949-1950.

# JACQUES PLANTE

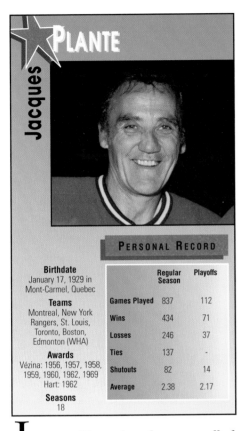

Jacques PLANTE

### PERSONAL RECORD

**Birthdate**
January 17, 1929 in
Mont-Carmel, Quebec

**Teams**
Montreal, New York
Rangers, St. Louis,
Toronto, Boston,
Edmonton (WHA)

**Awards**
Vézina: 1956, 1957, 1958,
1959, 1960, 1962, 1969
Hart: 1962

**Seasons**
18

|  | Regular Season | Playoffs |
|---|---|---|
| Games Played | 837 | 112 |
| Wins | 434 | 71 |
| Losses | 246 | 37 |
| Ties | 137 | - |
| Shutouts | 82 | 14 |
| Average | 2.38 | 2.17 |

Jacques Plante has the unequalled distinction of winning the Vézina Trophy seven times in the course of an outstanding career that spanned 18 seasons. Most notably, he was awarded the trophy five consecutive times between 1956 and 1960 while playing with the fabulous Canadiens, who won the Stanley Cup in each of the same five years.

Plante made his mark very early in his career with the Canadiens. After a three-game tryout in the 1952-1953 season, management called him back to the team during the playoffs. The team coached by Dick Irvin had won the first two semifinal games against Chicago, but the Black Hawks had taken a 3-2 lead in the series and were threatening to eliminate the Habs, who had not won the Stanley Cup since 1946. Plante made his appearance in the midst of this scenario and, to the astonishment of many, took Gerry McNeil's place in front of the net. He led his team to a 3-0 win, the very first shutout of his career. Montreal won the seventh game 4-1, still relying on Plante's talent. The Boston Bruins faced off with the Habs in the finals.

Plante minded the net during the first two games (a 4-2 win and a 4-1 loss), then McNeil won the next three games to bring the Canadiens to the Cup. At 24, Plante won his first of six Stanley Cups, an exploit matched only by Ken Dryden.

When Gerry McNeil retired at the end of the 1953-1954 season, Plante became the lead goalie for the Canadiens.

It has been said time and time again: Jacques Plante was an innovator and a role model for other

Pictured for the last time in the Canadiens uniform, Jacques Plante with the Stanley Cup, a trophy that bears his name six times.

In 1970-1971, after two brilliant years in the St. Louis Blues uniform, Jacques Plante joined the Toronto Maple Leafs. He won 24 out of 40 games, maintaining a 1.88 average, the best in the League. He played almost three seasons with Toronto before going to the Boston Bruins.

goaltenders. He was the first player to wear a mask regularly, following a facial injury during a game against the New York Rangers. He also astonished onlookers with his habit of skating away from the crease to find the puck and pass it to a teammate; he even dared to skate behind his net. Plante believed that goalies should do more than stop shots and preferred to play an active role in the game in order to control traffic around his net.

Plante played 11 seasons with the Canadiens. His best year was in 1955-1956, with an average of 1.86 in 64 games. In 1961-1962, he led the League for most wins (42), and maintained the best average (2.37 in 70 games), earning the Vézina Trophy for the sixth time. In addition, he won the Hart Trophy, awarded to the most valuable player; to date, he is the last goaltender selected for the Hart.

After being traded to the New York Rangers in 1963, Plante played with that team for two seasons, retired, but came back in 1968-1969 with the St. Louis Blues. Experienced and still very agile, he won the Vézina Trophy jointly with Glenn Hall. He went on to play in Toronto, Boston, and Edmonton with the World Hockey Association before permanently retiring in 1975 at the age of 46.

A legend in his own time: Jacques Plante suffered only 246 losses in 837 games during his 18-year career in the National League. Plante was inducted into the Hall of Fame in 1978, and to date remains the only goaltender whose name appears on the Vézina Trophy seven times.

# TERRY SAWCHUK

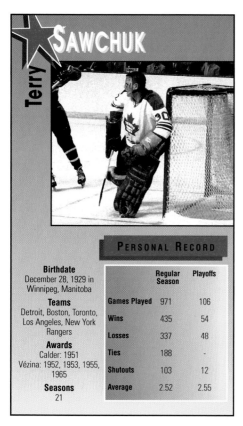

**SAWCHUK**

Terry

## PERSONAL RECORD

**Birthdate**
December 28, 1929 in
Winnipeg, Manitoba

**Teams**
Detroit, Boston, Toronto,
Los Angeles, New York
Rangers

**Awards**
Calder: 1951
Vézina: 1952, 1953, 1955,
1965

**Seasons**
21

|  | Regular Season | Playoffs |
|---|---|---|
| Games Played | 971 | 106 |
| Wins | 435 | 54 |
| Losses | 337 | 48 |
| Ties | 188 | - |
| Shutouts | 103 | 12 |
| Average | 2.52 | 2.55 |

Terry Sawchuk is the only goaltender in the National League to hold a record of more than 100 shutouts in his career, which spanned 21 years and five teams.

In 1950, his style in the junior leagues led the Detroit Red Wings to sign him at the age of 17 and to trade veteran Harry Lumley to the Chicago Black Hawks. Sawchuk was sensational in his first season, playing 70 of his team's games, with 44 wins and 11 shutouts. His 1.99 average earned him the Calder Trophy.

Sawchuk is also the only goalie in history to boast three 12-shutout seasons to his credit. In 1952, he allowed only five goals in eight

Terry Sawchuk looks on as defenceman Larry Hillman keeps an eye on Léon Rochefort of the Canadiens.

playoff games, even managing four shutouts on Detroit ice. His team won the Stanley Cup for the fifth time in its history, eliminating Toronto and Montreal.

Sawchuk won the Stanley Cup three times with Detroit (1952, 1954 and 1955), where he played for 14 seasons. Donning the Maple Leafs uniform from 1964-1965 to 1966-1967, he joined forces with Johnny Bower to win his fourth Stanley Cup in 1967.

That year the Leafs played the Chicago Black Hawks during the semifinals. Sawchuk proved that at 37, he was still a great goalie. During the fifth game in Chicago, he replaced Bower after the first period when the score was tied 2-2. The veteran handled the onslaught from Hull, Mikita and company, who sent 37 shots in his direction over the next two periods. He did not allow a single goal and the Leafs won the game 4-2. Toronto went on to eliminate Chicago in six games before defeating the Canadiens and winning the Stanley Cup.

"In my career I saw a lot of excellent goaltenders, including Jacques Plante, Glenn Hall, Ken Dryden and Vladislav Tretiak, but in my opinion Terry Sawchuk was the best," said Frank Mahovlich, who played four seasons with Sawchuk. "In 1967 he played a major role in our Stanley Cup victory. I remember the fifth game against Chicago. He was sensational, particularly against Bobby Hull. Even his own teammates could hardly believe some of the saves he made!"

Terry Sawchuk was the first player selected during the 1967 expansion draft by the Los Angeles Kings, but he played only one season with the team before going back to Detroit. He ended his career with the New York Rangers in 1969-1970, accomplishing his 103rd shutout in the process.

The League's leading goalie for most wins (435, one more than Jacques Plante), Terry Sawchuk died in 1970 and was inducted into the Hall of Fame the following year.

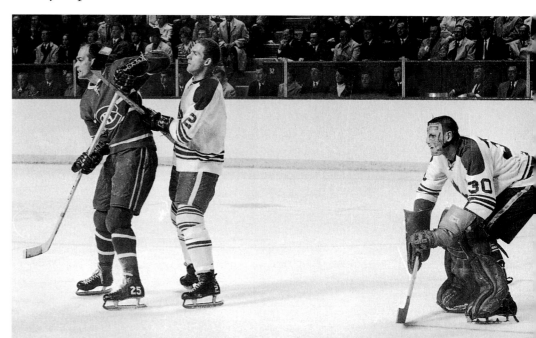

# LORNE WORSLEY

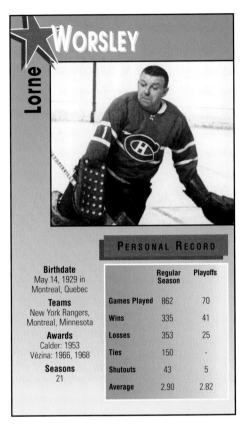

Lorne WORSLEY

### PERSONAL RECORD

**Birthdate**
May 14, 1929 in
Montreal, Quebec

**Teams**
New York Rangers,
Montreal, Minnesota

**Awards**
Calder: 1953
Vézina: 1966, 1968

**Seasons**
21

| | Regular Season | Playoffs |
|---|---|---|
| Games Played | 862 | 70 |
| Wins | 335 | 41 |
| Losses | 353 | 25 |
| Ties | 150 | - |
| Shutouts | 43 | 5 |
| Average | 2.90 | 2.82 |

Born in Montreal on May 14, 1929, Lorne Worsley began his professional hockey career in a very strange way. In 1952, the Rangers were eliminated from the playoffs for a second consecutive year despite a solid performance from veteran goalie Chuck Rayner. At 31, Rayner had maintained a very respectable average of 3.00 in 53 games. Still, Rangers management decided to call on Worsley, who was playing for Vancouver in the Western Hockey League. Rayner and Worsley shared goaltending duties in 1952-1953, but the Rangers had an even more disastrous season! The team won only 17 of its 70 games; Worsley and Rayner allowed 211 goals, the worst record in the League. Worsley had played 50 games, Rayner 20. Nonetheless,

Worsley won the Calder Trophy for rookie of the year; his performance was considered excellent given the holes in his team's defense.

Surprisingly, he was sent down to the minors early in the following season, leaving room for another rookie, Johnny Bower. Worsley came back to the Rangers for the 1954-1955 season after being chosen as best goalie in the Western Hockey League. He was the team's lead goalie for nine seasons before being traded to the Montreal Canadiens in the summer of 1963.

Backed by such ace defensemen as Jean-Claude Tremblay, Jacques Laperrière, Ted Harris and Jean-Guy Talbot, Worsley had a considerably easier time in the Canadiens net. More agile than he looked, he

became the backup goalie to Charlie Hodge and later shared the goaltending job with Rogatien Vachon in 1966-1967 and 1969-1970.

In the red, white and blue uniform of the Habs, Worsley won the Stanley Cup four times (1965, 1966, 1968 and 1969). He shared the Vézina Trophy with Charlie Hodge in 1966 and with Rogatien Vachon in 1968. He was particularly effective in the 1967-1968 season, maintaining an average of 1.98, with six shutouts in 40 games.

Nicknamed "Gump" because of his close resemblance to a comic strip character, Lorne Worsley ended his career in 1974 with the North Stars, at the age of 45. He was inducted into the Hall of Fame in 1980.

Despite falling to the ice, Lorne Worsley has his eye on the puck, at the feet of leftwinger Ab McDonald; meanwhile, Gordie Howe is a menacing presence in front of the net.

# The 60s

In the 60s, the National Hockey League decided to expand the organization, which had been limited to six teams for several decades. Six new teams were formed, giving dozens of promising players a chance to prove themselves and several "old time" stars the opportunity to prolong their careers.

Only one goaltender won the Calder Trophy in the 60s: Detroit's Roger Crozier, in 1965. Yet Johnny Bower, a veteran of the 50s, was still going strong; he had begun his playing career in 1953 and resurfaced in the 1960s to lead the Toronto Maple Leafs to four Stanley Cups.

Glenn Hall continued to demonstrate his goaltending prowess. Brilliant during the 50s, he won the Vézina Trophy three times—twice with Chicago and once while playing with the St. Louis Blues, one of the six 1967 expansion teams. The third time around he was sharing net-minding duties with none other than Jacques Plante!

The decade's most outstanding rookies were Gerry Cheevers, Bernard Parent, Ed Giacomin and Rogatien Vachon.

Sticks with curved blades were a major innovation as they significantly increased the power and accuracy of shots on goal. They also complicated the lives of goaltenders; most began to wear masks, and teams adopted the two-goalie system, using their goaltenders alternately.

After playing seven seasons with the Detroit Red Wings and winning the Calder and Conn-Smythe Trophies with them, Roger Crozier joined a new team admitted to the NHL in 1970: the Buffalo Sabres. The photo opposite shows Crozier using his stick to stop the puck, apparently unfazed by the heavy traffic in front of his net.

# GERRY CHEEVERS

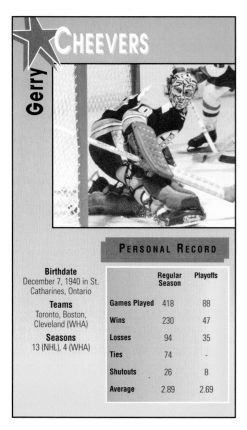

Gerry
CHEEVERS

## PERSONAL RECORD

**Birthdate**
December 7, 1940 in St.
Catharines, Ontario

**Teams**
Toronto, Boston,
Cleveland (WHA)

**Seasons**
13 (NHL), 4 (WHA)

| | Regular Season | Playoffs |
|---|---|---|
| Games Played | 418 | 88 |
| Wins | 230 | 47 |
| Losses | 94 | 35 |
| Ties | 74 | - |
| Shutouts | 26 | 8 |
| Average | 2.89 | 2.69 |

Gerry Cheevers wore the Bruins colours for 12 seasons and won two Stanley Cups.

Gerry Cheevers made his debut in 1965-1966 with the Boston Bruins. He played only six games that year, since the team's goaltending work was done mainly by Bernard Parent, a 20-year-old rookie, and Ed Johnston. When Parent was traded at the end of the 1966-1967 season—to the Philadelphia Flyers, one of the new expansion teams—Cheevers became the Bruins' lead goalie. Parent and Cheevers both won the Stanley Cup twice and both belong to the Hockey Hall of Fame.

Although Cheevers was never chosen for an All Star team and never won an individual award, he was a key player for the Bruins. Backed by Ed Johnston, he led the team to Stanley Cup wins in 1970 and 1972. During the 1971-1972 season he

Under defenseman Dallas Smith's stare, Gerry Cheevers stops a shot made by Mario Tremblay of the Montreal Canadiens.

Gerry Cheevers stretches out to the right of his net, anticipating a move by the Canadiens player making his way around the net.

played 32 consecutive games without suffering a single loss (a total of 24 wins), a streak that still stands as a League record.

When the World Hockey Association began its first season in 1972-1973, Cheevers, like many other NHL stars (notably, Bobby Hull, Frank Mahovlich and Dave Keaton) decided to join one of its teams. He played with the Cleveland Barons for four seasons and returned to the Bruins in 1975-1976.

In 1976-1977, the Boston Bruins finished first in the Adams Division and Cheevers played 45 games, maintaining an average of 3.04. The Bruins made it all the way to the Stanley Cup finals, but Cheevers missed the chance to win a third Cup when his team lost a six-game series against the Canadiens. Hockey fans who have seen Cheevers play will remember his habit of drawing stitches on his mask in the spots where he would have been injured had he played without it. From 1980 to 1985, Cheevers was the Bruins' head coach and won 204 of 376 games at the team's helm.

Although he was never chosen to play on any of the League's All Star teams, Gerry Cheevers was asked to play in the All Star game held in Montreal on January 21, 1969. Cheevers was the backup goalie for Ed Giacomin on the Eastern Division team and the game ended in a 3-3 tie.

Gerry Cheevers uses his stick to stop the puck, while defenceman Bobby Orr tries to help his goalie.

Gerry Cheevers deflects a shot by Steve Shutt.

# ROGER CROZIER

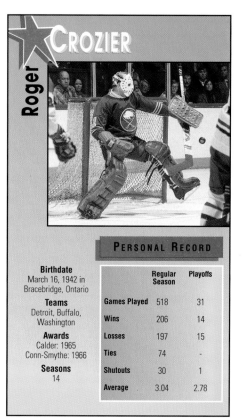

### PERSONAL RECORD

| Birthdate March 16, 1942 in Bracebridge, Ontario | | Regular Season | Playoffs |
|---|---|---|---|
| **Teams** Detroit, Buffalo, Washington | Games Played | 518 | 31 |
| | Wins | 206 | 14 |
| **Awards** Calder: 1965 Conn-Smythe: 1966 | Losses | 197 | 15 |
| | Ties | 74 | - |
| **Seasons** 14 | Shutouts | 30 | 1 |
| | Average | 3.04 | 2.78 |

Roger Crozier made his debut with the Detroit Red Wings during the 1963-1964 season, after the Chicago Black Hawks traded him for defenseman Howie Young. Recognized as one of the most promising players in the minor leagues, he played only 15 games that season. But the next year he was in front of the net for all 70 of his team's games, capitalizing on Terry Sawchuk's departure for Toronto.

At 22, he was a major factor in the Red Wings' first-place finish in the regular season for the first time since 1957, four points ahead of the Canadiens. Leading the League with an average of 2.42 and six shutouts, Crozier was awarded the Calder Trophy. He became the third goaltender in Red Wings history to win the Calder, after Glenn Hall (1956) and Terry Sawchuk (1951). He was also picked to play on the first All Star team.

In 1965-1966, the Red Wings played in the finals and faced Toe Blake's Canadiens. Detroit lost in seven games, but Crozier was so extraordinary that he won the Conn-Smythe Trophy as the best player in the playoffs. Besides Crozier, only Reggie Leach in 1976 and Ron Hextall in 1987—both with the Philadelphia Flyers—were chosen for the Conn-Smythe although they were not on the winning playoff team.

After seven seasons with Detroit, Crozier went to the Buffalo Sabres in 1970, when the team made its debut in the National League. He spent six seasons under general manager Punch Imlach and finished his playing career in 1976-1977 with the Washington Capitals. He was general manager of the Capitals for the 1981-1982 season.

A one-on-one encounter: Roger Crozier comes out of the net to ward off an attack by Pete Mahovlich of the Canadiens.

During the 1972-1973 season, Roger Crozier's brilliant showing made it possible for the Sabres to advance to the playoffs for the first time ever. That year Crozier played 49 games and maintained an average of 2.76. In the quarter finals for the Stanley Cup, Buffalo lost in a six-game series against the Canadiens.

Steve Shutt of the Canadiens, Jerry Korab of the Sabres and Roger Crozier seem to be searching for the puck, which the goaltender has deflected.

# DENIS DEJORDY

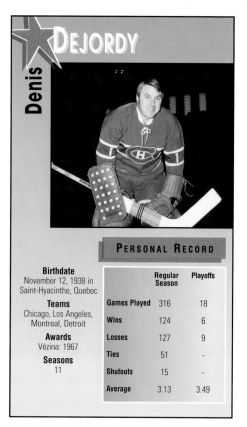

Denis Dejordy

**PERSONAL RECORD**

**Birthdate**
November 12, 1938 in
Saint-Hyacinthe, Quebec

**Teams**
Chicago, Los Angeles,
Montreal, Detroit

**Awards**
Vézina: 1967

**Seasons**
11

| | Regular Season | Playoffs |
|---|---|---|
| Games Played | 316 | 18 |
| Wins | 124 | 6 |
| Losses | 127 | 9 |
| Ties | 51 | - |
| Shutouts | 15 | - |
| Average | 3.13 | 3.49 |

Denis Dejordy made his National League debut in 1962-1963 with the Chicago Black Hawks. Glenn Hall had played 502 consecutive games with Detroit and Chicago (a record that still stands) when he was forced to make way for a replacement on November 7, 1962 after injuring his back in the first period of play against the Boston Bruins. Dejordy stepped in for his first game in the League.

During his first two seasons, Dejordy played only 11 games since Hull was the Hawks' lead goalie. Then, as the practice of alternating goalies became more common, he shared the goaltending job with Hall. Together, they won the Vézina Trophy for the 1966-1967 season.

That season was Dejordy's best; he played 44 games and maintained an average of 2.46.

Chicago traded Dejordy to the Los Angeles Kings during the 1969-1970 season while rookie Tony Esposito was doing dazzling work in his team's net. The following season, 1970-1971, Dejordy played 60 of his team's 78 games—a career high—and maintained a 3.80 average. Along with Dale Hoganson, Doug Robinson and Noël Price, Dejordy was sent to the Canadiens in 1971 in exchange for Rogatien Vachon. Dejordy played only seven games with the Canadiens in 1971-1972 before being traded to the Detroit Red Wings. The veteran goalie played 24 games in 1972-1973 and only one game in 1973-1974, his last season.

Denis Dejordy and Tony Esposito were teammates only during the 1969-1970 season, Number 35's first year with Chicago. Dejordy was traded during the season to the Los Angeles Kings.

# DAVE DRYDEN

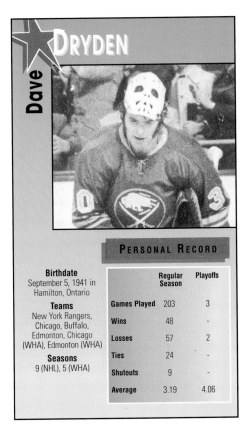

Dave

## DRYDEN

### PERSONAL RECORD

**Birthdate**
September 5, 1941 in
Hamilton, Ontario

**Teams**
New York Rangers,
Chicago, Buffalo,
Edmonton, Chicago
(WHA), Edmonton (WHA)

**Seasons**
9 (NHL), 5 (WHA)

| | Regular Season | Playoffs |
|---|---|---|
| Games Played | 203 | 3 |
| Wins | 48 | - |
| Losses | 57 | 2 |
| Ties | 24 | - |
| Shutouts | 9 | - |
| Average | 3.19 | 4.06 |

Dave Dryden—older brother to Ken, the famous Montreal Canadiens goalie—played his first NHL game in 1961-1962 with the New York Rangers. That was the only game he played that year, as he was sent back to the minors. After three seasons he returned to the NHL with the Chicago Black Hawks. He played three seasons with the Hawks, but was unable to secure the lead goalie position.

During his nine-season career, Dryden played with four teams. His finest moments came while he was with the Buffalo Sabres from 1970 to 1974. In 1972-1973 he played 37 games and maintained an average of 2.65, his career best.

In 1974 he jumped to the World Hockey Association, playing with the Chicago Cougars in 1974-1975 and with the Edmonton Oilers during the four subsequent seasons. In 1978-1979 Dryden was the lead goalie for the Oilers, playing 63 games and maintaining an excellent average of 2.89. When the WHA was dissolved Dryden stayed with the Oilers, but played only 14 games with the team in the NHL before hanging up his goalie pads for good.

The two Dryden brothers played in opposite nets for the first time in the National League during a 1971-1972 season game. After the siren signalled the end of the game between the Canadiens and the Sabres, Ken and Dave skated to center ice and shook hands, to the delight of the spectators in the stands.

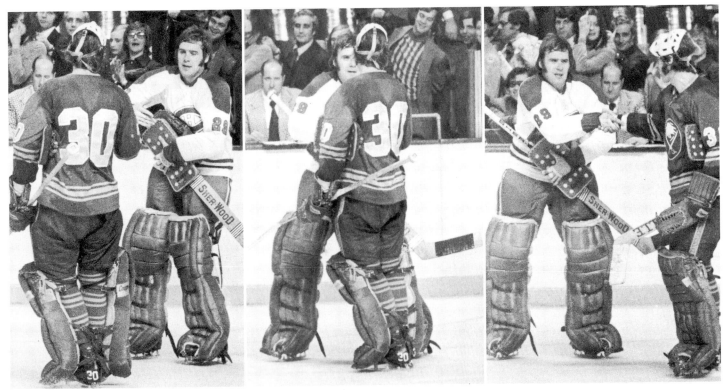

# ED GIACOMIN

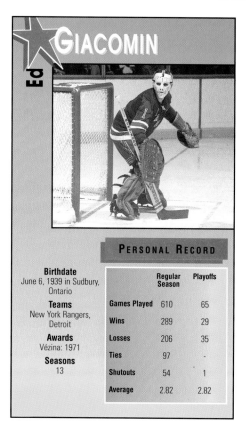

GIACOMIN
Ed

## PERSONAL RECORD

**Birthdate**
June 6, 1939 in Sudbury,
Ontario

**Teams**
New York Rangers,
Detroit

**Awards**
Vézina: 1971

**Seasons**
13

| | Regular Season | Playoffs |
|---|---|---|
| Games Played | 610 | 65 |
| Wins | 289 | 29 |
| Losses | 206 | 35 |
| Ties | 97 | - |
| Shutouts | 54 | 1 |
| Average | 2.82 | 2.82 |

Ed Giacomin was 26 when he made his debut in a New York Rangers uniform in 1965-1966. The previous season, the Rangers had relied on the goaltending talents of Jacques Plante and Marcel Paillé, but both players had decided to retire. So Giacomin was called up from the minors, where he had spent seven years playing backup to Cesare Maniago and Don Simmons. He played 36 games that year and became the Rangers' lead goalie the following season.

His solid performance made it possible for the team to get to the

During two consecutive seasons, 1968-1969 and 1969-1970, Ed Giacomin played 70 of his team's 76 games. In the 1970-1971 season the Rangers decided to alternate Giacomin and Gilles Villemure in the net.

playoffs after a four-season drought. He led the League in wins, with 30, and maintained an average of 2.61 while managing nine shutouts. Although the Rangers lost to the Canadiens in the semifinals, the team had a first-rate goalie on their side.

In 1970-1971, the Rangers began using goalies on an alternating basis and Giacomin shared his job with Gilles Villemure. In 45 games he achieved the best average of his career (2.16) and the duo won the Vézina Trophy. That season the Rangers allowed only 177 goals, the only team besides Chicago (194 goals) with a goals-against record of under 200.

Giacomin led the Rangers to the playoffs only once, in 1971-1972.

New York fell to the Bruins in a best-of-six.

After being selected for the second All Star team three years in a row beginning in 1967-1968, and twice for the first team, in 1966-1967 and 1970-1971, Giacomin was traded to the Detroit Red Wings during the 1975-1976 season. At the age of 38, he retired after playing only nine games in the 1977-1978 season.

The Rangers retired his sweater—Number 1—in recognition of his popularity with New York fans. Giacomin holds the Rangers team record for career shutouts, with 49.

Ed Giacomin's career record of 54 shutouts, including 49 while playing with the Rangers, ranks him fifth among National League goaltenders.

Ed Giacomin makes a save for the Rangers while Canadiens player Claude Larose waits in vain for a pass.

# CHARLIE HODGE

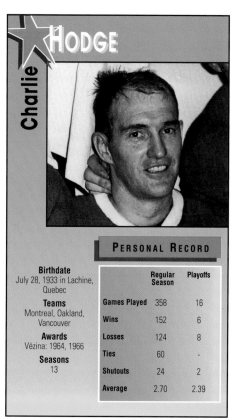

**Charlie HODGE**

### PERSONAL RECORD

**Birthdate**
July 28, 1933 in Lachine, Quebec

**Teams**
Montreal, Oakland, Vancouver

**Awards**
Vézina: 1964, 1966

**Seasons**
13

|  | Regular Season | Playoffs |
|---|---|---|
| Games Played | 358 | 16 |
| Wins | 152 | 6 |
| Losses | 124 | 8 |
| Ties | 60 | - |
| Shutouts | 24 | 2 |
| Average | 2.70 | 2.39 |

The least we can say for Charlie Hodge is that he was patient during his National League career, particularly with the Canadiens. Only 5"6", he made his debut with the Habs in 1954-1955 and played 14 games. Unfortunately for him at the time, the Canadiens were relying on the excellent Jacques Plante, which curtailed Hodge's playing possibilities. From the next season until 1960-1961, he played a total of only 15 games.

As Plante was injured that season and played only 40 games, Hodge was in the net for the remaining 30 and maintained a lower average than Plante (2.53 compared to 2.80). Still, Hodge became the lead goalie for Toe Blake's team only after Plante was

traded to the New York Rangers in the summer of 1963. Almost 10 years had gone by since he first joined the Canadiens!

By then 30, Hodge made the most of his golden opportunity. He maintained an excellent average of 2.26 in 62 games, managing eight shutouts and winning the Vézina Trophy. In 1965-1966 he joined forces with Lorne Worsley and the duo won the Vézina Trophy in addition to leading the Canadiens to a second consecutive Stanley Cup.

During his career with the Canadiens, Hodge had his name added to the Stanley Cup four times. In 1967-1968, he became the lead goalie for the Oakland Seals, an expansion team. Although the

Seals won only 15 games during their first season, Hodge maintained a respectable average of 2.86.

He hung up his skates at the end of the 1970-1971 season, the only one in which he played as a member of the Vancouver Canucks. Today he is a scout for the Pittsburgh Penguins, and his name was added to the Stanley Cup once again after the 1992 win by Mario Lemieux and his teammates.

In the Canadiens dressing room after one of his best games, Charlie Hodge shares a few minutes of glory with teammates Yvan Cournoyer, John Ferguson and Claude Provost. Together, the four players won 28 Stanley Cups!

# ED JOHNSTON

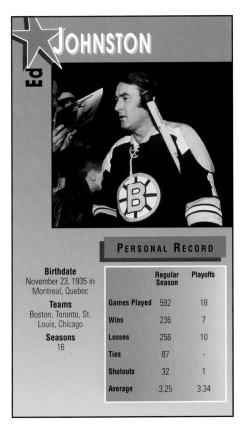

**JOHNSTON**

Ed

### PERSONAL RECORD

**Birthdate**
November 23, 1935 in
Montreal, Quebec

**Teams**
Boston, Toronto, St.
Louis, Chicago

**Seasons**
16

| | Regular Season | Playoffs |
|---|---|---|
| Games Played | 592 | 18 |
| Wins | 236 | 7 |
| Losses | 256 | 10 |
| Ties | 87 | - |
| Shutouts | 32 | 1 |
| Average | 3.25 | 3.34 |

A tense moment in front of the net as John Ferguson of the Canadiens tries to nab the puck that Ed Johnston has deflected with his pad.

Head coach of the Pittsburgh Penguins, Ed Johnston spent most of his National League career with the Boston Bruins. He led the team to Stanley Cup victories twice, in 1970 and in 1972.

Johnston started out with the Bruins in 1962-1963. He became the team's lead goalie but shared duties with Robert Perreault, a former Canadiens and Red Wings goalie. In 1963-1964, he was the last goaltender in history to play in every one of his team's 70 regular-season games. The Bruins weren't very formidable, however: from 1961 to 1967 they finished in last place six times out of seven.

Beginning in the 1967-1968 season, Johnston shared his job with Gerry Cheevers. Then after 11 seasons with the Bruins, he joined the Toronto Maple Leafs, playing only one season with that team. After a little over three years with St. Louis, he hung up his skates in Chicago at the age of 42.

Johnston decided to stay in hockey and worked as the Pittsburgh Penguins' head coach from 1980 to 1983 and as the team's general manager from 1983 to 1988. After a stint as the Hartford Whalers' general manager from 1989 to 1992, he eventually returned to Pittsburgh and resumed his functions as head coach.

Ed Johnston played 11 seasons with the Boston Bruins. He was 26 years old when he joined the team in 1962-1963. He won the Stanley Cup with the Bruins in 1970 and 1972.

# CESARE MANIAGO

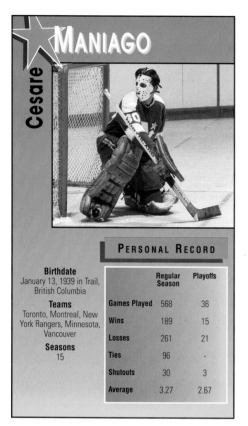

Cesare MANIAGO

### PERSONAL RECORD

**Birthdate**
January 13, 1939 in Trail,
British Columbia

**Teams**
Toronto, Montreal, New
York Rangers, Minnesota,
Vancouver

**Seasons**
15

|  | Regular Season | Playoffs |
|---|---|---|
| Games Played | 568 | 36 |
| Wins | 189 | 15 |
| Losses | 261 | 21 |
| Ties | 96 | - |
| Shutouts | 30 | 3 |
| Average | 3.27 | 2.67 |

Like many others, Cesare Maniago had to wait several seasons before getting his first real chance in the National League. He made his debut with the Toronto Maple Leafs in 1960-1961. He played only seven games at the time, but they were enough for his name to go down in history as the goalie who gave Bernard Geoffrion his 50th goal of the season, on March 16, 1961. Geoffrion became the second player to score 50 goals in a season, an honour he shared with his illustrious teammate Maurice Richard.

Maniago was sent back to the minors but returned to the Montreal Canadiens in 1962-1963, playing 14 games. Later, after two seasons with the Rangers, he was drafted by one of the six new expansion teams in 1967 and joined the Minnesota North Stars. During his first season with the team, Maniago managed six shutouts and led the North Stars to a playoff berth. The team lost in the semifinals, but with an average of 2.77 in regular-season play, Maniago had finally carved out a niche of his own in the NHL.

In 1971-1972 he enjoyed the best season of his career, maintaining an average of 2.65 in 43 games. His performance hoisted the North Stars to second place in the West Division, behind Chicago.

"Maniago was one of the good goalies I played against when I started in the National League," says Guy Lafleur, the former Canadiens star.

"He was an experienced player with a gift for guessing what moves players would try as they approached his net."

Maniago holds two records with the North Stars (which became the Dallas Stars in 1993-1994): most shutouts in one season (six in 1967-1968), and most shutouts overall (a total of 27).

Chicago Black Hawks star Bobby Hull has a very vivid memory of Maniago: it was at his expense that on March 12, 1966 Hull scored his 51st goal of the season, becoming the first player to score more than 50 goals in a single season. At the time, Maniago was playing with the New York Rangers.

Cesare Maniago was given the chance to play regularly in the National League when the Minnesota North Stars, one of six expansion teams, joined the Campbell Conference in 1967. On this play he makes a save while Jean Béliveau tries to retrieve the puck.

# BERNARD PARENT

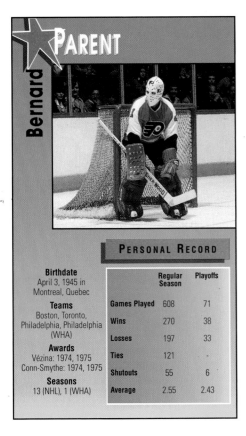

Bernard PARENT

## PERSONAL RECORD

**Birthdate**
April 3, 1945 in
Montreal, Quebec

**Teams**
Boston, Toronto,
Philadelphia, Philadelphia
(WHA)

**Awards**
Vézina: 1974, 1975
Conn-Smythe: 1974, 1975

**Seasons**
13 (NHL), 1 (WHA)

| | Regular Season | Playoffs |
|---|---|---|
| Games Played | 608 | 71 |
| Wins | 270 | 38 |
| Losses | 197 | 33 |
| Ties | 121 | - |
| Shutouts | 55 | 6 |
| Average | 2.55 | 2.43 |

The Philadelphia Flyers won the Stanley Cup twice during their history and in large part, they owe both victories to Bernard Parent. In 1973-1974, Parent maintained an average of 1.89 in 73 games, managing 12 shutouts. The following season his record included 12 shutouts again and he maintained an average of 2.03 and won 40 of his 68 games.

His performance during those two seasons earned him the Vézina Trophy (which he shared with Tony Esposito in 1974) and the Conn-Smythe Trophy for the most valuable player in the playoffs. During the 1974 playoffs Parent won 12 games, including two shutouts, for an average of 2.02. He did even better in the 1975 playoffs, with an average of 1.89.

Parent had started his career in the National League in 1965-1966, with Boston. In 1967, he and goalie Doug Favell were the first players drafted by the Flyers, a new expansion team. He played three full seasons with Philadelphia, going to the Toronto Maple Leafs during the 1970-1971 season. In 1972-1973 he joined the WHA as a member of the Philadelphia Blazers. He remained there for only one year, becoming the first player to return to the NHL when he signed a new contract with the Flyers.

He stayed with the team until the end of his career, in 1979. He was inducted into the Hockey Hall of Fame in 1984.

Bernard Parent makes a save at the expense of Canadiens player Yvan Cournoyer, known as "Roadrunner."

Lightning-quick, Bernard Parent positions his pad in exactly the right spot to block a shot by Frank Mahovlich.

While the Philadelphia Flyers were feared by all in the mid-1970s, notably because of the infamous Dave Schultz, the team could also count on Bernard Parent, who was considered the best goalie in the League.

Bernard Parent's Number 1 sweater was retired by the Flyers organization when his career came to an end. Parent managed 55 shutouts in his 13 seasons in the National League.

# GARY SMITH

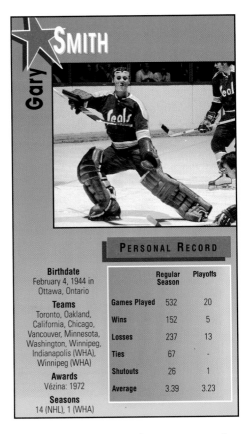

### PERSONAL RECORD

**Birthdate**
February 4, 1944 in
Ottawa, Ontario

**Teams**
Toronto, Oakland,
California, Chicago,
Vancouver, Minnesota,
Washington, Winnipeg,
Indianapolis (WHA),
Winnipeg (WHA)

**Awards**
Vézina: 1972

**Seasons**
14 (NHL), 1 (WHA)

|  | Regular Season | Playoffs |
|---|---|---|
| **Games Played** | 532 | 20 |
| **Wins** | 152 | 5 |
| **Losses** | 237 | 13 |
| **Ties** | 67 | - |
| **Shutouts** | 26 | 1 |
| **Average** | 3.39 | 3.23 |

After Gary Smith came to the National League, it wasn't long before he earned the nickname "Suitcase." Appropriate, since he played with no less than eight different teams in 14 years. Sadly, none of his teams won the Stanley Cup while he was with them.

Smith got his start with the Toronto Maple Leafs in 1965-1966, playing only five games in his two-year stay. After three seasons with the Oakland Seals and another with the California Golden Seals, he was traded to the Chicago Black Hawks, where he played backup to Tony Esposito for two seasons.

The imposing 6"5", 215-pound Smith enjoyed his glory days in 1971-1972, winning the Vézina Trophy along with Esposito. The Black Hawks boasted the best defense record in the League with Smith managing five shutouts in 28 games and maintaining an average of 2.42, the best among professional goalies.

Smith packed his suitcase a number of times in subsequent years, notably playing with Indianapolis and Winnipeg in the WHA during the 1978-1979 season. He ended his career in 1979-1980 with the Winnipeg Jets, one of four WHA teams admitted to the NHL.

Gary Smith in an Oakland Seals uniform, a team he played with for three seasons. In 14 years, he played 532 games in the NHL and 22 in the WHA.

# ROGATIEN VACHON

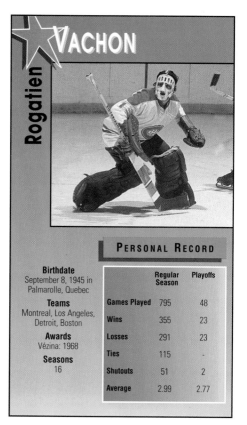

**Rogatien**
**VACHON**

### PERSONAL RECORD

**Birthdate**
September 8, 1945 in
Palmarolle, Quebec

**Teams**
Montreal, Los Angeles,
Detroit, Boston

**Awards**
Vézina: 1968

**Seasons**
16

| | Regular Season | Playoffs |
|---|---|---|
| Games Played | 795 | 48 |
| Wins | 355 | 23 |
| Losses | 291 | 23 |
| Ties | 115 | - |
| Shutouts | 51 | 2 |
| Average | 2.99 | 2.77 |

Rogatien Vachon, appointed president of the Los Angeles Kings in 1995, played a little over six seasons with the team, which recognized his talent by retiring his sweater, Number 30. However, his most exciting years were spent with the Canadiens and as that team's goalie, his name was added to the Stanley Cup three times, in 1968, 1969 and 1971.

While goaltending with the Houston team in the Central League—where Serge Savard and Jacques Lemaire were his teammates—Vachon was called up by the Canadiens during the 1966-1967 season. The 5"7" rookie did so well in 19 games that the team decided to trade Charlie Hodge. At age 22, Vachon shared the team's goaltending duties with veteran Lorne Worsley.

When the extremely talented Ken Dryden arrived on the scene during the 1970-1971 season, the Canadiens decided to trade Vachon to the Los Angeles Kings for the next season. He stayed with the Kings until the end of the 1977-1978 season, when he was traded to the Detroit Red Wings. He experienced the best season of his career in 1974-1975—with an average of 2.24—as the Kings moved beyond the 100-point mark for the first time since they had joined the League. The team finished second in the Norris Division with 105 points, eight less than the Canadiens. Vachon and the Kings had allowed only 185 goals.

In 1976 Vachon was particularly spectacular during the Canada Cup tournament, ensuring an astounding win for Team Canada. Selected to play on the second All Star team twice (1974-1975 and 1976-1977), his name was added to the Vézina Trophy in 1968, an honour he shared with Lorne Worsley. He retired at the end of the 1981-1982 season after playing two seasons with Boston.

Rogatien Vachon played with the Canadiens for five seasons before being traded to Los Angeles in November 1971. He became a major star with the Kings and in recognition, the team retired his sweater, Number 30.

Rogatien Vachon reaches out to stop a shot from Frank Mahovlich of the Canadiens.

A goaltender who stood only 5"7", Vachon played 795 games in his 16 years in the National League.

As the play moves out of the Canadiens zone, Rogatien Vachon tries to distract an opponent.

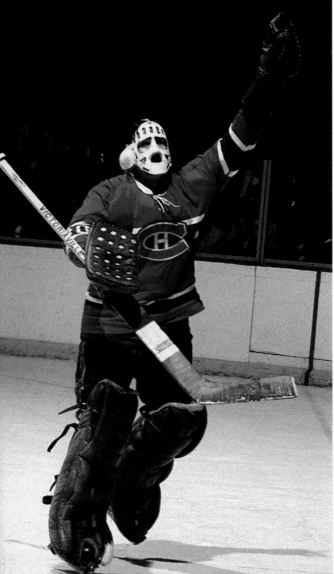

Alone with Rogatien Vachon, winger Murray Wilson of the Canadiens is foiled by the Kings' diminutive goalie.

Rogatien Vachon and Philippe Myre were teammates for two seasons with the Canadiens. This photo was taken by Denis Brodeur during a Canadiens practice at the Forum.

Vachon made his start in the National League with the Canadiens during the 1966-1967 season. Ken Dryden's outstanding performance with the Habs in the spring of 1971 led to Vachon's departure from Montreal.

# ERNIE WAKELY

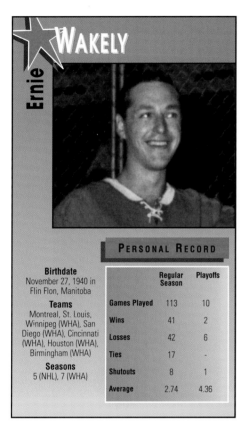

**PERSONAL RECORD**

**Birthdate**
November 27, 1940 in
Flin Flon, Manitoba

**Teams**
Montreal, St. Louis,
Winnipeg (WHA), San
Diego (WHA), Cincinnati
(WHA), Houston (WHA),
Birmingham (WHA)

**Seasons**
5 (NHL), 7 (WHA)

| | Regular Season | Playoffs |
|---|---|---|
| Games Played | 113 | 10 |
| Wins | 41 | 2 |
| Losses | 42 | 6 |
| Ties | 17 | - |
| Shutouts | 8 | 1 |
| Average | 2.74 | 4.36 |

As a professional, Ernie Wakely played twice as many games in the World Hockey Association as he did in the National League. He played his first NHL game with the Canadiens, during the 1962-1963 season, and later was sent down to the minors before getting his next chance to play for Montreal in 1968-1969. Traded to the St. Louis Blues in June 1969 in return for Bobby Schmautz and Norm Beaudin, he stayed with that team for three years.

With the Blues, who made it to the Stanley Cup finals in their first two seasons in the League, Wakely had the opportunity to prove himself. In 30 games in 1969-1970, he managed four shutouts and maintained an average of 2.11, the best in the League. That year he shared his job with veterans Jacques Plante and Glenn Hall.

The following season Jacques Plante was traded to Toronto and Wakely became the team's lead goalie. In 51 games he maintained an average of 2.79. In 1971, he took part in his only All Star game, backing up Tony Esposito for the West Division's team, which won 2-1. Wakely played a third and final season with the Blues (1971-1972, 3.42 average in 30 games) before joining the World Hockey Association.

In 1972-1973 the goalie went to the Winnipeg Jets, where he stayed for two years. When the WHA was dissolved at the end of the 1978-1979 season, Wakely played with four other teams but never experienced the thrill of a championship. In 1979, at 39, he decided to retire.

Ernie Wakely in the Canadiens uniform. During his career, the goaltender played only two games with Montreal.

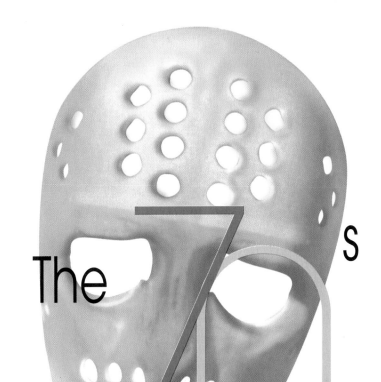

# The 70s

T he 70s were especially memorable because of the famous Super Series: the 1972 showdown between a Canadian team composed of National League professionals and the Soviet Union's national team. A 20-year-old Soviet goaltender for the Soviets made a very strong impression during that series. His name was Vladislav Tretiak, but he was never to play in the National League.

Ken Dryden was the League's dominant figure among this decade's goalies. In 1971, he made a spectacular debut with the Canadiens, beginning an eight-year career during which he won the Vézina Trophy five times.

The Philadelphia Flyers were the first 1967 expansion team to win the Stanley Cup. They came out on top in two consecutive years, notably thanks to their brilliant veteran goalie, Bernard Parent.

The other major stars of the 70s were Tony Esposito in Chicago and Rogatien Vachon, who had gone from the Canadiens to the Los Angeles Kings.

The decade was also marked by the 1972 founding of a new professional circuit, the World Hockey Association (WHA), which lasted until 1979. The advent of the new league created a great deal of upheaval, including salary inflation and, for some stars, a round of "musical teams." The new league gave veterans a chance to prolong their careers and newcomers an opportunity to hone their skills.

Gerry Cheevers was one of several who added a few jewels to their crowns, and Richard Brodeur, John Garrett, Michel Dion, Ed Mio and Mike Liut made very interesting debuts that proved to be their passports to the National League.
When the WHA was dissolved, the National League picked up four teams: the Edmonton Oilers, the Winnipeg Jets, the Quebec Nordiques and the Hartford Whalers.

Defenceman Miles Zaharko of the Chicago Black Hawks rescues teammate Tony Esposito, in a precarious position after stopping an attack launched by Mark Napier of the Canadiens.

# DANIEL BOUCHARD

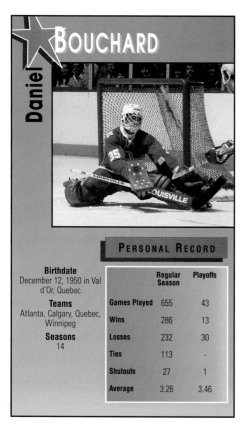

**PERSONAL RECORD**

**Birthdate**
December 12, 1950 in Val d'Or, Quebec

**Teams**
Atlanta, Calgary, Quebec, Winnipeg

**Seasons**
14

| | Regular Season | Playoffs |
|---|---|---|
| Games Played | 655 | 43 |
| Wins | 286 | 13 |
| Losses | 232 | 30 |
| Ties | 113 | - |
| Shutouts | 27 | 1 |
| Average | 3.26 | 3.46 |

Picked by the Boston Bruins during the second round of the 1970 draft, Daniel Bouchard made his start in the National League in 1972-1973 with another team, the Atlanta Flames. Under head coach Bernard Geoffrion, Bouchard and former Canadiens goalie Philippe Myre were a formidable duo in the net. In both goalies' second season with Atlanta, the Flames made it to the playoffs, but were stopped in the quarter finals by the Philadelphia Flyers.

In 1975-1976 Bouchard achieved the best average in his career: 2.54 in 47 games. He led the League in 1978-1979, with 32 wins in 64 games.

He played eight full seasons with the Flames before being traded to the Quebec Nordiques in January 1981 in exchange for rightwinger Jamie Hislop. The Nordiques finished fourth in the Adams Division and took on the Canadiens, who had finished in first place with 27 points more than Quebec. Naturally the Habs were heavy favourites, but the Nordiques surprised everyone by beating the Canadiens in five games, thanks to an overtime goal by Dale Hunter. Bouchard's solid performance made it possible for his team to eliminate the Boston Bruins in seven games, but the Nordiques finally fell in the conference finals after four games against the New York Islanders.

Bouchard played his worst season in 1982-1983, with an average of 4.01 in 50 games. But he had spunk, rebounding spectacularly the following season and achieving an average of 3.20 in 57 games. That year the Nordiques' goalies, Daniel Bouchard, Clint Malarchuk and Mario Gosselin, gave away 58 fewer goals than the previous year. The Canadiens eliminated the Nordiques in the Adams Division final, in six games, a series that included the infamous "Good Friday match." In 1984-1985 Bouchard played only 29 games when Mario Gosselin and Richard Sévigny were the team's other goaltenders. The next season Bouchard went to the Winnipeg Jets, where he played for one year before hanging up his pads at age 36.

Daniel Bouchard, a butterfly-style goaltender, makes a great save against Pierre Mondou of the Canadiens.

(Opposite page) Acquired by the Atlanta Flames from the Boston Bruins during the June 1972 expansion draft, Daniel Bouchard played eight seasons with the team. In this photo, Canadiens Murray Wilson and Peter Mahovlich test his mettle.

# RICHARD BRODEUR

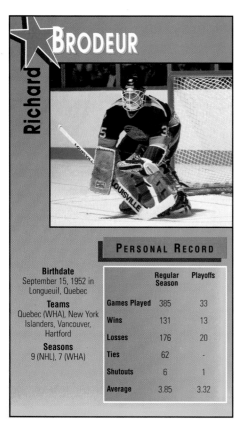

## Richard BRODEUR

### PERSONAL RECORD

**Birthdate**
September 15, 1952 in
Longueuil, Quebec

**Teams**
Quebec (WHA), New York
Islanders, Vancouver,
Hartford

**Seasons**
9 (NHL), 7 (WHA)

| | Regular Season | Playoffs |
|---|---|---|
| Games Played | 385 | 33 |
| Wins | 131 | 13 |
| Losses | 176 | 20 |
| Ties | 62 | - |
| Shutouts | 6 | 1 |
| Average | 3.85 | 3.32 |

Richard Brodeur was 20 when he began his career as a professional hockey player with the Quebec Nordiques in the World Hockey Association. Considered to be one of the best goaltenders in Canadian junior hockey, he had won the Memorial Cup with the Cornwall Royals the previous season.

He played seven seasons with the Nordiques. In 1976-1977, he helped them win the Avco Cup. His best average came in 1973-1974: 3.32 in 30 games.

When the WHA was dissolved, Brodeur joined the New York Islanders for the 1979-1980 season, playing only two games. The following season he went to the Vancouver Canucks, where he would be one of the team's biggest stars for the next seven seasons.

Nicknamed "King Richard," Brodeur was particularly stupendous in 1981-1982 when he led the Canucks to the Stanley Cup playoffs against the New York Islanders. To everyone's amazement, the Canucks had managed to eliminate Calgary, Los Angeles and Chicago along the way.

"The highlight of my career came during those playoffs, when we beat Chicago in five games in the conference finals," remembers Richard Brodeur. "It was something very special because Tony Esposito, the other team's goalie, had been my idol since childhood." Brodeur played five more seasons with the Canucks, although the team never made it all the way to

the Stanley Cup finals again. The team's fans would have to wait until 1994 to once again dream of capturing the coveted Cup, when Vancouver met the New York Rangers but lost in a seven-game final series. When rookie Kirk McLean came to the Canucks in 1987-1988, Brodeur was traded to the Hartford Whalers. At the end of that season, he decided to hang up his skates for good. "When Richard was playing for the National League," comments Denis Brodeur, "a lot of people thought that he was my son and he had a lot of fun calling out "Hi, Dad!' each time our paths crossed. He was always a joker, and he was well-liked by his teammates."

Richard Brodeur was only 20 when he began his career as a professional hockey player with the Quebec Nordiques, in the World Hockey Association.

During a game at the Montreal Forum, Richard Brodeur robs Guy Carbonneau of a goal, under referee Dan Marouelli's nose.

After playing with the Nordiques in the World Hockey Association from its founding until it was dismantled in 1979, Richard Brodeur came very close to winning the Stanley Cup with the Canucks in 1982. Vancouver lost in a four-game series against the New York Islanders, who won their third consecutive Stanley Cup in the process.

# ANDY BROWN

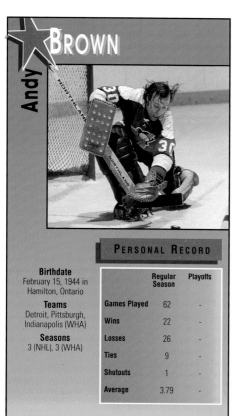

**BROWN**

Andy

NORTHLAND

**PERSONAL RECORD**

**Birthdate**
February 15, 1944 in
Hamilton, Ontario

**Teams**
Detroit, Pittsburgh,
Indianapolis (WHA)

**Seasons**
3 (NHL), 3 (WHA)

| | Regular Season | Playoffs |
|---|---|---|
| Games Played | 62 | - |
| Wins | 22 | - |
| Losses | 26 | - |
| Ties | 9 | - |
| Shutouts | 1 | - |
| Average | 3.79 | - |

Andy Brown played only 62 games in his three years in the National League. He began playing as a professional in 1971-1972 with the Detroit Red Wings. He played only 10 games and was traded to the Pittsburgh Penguins the next season. With his new team Brown was the goalie who played the most games in the 1973-1974 season, a total of 36, compared to 20 for rookie Gary Inness. He maintained an average of 3.53 and the Penguins finished fifth in their division, missing the playoffs for the fifth time in seven seasons.

The next season Brown decided to jump to the World Hockey Association, playing for the Indianapolis Racers.

He became the team's lead goalie, but maintained a fairly poor average of 4.15 in 52 games. In the next two seasons with the Racers, Brown played 24 and 10 games respectively before ending his career.

Andy Brown in the Pittsburgh Penguins uniform makes a nice save in Peter Mahovlich. Also in the photo is Guy Lafleur, in the background.

# JACQUES CARON

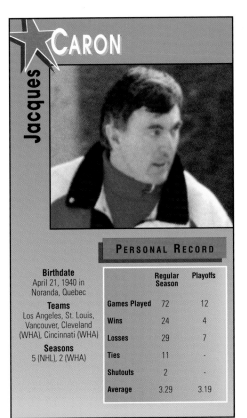

**Jacques CARON**

### PERSONAL RECORD

**Birthdate**
April 21, 1940 in
Noranda, Quebec

**Teams**
Los Angeles, St. Louis,
Vancouver, Cleveland
(WHA), Cincinnati (WHA)

**Seasons**
5 (NHL), 2 (WHA)

|  | Regular Season | Playoffs |
|---|---|---|
| Games Played | 72 | 12 |
| Wins | 24 | 4 |
| Losses | 29 | 7 |
| Ties | 11 | - |
| Shutouts | 2 | - |
| Average | 3.29 | 3.19 |

Jacques Caron enjoyed a brief moment of glory at age 19, when the Peterborough Petes won the Ontario Hockey Association Championship in 1959; at the time, he was sharing goaltending duties with Denis Dejordy. He came to the National League only in 1967-1968; that year, he played only one game with the Los Angeles Kings. He played three other games with the team the following season, then joined the St. Louis Blues in 1971-1972. In two seasons there he played only 58 games, subsequently joining the Vancouver Canucks briefly before switching to the World Hockey Association in 1975-1976; he played two seasons in the WHA.

Although he played only 72 games in the NHL and 26 in the WHA, Jacques Caron is one of the most highly regarded goaltending coaches in the National League today. He has held the position with the New Jersey Devils since the 1993-1994 season, after working with the Whalers organization. Notably, his teaching contributed to making Martin Brodeur one of the best goalies in the League and in his capacity as a coach he experienced the thrill of winning a Stanley Cup in 1995, with the Devils.

Jacques Caron, playing with the St. Louis Blues, stops speedy rightwinger Yvan Cournoyer as centre Garry Unger watches.

# JOE DALEY

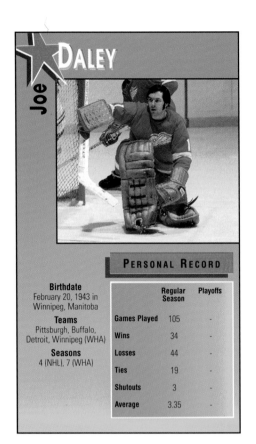

## PERSONAL RECORD

| **Birthdate**<br>February 20, 1943 in<br>Winnipeg, Manitoba | Regular<br>Season | Playoffs |
|---|---|---|
| **Teams**<br>Pittsburgh, Buffalo,<br>Detroit, Winnipeg (WHA) | Games Played | 105 | - |
| **Seasons**<br>4 (NHL), 7 (WHA) | Wins | 34 | - |
| | Losses | 44 | - |
| | Ties | 19 | - |
| | Shutouts | 3 | - |
| | Average | 3.35 | - |

Joe Daley played almost three times more games in the World Hockey Association than he did in the National League, where he made his debut in 1968-1969 with the Pittsburgh Penguins. He played only two seasons and 38 games with the Penguins before joining the Buffalo Sabres. During his one and only season with Buffalo, in 1970-1971, he played the most games in a single season (38), maintaining an average of 3.70.

In 1972-1973, after one year with Detroit, he became the lead goalie for the Winnipeg Jets in the WHA. He played seven seasons with the team. In 1975-1976, he played 62 games and maintained an average of 2.84, the best in his career. The Jets won the division championship and beat the Houston Aeros in the finals. Daley and the Jets took top honours in the WHA again in 1978 and in 1979, the Association's last year of existence. Aged 36 at the time, Daley decided to end his career.

# JOHN DAVIDSON

John Davidson was only 19 years old when he joined the St. Louis Blues in 1973-1974. He played 39 games, maintaining an average of 3.08, the best in his career. After another season with the Blues he went to the New York Rangers, where he quickly became a crowd favourite. In 1978-1979, his performance helped the Rangers reach the Stanley Cup finals for the first time since 1972. Davidson maintained an average of 2.28 during the playoffs and was one of the heros in his team's win against the New York Islanders in the semifinals. In the final round, however, the Rangers were easy prey for the Montreal Canadiens, who won the Stanley Cup for the fourth consecutive year.

With two injured knees, Davidson underwent surgery and came back to play 10 games in 1980-1981. He was in the net for the Rangers only three times in the next two seasons. After his retirement, he began a new career as a television commentator for the Rangers.

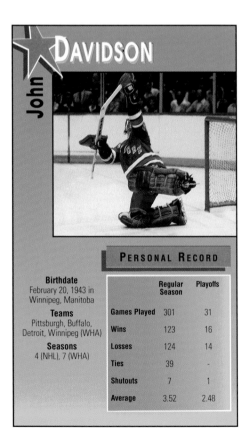

## PERSONAL RECORD

| **Birthdate**<br>February 20, 1943 in<br>Winnipeg, Manitoba | Regular<br>Season | Playoffs |
|---|---|---|
| **Teams**<br>Pittsburgh, Buffalo,<br>Detroit, Winnipeg (WHA) | Games Played | 301 | 31 |
| **Seasons**<br>4 (NHL), 7 (WHA) | Wins | 123 | 16 |
| | Losses | 124 | 14 |
| | Ties | 39 | - |
| | Shutouts | 7 | 1 |
| | Average | 3.52 | 2.48 |

# GERRY DESJARDINS

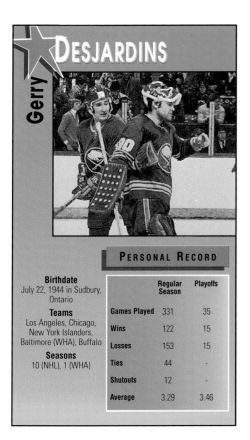

**PERSONAL RECORD**

**Birthdate**
July 22, 1944 in Sudbury, Ontario

**Teams**
Los Angeles, Chicago, New York Islanders, Baltimore (WHA), Buffalo

**Seasons**
10 (NHL), 1 (WHA)

| | Regular Season | Playoffs |
|---|---|---|
| Games Played | 331 | 35 |
| Wins | 122 | 15 |
| Losses | 153 | 15 |
| Ties | 44 | - |
| Shutouts | 12 | - |
| Average | 3.29 | 3.46 |

Gerry Desjardins played 10 seasons in the National League. He began his career with the Los Angeles Kings in 1968-1969, playing 60 of the team's 76 games. Traded to the Chicago Black Hawks during the following season, he played 22 games with his new team and helped earn the Vézina Trophy by maintaining an average of 2.42.

After two seasons in the New York Islanders uniform, Desjardins played 41 games in the WHA with the Baltimore Blades in 1974-1975, returning to the National League with the Buffalo Sabres to end the season. In 1975-1976, Desjardins was the team's lead goalie, playing 55 games and maintaining an average of 2.95. The Sabres, who had lost a six-game series to the Philadelphia Flyers in the previous spring's Stanley Cup finals, lost again in six games, this time to the New York Islanders in the quarter finals. The next season's scenario was identical, with Desjardins playing 49 of his team's 80 games. In 1977-1978, Desjardins played only three games with the Sabres, a factor in his decision to retire.

# MICHEL DION

In 12 years with the professionals, Michel Dion played with five teams, including two in the World Hockey Association when he was still a very young player. In 1975-1976 with Indianapolis, his second season in the WHA, he enjoyed his best year, maintaining an average of 2.74 in 31 games.

When the WHA was dissolved at the end of the 1978-1979 season, Dion came to the National Hockey League with the Quebec Nordiques, where he played 50 games.

The following season, 1980-1981, Michel Dion was traded to the Winnipeg Jets, playing only 26 games. His stay in the West was short-lived and he became the Pittsburgh Penguins' lead goalie in 1981-1982. He played 62 games and maintained an average of 3.79, earning the privilege of playing in the February 9, 1982 All Star game along with Don Edwards of the Buffalo Sabres. Dion played three more seasons with Pittsburgh before retiring in 1985.

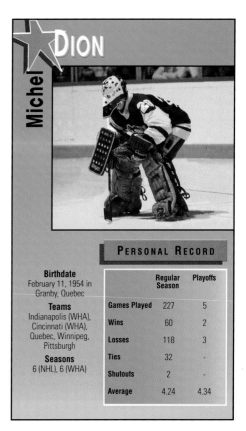

**PERSONAL RECORD**

**Birthdate**
February 11, 1954 in Granby, Quebec

**Teams**
Indianapolis (WHA), Cincinnati (WHA), Quebec, Winnipeg, Pittsburgh

**Seasons**
6 (NHL), 6 (WHA)

| | Regular Season | Playoffs |
|---|---|---|
| Games Played | 227 | 5 |
| Wins | 60 | 2 |
| Losses | 118 | 3 |
| Ties | 32 | - |
| Shutouts | 2 | - |
| Average | 4.24 | 4.34 |

# KEN DRYDEN

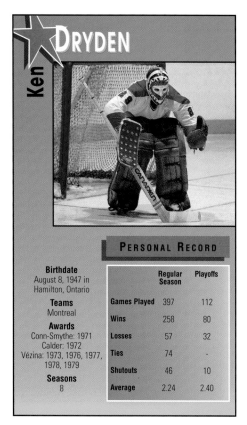

**Ken Dryden**

### PERSONAL RECORD

**Birthdate**
August 8, 1947 in
Hamilton, Ontario

**Teams**
Montreal

**Awards**
Conn-Smythe: 1971
Calder: 1972
Vézina: 1973, 1976, 1977,
1978, 1979

**Seasons**
8

|  | Regular Season | Playoffs |
|---|---|---|
| Games Played | 397 | 112 |
| Wins | 258 | 80 |
| Losses | 57 | 32 |
| Ties | 74 | - |
| Shutouts | 46 | 10 |
| Average | 2.24 | 2.40 |

Ken Dryden's record is very impressive considering that his career in the National League spanned only eight years. He was the star goalie of only one team, the Montreal Canadiens. He had his name engraved on the Stanley Cup six times, won the Vézina Trophy five times, and was selected for the first All Star team five times. Only four years after announcing his retirement, at the age of 32, he was inducted into the Hockey Hall of Fame. A truly fabulous career!

As soon as he began playing for the Canadiens in late 1971, Dryden

To everyone's amazement, and particularly that of the Boston Bruins who were eliminated by the Canadiens, Ken Dryden consistently worked wonders in the net in the spring of 1971. The rookie goalie was just beginning what was to be a short but glorious career in the National League.

demonstrated his exceptional talent. "He was consistent, his teammates knew that they could count on him," says former team captain Yvan Cournoyer.

Dryden was indeed spectacular during the 1971 playoffs, first helping the Canadiens to get rid of their arch rivals, the Boston Bruins, in the preliminary round. Very calm, quicker than he appeared, he was the driving force behind the Stanley Cup win against the Chicago Black Hawks in the finals. He richly deserved the Conn-Smythe Trophy, and was the first goalie to earn the honour.

"Ken Dryden and Jacques Plante are undoubtedly the two best goaltenders I saw playing during my career in the National League," observes Henri Richard.

Screened by a flawless defence known as the "Big Three"—which notably included Serge Savard, Guy Lapointe and Larry Robinson—

Dryden enjoyed a real dream year in 1976-1977. The Canadiens suffered only eight losses in 70 games and won the nineteenth Stanley Cup in their history. When the regular season ended, Dryden's could boast the fantastic average of 2.14.

"Ken's biggest strength was his ability to concentrate, and he was a hard worker," comments Pierre Larouche, the first NHL player to score 50 goals with two teams, Pittsburgh and Montreal. "He'd often ask me and Pierre Mondou to stay on the ice after practice to help him put in more time stopping pucks."

Hockey fans have vivid memories of Dryden's signature pose, which he struck whenever play was stopped for one reason or another: leaning on his stick, ramrod straight, totally immobile! He and Jacques Plante are the only goaltenders with six Stanley Cups to their credit.

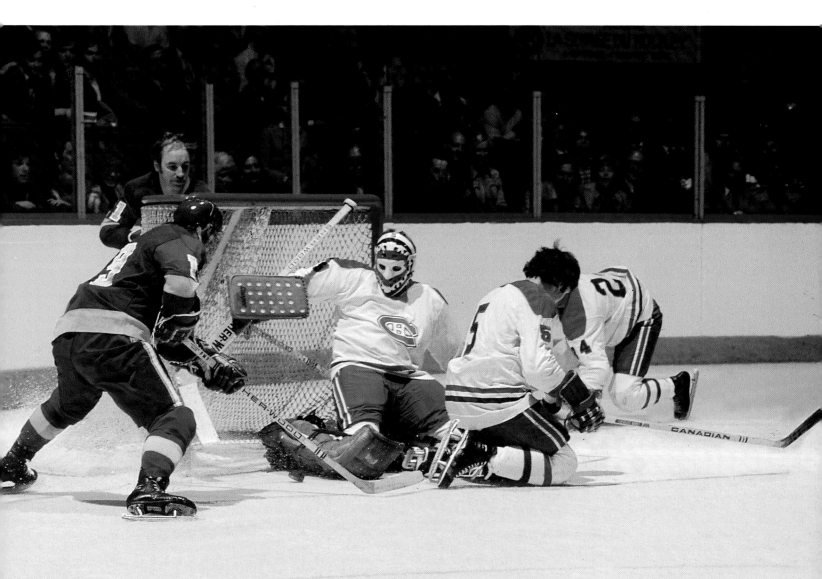

With a little help from defenceman Guy Lapointe, one of the Big Three, Ken Dryden withstands an onslaught led by Butch Goring of the New York Islanders.

# GOALIES, GUARDIANS OF THE NET

Ken Dryden holds off a Russian player during a game at the Forum in Montreal.

In 1983, only four years after his retirement, Ken Dryden was inducted into the Hockey Hall of Fame. He became the sixth goaltender to receive the honour, following in the footsteps of Georges Vézina, George Hainsworth, Bill Durnan, Jacques Plante and Lorne Worsley.

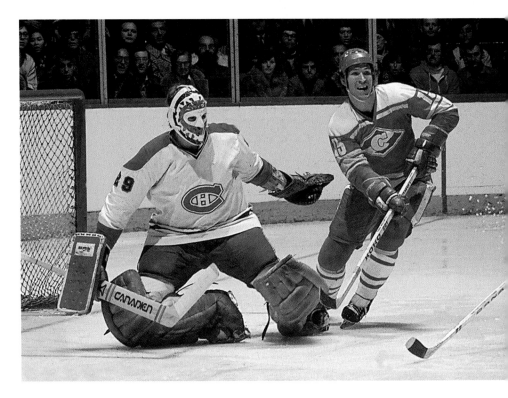

Alone in front of Ken Dryden, forward Pierre Jarry of the Toronto Maple Leafs fails to slip the puck by the Habs star. Ken Dryden was definitely one of the greatest goalies of the 70s, as his astounding personal record attests.

# DON EDWARDS

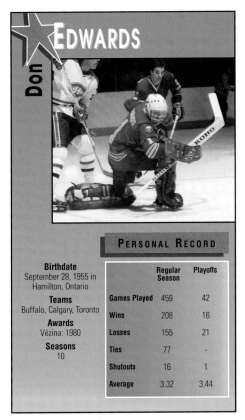

### PERSONAL RECORD

**Birthdate**
September 28, 1955 in
Hamilton, Ontario

**Teams**
Buffalo, Calgary, Toronto

**Awards**
Vézina: 1980

**Seasons**
10

| | Regular Season | Playoffs |
|---|---|---|
| Games Played | 459 | 42 |
| Wins | 208 | 16 |
| Losses | 155 | 21 |
| Ties | 77 | - |
| Shutouts | 16 | 1 |
| Average | 3.32 | 3.44 |

In 1980, four years after his start in the National Hockey League, Don Edwards, goaltender for the Buffalo Sabres, won the Vézina Trophy along with Robert Sauvé. He had played 49 games, 17 more than Sauvé, and had maintained an average of 2.57. For the first time ever, the Sabres finished at the top of the Adams Division.

In 1977-1978, in his second NHL season with Buffalo, Edwards led the League for the most wins (38 in 72 games), maintaining an average of 2.64. He had also managed five shutouts, his career high for a single season.

After playing less than 50 games in the two previous seasons, Edwards was a key player for coaches Scotty Bowman and Jim Roberts in 1981-1982. He played 62 games and finished the season with an average of 3.51.

At the end of the 1981-1982 season, he was traded to the Calgary Flames. He stayed with the team for three years and ended his career with the Toronto Maple Leafs in 1985-1986.

After the 1995-1996 season, Edwards and Dominik Hasek share the Sabres' team record for most career shutouts, with 14.

Don Edwards makes a quick move in his net, anticipating a duel with Guy Lafleur of the Canadiens.

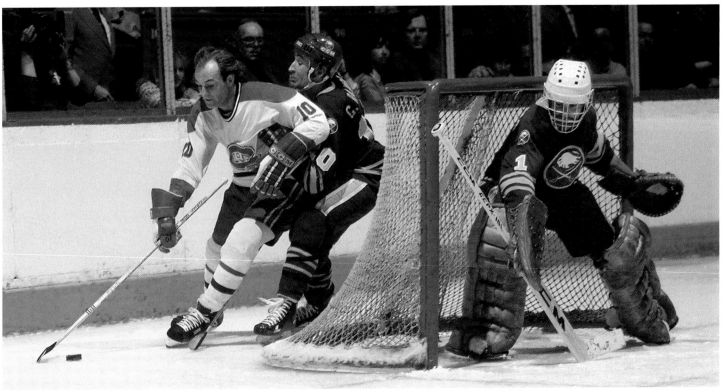

# TONY ESPOSITO

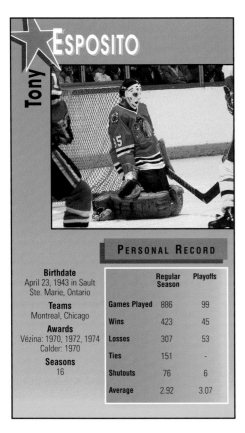

**Tony Esposito**

### PERSONAL RECORD

**Birthdate**
April 23, 1943 in Sault
Ste. Marie, Ontario

**Teams**
Montreal, Chicago

**Awards**
Vézina: 1970, 1972, 1974
Calder: 1970

**Seasons**
16

| | Regular Season | Playoffs |
|---|---|---|
| Games Played | 886 | 99 |
| Wins | 423 | 45 |
| Losses | 307 | 53 |
| Ties | 151 | - |
| Shutouts | 76 | 6 |
| Average | 2.92 | 3.07 |

During the Montreal Canadiens' training camp in September 1968, Tony Esposito, a 25-year-old rookie, was very impressive alongside Lorne Worsley and Rogatien Vachon. He played only 13 games during the season, but made his mark by managing two shutouts and maintaining an average of 2.73. In 1969, he helped the team win the Stanley Cup before being traded to the Chicago Black Hawks. He was never again to see his name added to the Cup, but he had an illustrious career with his new team, nonetheless.

Tony Esposito tries to regain his balance after making a save; meanwhile, defenceman Doug Hicks of the Black Hawks is busy keeping Steve Shutt away from the puck.

In 1969-1970, he set a record that still stands: 15 shutouts in a single season. Based on his average of 2.17 in 63 games, he was awarded the Calder and Vézina Trophies. He reprised his Vézina win again in 1972 and 1974.

Esposito holds the League record for most seasons with 30 wins or more, a total of eight in 16 years. He led his team to the Stanley Cup finals twice and ranks third behind Terry Sawchuk and Jacques Plante for most career wins by a goalie, with 423.

The Hawks' Number 35 had his best year in 1971-1972, with an average of 1.77 in 48 games.

Goalie Richard Brodeur, who played with the Vancouver Canucks, was one of Esposito's biggest admirers. "I remember what he told me when I was starting out, "Richard, being a goalie isn't complicated: stay between the puck and the net!" His explanation was simple, but so accurate! Tony could predict a play, he had a nice butterfly style, and his strength was his concentration."

Tony Esposito was inducted into the Hockey Hall of Fame in 1988, four years after his brother, Phil. The two Espositos never played for the same team in the National League, but they played together several times, notably in the 1972 games between Team Canada and the USSR.

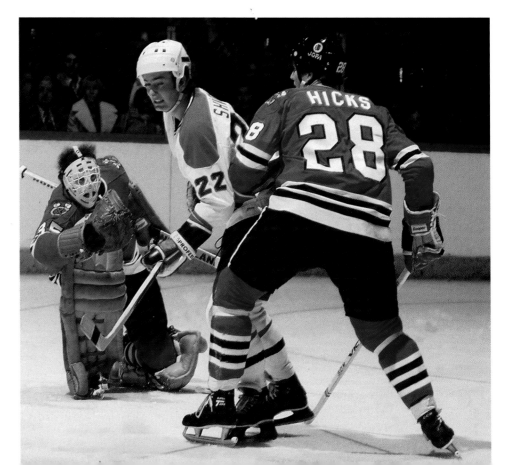

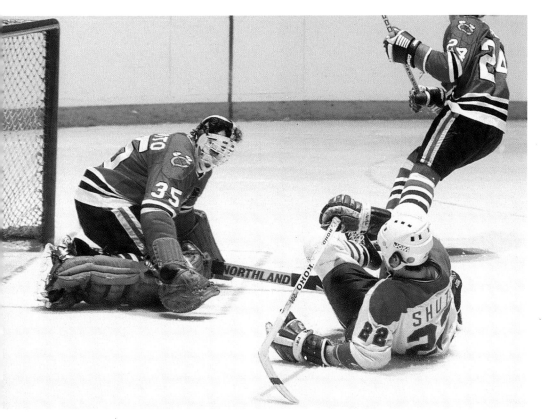

Tony Esposito makes a save on Steve Shutt of the Canadiens, who falls to the ice after a powerful shot on the Black Hawks goaltender.

With 76 shutouts in 16 seasons, Tony Esposito ranks seventh for career shutouts by goalies in the National League.

Photos of Tony Esposito in a Canadiens uniform are rare since he played only 13 games with the Montreal team. Denis Brodeur took this shot during a Montreal-Chicago game. Behind Esposito is defenceman Jean-Claude Tremblay.

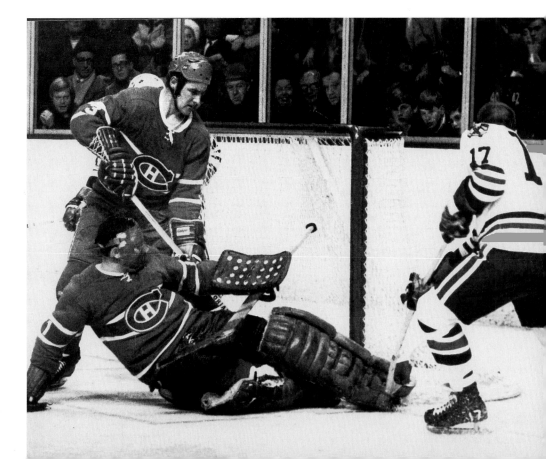

Tony Esposito makes a nice save while leftwinger Yvon Lambert waits in vain for the puck to reach his stick.

In 1973-1974, Tony Esposito played in 70 of his team's 78 games. He was responsible for 34 wins, managed 10 shutouts and maintained an average of 2.04.

(Opposite page) On this play Tony Esposito stops both the puck and Pierre Mondou of the Canadiens; defenceman Doug Wilson rushes to his goalie's rescue.

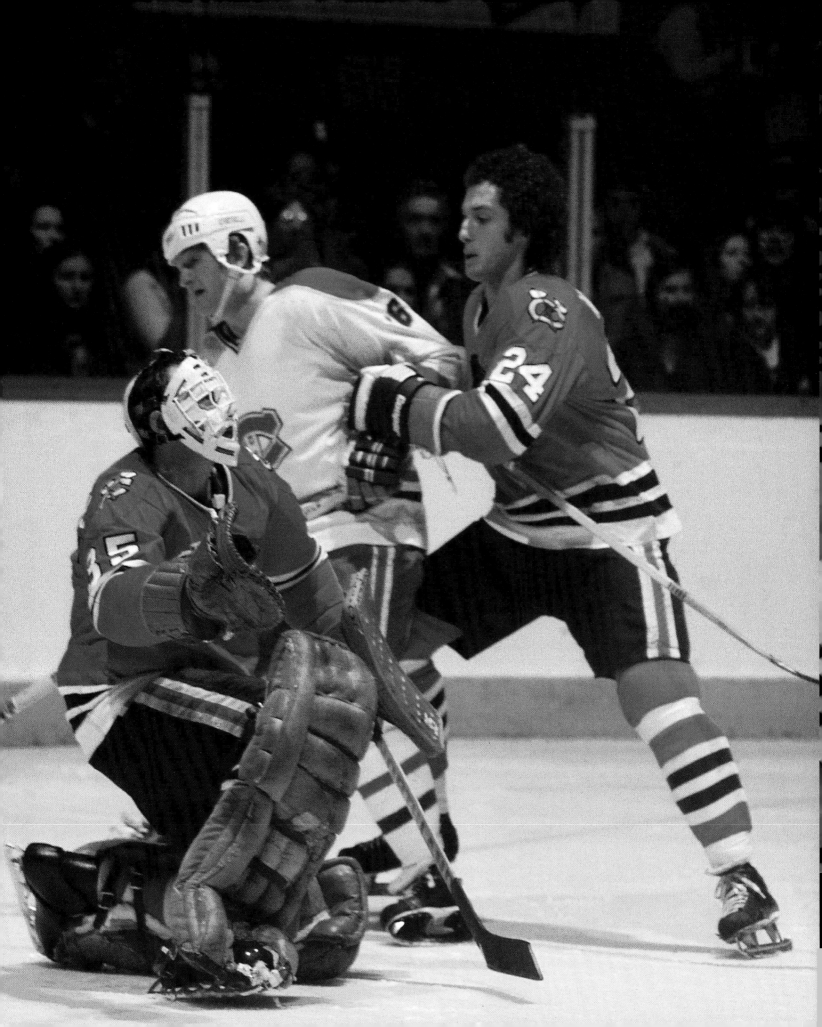

# DOUG FAVELL

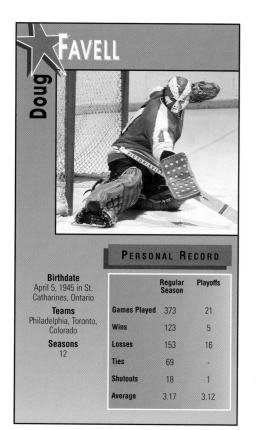

**FAVELL**

**Doug**

### PERSONAL RECORD

**Birthdate**
April 5, 1945 in St.
Catharines, Ontario

**Teams**
Philadelphia, Toronto,
Colorado

**Seasons**
12

| | Regular Season | Playoffs |
|---|---|---|
| Games Played | 373 | 21 |
| Wins | 123 | 5 |
| Losses | 153 | 16 |
| Ties | 69 | - |
| Shutouts | 18 | 1 |
| Average | 3.17 | 3.12 |

When the Philadelphia Flyers came into the National League in 1967-1968, the team recruited two goaltenders, Bernard Parent and Doug Favell. Both were 22 years old, but Parent had two years of experience in the NHL, with Boston, while Favell was a rookie.

Favell played six seasons with the Flyers and was at his best during the first year, with an average of 2.27 in 37 games. That same season, on November 7, 1968, he also went down in history by giving up eight goals to Red Berenson of the St. Louis Blues. Berenson's exploit set a modern-day record that would be tied in 1976 by Darryl Sittler of the Toronto Maple Leafs.

In 1973-1974, Favell was traded by the Flyers and consequently missed the chance to take part in winning the Stanley Cup with the team known as the "Broad Street Bullies." In his last season with Philadelphia Favell had done well, playing 44 games for an average of 2.83. To make up for Favell's departure to play for Toronto, the Flyers acquired Wayne Stephenson, who played only 12 games that season.

Favell played only three seasons with the Maple Leafs before joining the Colorado Rockies for the 1976-1977 season. Three years later, the goalie decided it was time to retire.

# JOHN GARRETT

John Garrett began his professional hockey career in 1973-1974 with the Minnesota Fighting Saints, during the World Hockey Association's second season. During the 1975-1976 season, he was traded to the Toronto Toros. One season later, he joined the Birmingham Bulls and played 65 games with that team—his highest career total—maintaining an average of 3.53. Garrett played with four different teams in the WHA until it was dissolved in 1978-1979. After becoming the goalie for the New England Whalers in 1978-1979, Garrett stuck with the team, which later joined the National Hockey League as the Hartford Whalers.

For two years he was the lead goalie for that team, which made it to the playoffs in its first year in the NHL. However, the Whalers were defeated in the first round by the Montreal Canadiens.

During the 1981-1982 season, Garrett was traded to the Quebec Nordiques, where he played only briefly before going to the Vancouver Canucks the following year. As a backup to Richard Brodeur, who had also made his debut in the WHA, Garrett ended his career with the team in 1984-1985, after playing only 10 games and allowing 44 goals.

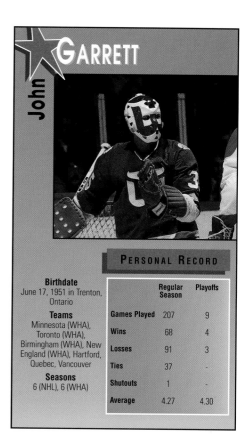

**GARRETT**

**John**

### PERSONAL RECORD

**Birthdate**
June 17, 1951 in Trenton,
Ontario

**Teams**
Minnesota (WHA),
Toronto (WHA),
Birmingham (WHA), New
England (WHA), Hartford,
Quebec, Vancouver

**Seasons**
6 (NHL), 6 (WHA)

| | Regular Season | Playoffs |
|---|---|---|
| Games Played | 207 | 9 |
| Wins | 68 | 4 |
| Losses | 91 | 3 |
| Ties | 37 | - |
| Shutouts | 1 | - |
| Average | 4.27 | 4.30 |

# GILLES GILBERT

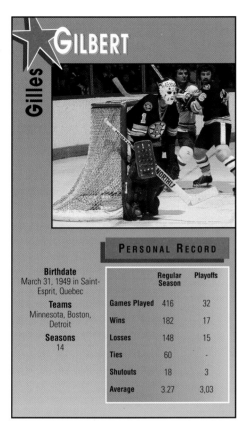

**PERSONAL RECORD**

**Birthdate**
March 31, 1949 in Saint-Esprit, Quebec

**Teams**
Minnesota, Boston, Detroit

**Seasons**
14

| | Regular Season | Playoffs |
|---|---|---|
| Games Played | 416 | 32 |
| Wins | 182 | 17 |
| Losses | 148 | 15 |
| Ties | 60 | - |
| Shutouts | 18 | 3 |
| Average | 3.27 | 3,03 |

After starting out in the National League in 1969-1970 and playing four seasons with the Minnesota North Stars, Gilles Gilbert was traded to the Boston Bruins, where he experienced the best years of his career.

He spent seven seasons with the Bruins, who made it to the Stanley Cup playoffs three times without ever coming out on top. In 1975-1976, he set a League record by winning 17 consecutive games in the Boston net. His glory days were in 1977-1978, when he maintained an average of 2.53 in 25 games.

During his time with Boston, from 1973 to 1980, the team finished at the top of the Adams Division five times and made it to the Stanley Cup finals three times. During his first three seasons in the Bruins uniform,

Gilbert played 54, 53 and 55 games, but the number dropped with the return of Gerry Cheevers, who had gone to play in the World Hockey Association for four seasons.

Before the start of the 1980-1981 season, Gilbert was traded to the Detroit Red Wings. He played 48 games in his first year with his new team, but recorded an average of 4.01, the worst in his career. The

Wings' goaltenders allowed 339 goals in 80 games, 33 more than the previous year.

Gilbert played two more seasons with the Red Wings and ended his career with the team. He played only one All Star game, on January 29, 1974 in Chicago, sharing goaltending duties with Dave Dryden of the Buffalo Sabres.

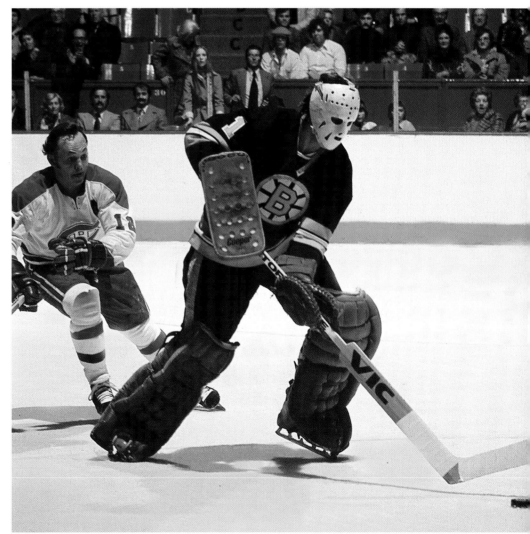

Gilles Gilbert's record includes 18 career shutouts, six of which he won during his first season with the Bruins, in 1973-1974. On this play, Gilbert rushes to the puck with speedy Yvan Cournoyer hot on his heels.

# Denis Herron

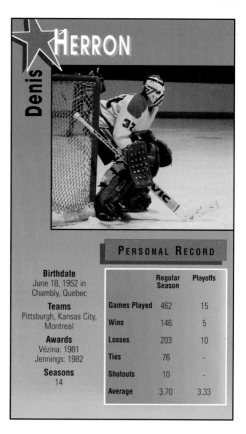

**Denis HERRON**

### PERSONAL RECORD

**Birthdate**
June 18, 1952 in
Chambly, Quebec

**Teams**
Pittsburgh, Kansas City,
Montreal

**Awards**
Vézina: 1981
Jennings: 1982

**Seasons**
14

| | Regular Season | Playoffs |
|---|---|---|
| Games Played | 462 | 15 |
| Wins | 146 | 5 |
| Losses | 203 | 10 |
| Ties | 76 | - |
| Shutouts | 10 | - |
| Average | 3.70 | 3.33 |

Denis Herron's career was a strange one. He played with the Pittsburgh Penguins for 10 years, at three different points in his career, but enjoyed his best times with the Montreal Canadiens, a team he stayed with for only three seasons.

He started with Pittsburgh in 1972-1973 before going to Kansas City for the 1974-1975 season. The Penguins recovered him before the start of the 1976-1977 season.

In 1979-1980, the Canadiens acquired him as a backup for Michel Larocque after Ken Dryden's unexpected retirement. Herron then experienced the finest moments of his career, maintaining an average of 2.51 in 34 games, and the Canadiens finished in first place

in the Norris Division for the sixth season in a row. In March of the following year, Michel Larocque was traded to the Toronto Maple Leafs and Herron shared goaltending duties with rookie Richard Sévigny. The duo was excellent, winning the Vézina Trophy, upon which Larocque's name also appeared.

During his third season with the Canadiens, in 1981-1982, Herron played only 27 games but he maintained the best average in the League, with 2.64. He and Rick Wamsley, the team's new lead goalie, were the first players to win the Jennings Trophy, awarded to a team's goalies who allowed the fewest goals in a season.

In September 1982, the Canadiens decided to trade Herron, by then aged 30, for Richard Sévigny, 25, and Rick Wamsley, who was just 23. Herron was traded back to the Pittsburgh Penguins. Without such experienced and effective defencemen as Larry Robinson, Rod Langway and Brian Engblom (his former teammates with the Canadiens) to support him, Herron played 31 games and finished the season with an average of 5.31. Pittsburgh won only 18 of 80 games, the team's worst showing since it joined the League in 1967. During the 1982-1983 season, Denis Herron, Michel Dion, Roberto Romano and Nick Ricci let in 394 goals, placing second to last for goals against, barely ahead of the Hartford Whalers, who had allowed 403 goals.

The following season was an even bigger disaster: only 16 wins in 80 games, with Herron playing 42 games for an average of 4.65. Denis Herron played only three games in 1985-1986, his last season in the National League.

Denis Herron uses his pads to make a save as defencemen Brian Engblom and Gaston Gingras look on.

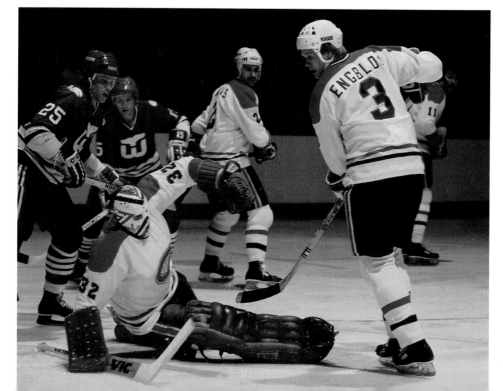

# MICHEL LAROCQUE

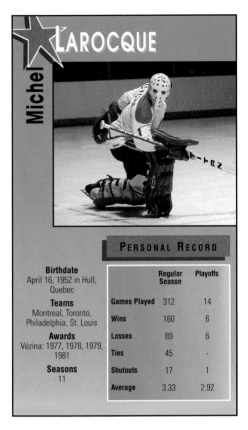

### PERSONAL RECORD

**Birthdate**
April 16, 1952 in Hull, Quebec

**Teams**
Montreal, Toronto, Philadelphia, St. Louis

**Awards**
Vézina: 1977, 1978, 1979, 1981

**Seasons**
11

|  | Regular Season | Playoffs |
|---|---|---|
| Games Played | 312 | 14 |
| Wins | 160 | 6 |
| Losses | 89 | 6 |
| Ties | 45 | - |
| Shutouts | 17 | 1 |
| Average | 3.33 | 2.92 |

In 1973, star goalie Ken Dryden of the Canadiens decided to take a year off, which left a job to fill with the glorious Montreal team. Team managers called on Michel Larocque, a first round pick during the 1972 draft. So Larocque made his debut in 1973-1974, playing 27 games and sharing the goaltending job with Wayne Thomas and Michel Plasse. Dryden came back to play the next season and Larocque became the backup goalie; the Canadiens won the first of four consecutive Stanley Cups.

In 1976-1977, Larocque and Dryden won the Vézina Trophy. Larocque had just played the best season of his career, maintaining an average of 2.09 in 26 games. Larocque and Dryden earned the coveted trophy the following two years as well.

Larocque never carved out a place as the team's lead goalie, even after Ken Dryden's retirement at the end of the 1978-1979 season. In March 1981 he was traded to the Toronto Maple Leafs in exchange for defenceman Robert Picard. That year the Canadiens' goalies won the Vézina Trophy again; since Larocque had spent most of the season in Montreal, he had his name added to the trophy for the fourth time, along with Denis Herron and Richard Sévigny.

In Toronto, Larocque had the opportunity to play many more games than he had with the Canadiens, but his average suffered a severe blow— 4.69 in 50 games. In 1982-1983, he was traded to the Philadelphia Flyers and he ended his career in 1983-1984 after playing only five games with the St. Louis Blues.

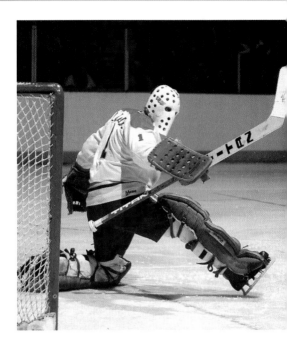

Michel Larocque began his career with the Canadiens in 1973-1974, when Ken Dryden sat out an entire season. Dryden came back the following year, and Larocque had to play second fiddle to the superstar.

Michel Larocque makes a spectacular save, to the frustration of a Boston Bruins forward.

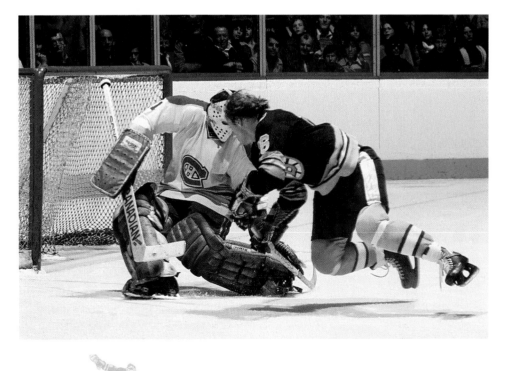

Michel Larocque gets hold of the puck, with solid backup from his defenceman Serge Savard.

The former Canadiens goalie played for the Philadelphia Flyers briefly in 1982-1983, after being traded from Toronto. He played only 18 games in the season.

Michel Larocque in a Maple Leafs uniform. In 1981-1982, he played 50 games with Toronto, a career high.

Alone in front of Michel Larocque's net, Marc Tardif of the Quebec Nordiques is kept at bay by the Canadiens goalie.

# MARIO LESSARD

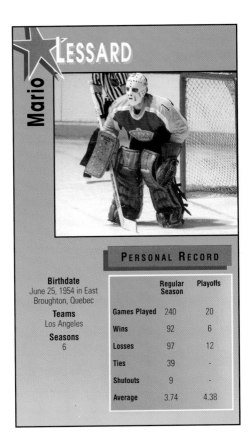

**LESSARD**

**Mario**

### PERSONAL RECORD

**Birthdate**
June 25, 1954 in East
Broughton, Quebec

**Teams**
Los Angeles

**Seasons**
6

| | Regular Season | Playoffs |
|---|---|---|
| Games Played | 240 | 20 |
| Wins | 92 | 6 |
| Losses | 97 | 12 |
| Ties | 39 | - |
| Shutouts | 9 | - |
| Average | 3.74 | 4.38 |

Mario Lessard spent his entire career in the National League in a Los Angeles Kings uniform, at the same time as centre Marcel Dionne was at his peak. The Kings' seventh pick in the 1974 draft, Lessard had made his mark in 1976-1977 with the Saginaw team in the International League. In 44 games, he had maintained the league's best average, with 3.47. The following season, he played for the Springfield Americans in the American League. In 1978-1979, along with veteran Ron Gilmore, he was called up to take over from Rogatien Vachon, who had been traded to the Detroit Red Wings. He did so well (an average of 3.10 in 49 games) that he became the team's lead goalie for the next three seasons.

In 1980-1981, he led the League in wins, with 35 in 64 games. The Kings finished in second place in the Norris Division with 99 points; it took until 1990-1991 for the team to improve on that.

Over the next two seasons, Lessard played 52 and 19 games respectively. In his last season with the National League, in 1983-1984, he played only six games with the Kings before deciding to retire.

# MIKE LIUT

After playing two years in the World Hockey Association with the Cincinnati Stingers, Mike Liut made his NHL debut with the St. Louis Blues in 1979-1980. He was off to an astonishing start, leading the League in wins, with 32, and maintaining an average of 3.18. He achieved as good an average again only in 1987-1988, with the Hartford Whalers.

In 1980-1981, Liut won 33 of 60 games and led the Blues to the Smythe Division championship for the first time in four years. He lost the Hart Trophy to Wayne Gretzky, but took some consolation in being chosen to play on the League's first All Star team. During the All Star game played in Los Angeles in February 1981, he stopped 18 shots in the first period and was named most valuable player. In 1986-1987, he was selected to play on the second All Star team.

Mike Liut played five full seasons with St. Louis before going to the Hartford Whalers for the 1984-1985 season. He was the team's lead goalie until he was traded to the Washington Capitals in 1989-1990. He played two seasons with the Capitals before hanging up his skates at age 36.

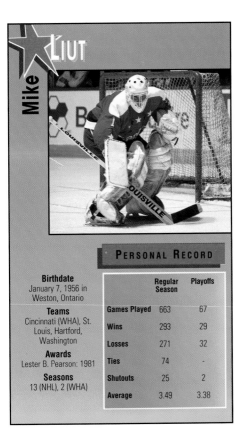

**LIUT**

**Mike**

### PERSONAL RECORD

**Birthdate**
January 7, 1956 in
Weston, Ontario

**Teams**
Cincinnati (WHA), St.
Louis, Hartford,
Washington

**Awards**
Lester B. Pearson: 1981

**Seasons**
13 (NHL), 2 (WHA)

| | Regular Season | Playoffs |
|---|---|---|
| Games Played | 663 | 67 |
| Wins | 293 | 29 |
| Losses | 271 | 32 |
| Ties | 74 | - |
| Shutouts | 25 | 2 |
| Average | 3.49 | 3.38 |

# RON LOW

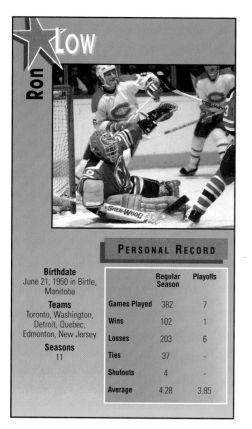

## PERSONAL RECORD

**Birthdate**
June 21, 1950 in Birtle, Manitoba

**Teams**
Toronto, Washington, Detroit, Quebec, Edmonton, New Jersey

**Seasons**
11

|  | Regular Season | Playoffs |
|---|---|---|
| Games Played | 382 | 7 |
| Wins | 102 | 1 |
| Losses | 203 | 6 |
| Ties | 37 | - |
| Shutouts | 4 | - |
| Average | 4.28 | 3.85 |

Ron Low never had it easy during his 11-year career in the National League. During his debut in 1972-1973, he tended the Toronto Maple Leafs' nets for 42 games, maintaining an average of 3.89. In 1974-1975, he had a horrendous year with a new team, the Washington Capitals. He and goalie Michel Belhumeur allowed 446 goals in 80 games—Low played 48 games—setting a most unenviable team record.

After playing five seasons with the Washington Capitals, Low enjoyed his best year in 1977-1978 with the Detroit Red Wings. In 32 games, he maintained an average of 3.37, and although his team made it to the playoffs for the first time in seven years, they lost to the Montreal Canadiens in the quarter finals.

After a brief stint with the Nordiques in 1979-1980, Low went to the Edmonton Oilers. In 1980-1981, as backup to Ed Mio, he played 24 games. The following year, he was Grant Fuhr's backup. His team won the Smythe Division championship, a first-time thrill for Low. When rookie Andy Moog arrived on the scene in 1982-1983, Low was traded to the New Jersey Devils. The veteran goalie played two more seasons with the team before retiring in 1985.

During a game at the Forum in Montreal with the Detroit Red Wings, Ron Low tries to make a save on Guy Lafleur.

# GILLES MELOCHE

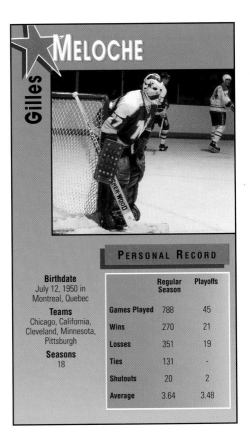

**MELOCHE**

Gilles

### PERSONAL RECORD

**Birthdate**
July 12, 1950 in
Montreal, Quebec

**Teams**
Chicago, California,
Cleveland, Minnesota,
Pittsburgh

**Seasons**
18

| | Regular Season | Playoffs |
|---|---|---|
| Games Played | 788 | 45 |
| Wins | 270 | 21 |
| Losses | 351 | 19 |
| Ties | 131 | - |
| Shutouts | 20 | 2 |
| Average | 3.64 | 3.48 |

Gilles Meloche played 18 years in the National League, but it was only while working as goaltending coach for the Pittsburgh Penguins in 1991 and 1992 that he saw his name added to the Stanley Cup.

He began his career with the Chicago Black Hawks in 1970-1971, followed by five seasons with the Atlanta Flames. Later, he went to the Cleveland Barons, where he played for two years before being traded to the Minnesota North Stars at the end of the 1977-1978 season. His six seasons with Minnesota were the best in his career. His finest hours came in 1977-1978, when he played 54 games for an average of 3.06. His performance led to two appearances in All Star games, in 1980 and 1982. In 1980-1981, he and rookie Don Beaupre led the North Stars to the Stanley Cup finals against the New York Islanders.

At the end of the 1984-1985 season, Meloche was traded to the Pittsburgh Penguins and played three seasons alongside Mario Lemieux, who was starting out in the National League. In 1986-1987, Meloche played 43 games and maintained an average of 3.43, his best since the 1980-1981 season. He ended his career with the Penguins in 1988 and has been one of the team's coaches since then.

# ED MIO

Ed Mio made his professional debut with the Indianapolis Racers, in the WHA, in 1977-1978. The following season the team made history by recruiting a certain 17-year-old named Wayne Gretzky, who played only eight games with the team, however. Gretzky, Mio and leftwinger Peter Driscoll were traded to Peter Pocklington's Edmonton Oilers, admitted to the NHL in 1979-1980.

Mio tended the Oilers net for two seasons until Grant Fuhr was chosen in the 1981 draft, the team's first pick and the eighth overall. Mio was traded to the New York Rangers and played two seasons with the team before going to the Detroit Red Wings in 1983. In three seasons, Mio played only 49 games; he ended his career in 1986.

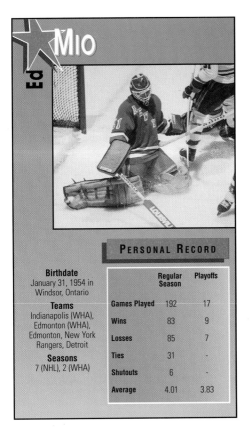

**MIO**

Ed

### PERSONAL RECORD

**Birthdate**
January 31, 1954 in
Windsor, Ontario

**Teams**
Indianapolis (WHA),
Edmonton (WHA),
Edmonton, New York
Rangers, Detroit

**Seasons**
7 (NHL), 2 (WHA)

| | Regular Season | Playoffs |
|---|---|---|
| Games Played | 192 | 17 |
| Wins | 83 | 9 |
| Losses | 85 | 7 |
| Ties | 31 | - |
| Shutouts | 6 | - |
| Average | 4.01 | 3.83 |

# PHILIPPE MYRE

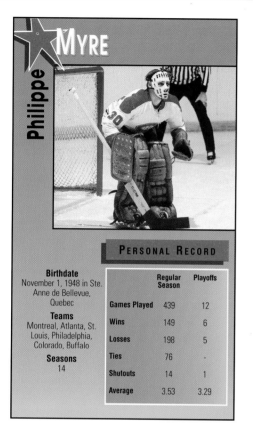

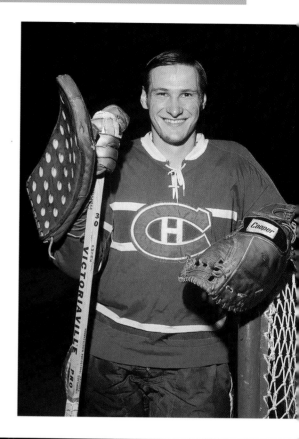

During the 1977-1978 season, he was traded to the St. Louis Blues and later played with four other teams before hanging up his skates in 1982-1983, after playing only five games with Buffalo.

Myre has stayed in hockey since his goaltending career came to an end, notably working as a goaltending coach with the Detroit Red Wings. In 1994-1995, he was in charge of player development with the Chicago Black Hawks.

Philippe Myre was the Canadiens' first pick and the fifth player selected in the 1966 draft.

## PERSONAL RECORD

**Birthdate**
November 1, 1948 in Ste. Anne de Bellevue, Quebec

**Teams**
Montreal, Atlanta, St. Louis, Philadelphia, Colorado, Buffalo

**Seasons**
14

| | Regular Season | Playoffs |
|---|---|---|
| Games Played | 439 | 12 |
| Wins | 149 | 6 |
| Losses | 198 | 5 |
| Ties | 76 | - |
| Shutouts | 14 | 1 |
| Average | 3.53 | 3.29 |

Philippe Myre made his debut in the National Hockey League with the Montreal Canadiens in 1969-1970. At the time, Rogatien Vachon was the rising star, but things changed in 1971 when Ken Dryden took the spotlight in the drive to the Stanley Cup. The following season, Vachon was traded to Los Angeles and Myre, Dryden's backup, played only nine games.

In 1972-1973, he headed for Atlanta, were he played five full seasons. In 1974-1975, he had the best year of his career, maintaining an average of 2.85 in 40 games.

Philippe Myre comes out of his crease to stop a shot by a Canadiens player while his teammates try their best to give him a helping hand.

# MIKE PALMATEER

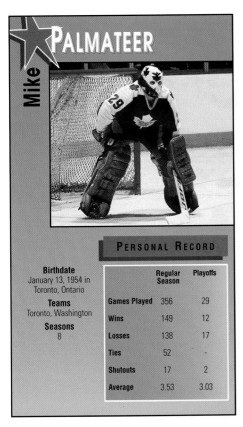

PALMATEER

Mike

### PERSONAL RECORD

| Birthdate<br>January 13, 1954 in<br>Toronto, Ontario | | Regular<br>Season | Playoffs |
|---|---|---|---|
| **Teams**<br>Toronto, Washington | Games Played | 356 | 29 |
| | Wins | 149 | 12 |
| **Seasons**<br>8 | Losses | 138 | 17 |
| | Ties | 52 | - |
| | Shutouts | 17 | 2 |
| | Average | 3.53 | 3.03 |

The star goalie of the Toronto Marlboros, winners of the 1973 Memorial Cup, Mike Palmateer was picked by the Toronto Maple Leafs in 1974 and had the chance to play six seasons with his hometown team.

Palmateer made his debut with the Leafs in 1976-1977 and in his very first season became a favourite of head coach Red Kelly. The previous season Wayne Thomas had played 64 games, but with Palmateer playing 50 of the year's games, the former Canadiens goalie was limited to 33. Palmateer maintained an average of 3.21 and by the next season, 1977-1978, he was a definite hit with

During his first season with Toronto, Palmateer played 50 games. In this photo he robs a goal from Canadiens Mark Napier.

Toronto fans. He experienced what was to be the best year of his career, with an average of 2.74 in 63 games. Toronto had chalked up a record of 81 points in 1976-1977 and now they added 11 more to finish third in the Adams Division. During the playoffs Palmateer's panache made it easy for the Maple Leafs to entertain Stanley Cup dreams. First, Toronto got rid of the Los Angeles Kings in two games. Then, in the quarter finals, Palmateer and the Maple Leafs surprised the so-called experts by eliminating the New York Islanders, the Patrick Division champions, in seven games. Toronto won a decisive victory in overtime thanks to Lanny McDonald's goal. The Maple Leafs were finally eliminated in four games during a semifinal battle with the Montreal Canadiens, who were unstoppable on their way to a third consecutive Stanley Cup.

After four seasons with Toronto, Palmateer was traded to the Washington Capitals, where he played for two years. In 1982-1983, Palmateer was back with the Maple Leafs, playing 53 games and ending the season with an average of 3.99.

Mike Palmateer played six of his eight seasons in the National League with the Toronto Maple Leafs.

Toronto was eliminated in the first round of the playoffs, in a four-game series against Minnesota. The goalie was only 30 years old when he retired at the end of the 1983-1984 season after playing 34 games.

# MICHEL PLASSE

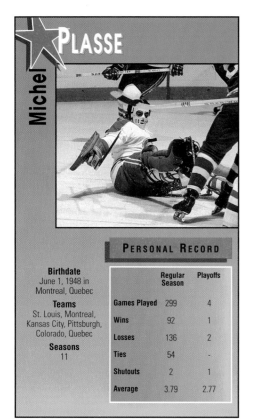

**PLASSE**

**Michel**

| PERSONAL RECORD | | |
|---|---|---|

**Birthdate**
June 1, 1948 in
Montreal, Quebec

**Teams**
St. Louis, Montreal,
Kansas City, Pittsburgh,
Colorado, Quebec

**Seasons**
11

| | Regular Season | Playoffs |
|---|---|---|
| Games Played | 299 | 4 |
| Wins | 92 | 1 |
| Losses | 136 | 2 |
| Ties | 54 | - |
| Shutouts | 2 | 1 |
| Average | 3.79 | 2.77 |

Michel Plasse was the first player chosen in the 1968 draft by the Montreal Canadiens. After being traded to the St. Louis Blues in 1970, Plasse played only one game with the team in 1970-1971 before going to the Canadiens in August 1971. He spent the 1971-1972 season with the Montreal farm team, the Nova Scotia Canadiens (recording an average of 2.77 in 36 games), and was promoted to the professional leagues the following year. In 1972-1973, he played 17 games and was fortunate enough to have his name engraved on the Stanley Cup for the one and only time in his career. Ken Dryden was the lead goalie, however, and Plasse couldn't hope to see much on-ice action. The following season he played 15 games and was recruited by a new team, the Kansas City Scouts, in June 1974. His stay with the team

Michel Plasse played two seasons with the Quebec Nordiques. In 1980-1981, he played 33 games and maintained an average of 3.66. That year, Quebec made it to the playoffs for the first time ever.

was short and in January 1975, he was traded to Pittsburgh for goalie Denis Herron and defenceman Jean-Guy Lagacé.

With the Pittsburgh Penguins in 1974-1975 and 1975-1976, Plasse had a chance to tend the net on a much more regular basis. In 1975-1976, he enjoyed his best season, maintaining an average of 3.45 in 55 games.

He spent the next four seasons with the Colorado Rockies and in 1980-1981, came back to Quebec to play for the Nordiques. He hung up his skates after playing eight games in Quebec in 1981-1982.

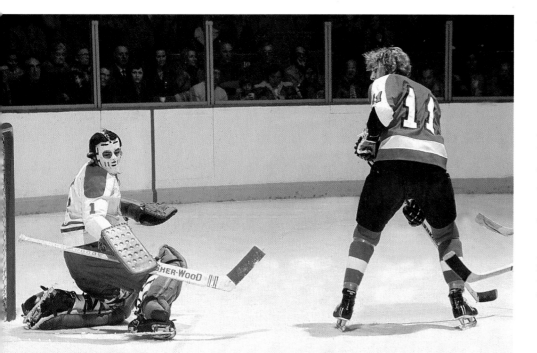

Michel Plasse in a Montreal Canadiens uniform. He played 32 games with the Habs.

# GLENN RESCH

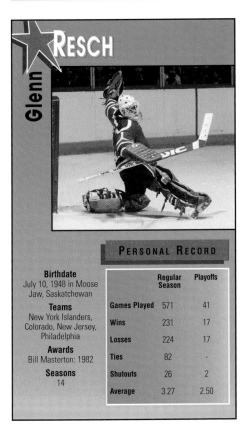

Glenn Resch

RESCH

## PERSONAL RECORD

**Birthdate**
July 10, 1948 in Moose Jaw, Saskatchewan

**Teams**
New York Islanders, Colorado, New Jersey, Philadelphia

**Awards**
Bill Masterton: 1982

**Seasons**
14

|  | Regular Season | Playoffs |
|---|---|---|
| Games Played | 571 | 41 |
| Wins | 231 | 17 |
| Losses | 224 | 17 |
| Ties | 82 | - |
| Shutouts | 26 | 2 |
| Average | 3.27 | 2.50 |

1977. He was also selected twice for the second All Star team, in 1975-1976 and 1978-1979.

In 1980-1981, Resch was traded to the Colorado Rockies. He became the team's lead goalie and in 1982, won the Bill Masterton Trophy, awarded to the player who demonstrates the most perseverance and dedication to hockey along with gentlemanly conduct. Mark Fitzpatrick of the Islanders is the only other goalie to have won that trophy, in 1992.

The Rockies moved to New Jersey early in the 1982-1983 season, where they were renamed the Devils. Resch went to the Philadelphia Flyers in 1985-1986 and he ended his career there one season later.

In 1975-1976, Glenn Resch managed seven shutouts, one less than the League's leader, Ken Dryden. His 2.07 average was the best of his career.

Glenn "Chico" Resch made his debut with the New York Islanders in 1973-1974; he played only two games that season, but was promoted to the lead goaltending position the following year. He shared goaltending duties with Billy Smith for six seasons and was a key factor in the Islanders' Stanley Cup victory in 1980.

During the 1975-1976 season, he had the second best average in the League, after Ken Dryden, with 2.07 in 44 games. He was brilliant once again in the next season, with an average of 2.28, better than Billy Smith's record. In view of his steady performance, he was invited to play in the All Star game in Vancouver in January

In 1982-1983, Resch played 65 games with the New Jersey Devils, his career high. He was the team's lead goalie for three seasons before joining the Philadelphia Flyers.

# JIM RUTHERFORD

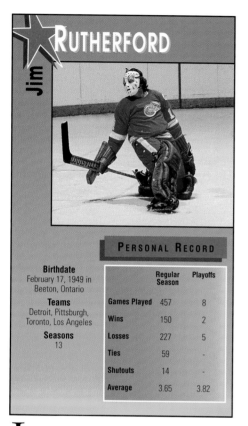

**Jim**
**RUTHERFORD**

### PERSONAL RECORD

**Birthdate**
February 17, 1949 in Beeton, Ontario

**Teams**
Detroit, Pittsburgh, Toronto, Los Angeles

**Seasons**
13

|  | Regular Season | Playoffs |
|---|---|---|
| Games Played | 457 | 8 |
| Wins | 150 | 2 |
| Losses | 227 | 5 |
| Ties | 59 | - |
| Shutouts | 14 | - |
| Average | 3.65 | 3.82 |

Jim Rutherford spent most of his career with the Detroit Red Wings, where he made his debut in 1970-1971 as the team's first choice in the 1969 draft. Rutherford moved on to the Pittsburgh Penguins in June 1971 and was lead goalie for that team, which made it to the playoffs for the second time in its history in the spring of 1972. Rutherford couldn't keep the Chicago Black Hawks from eliminating his team in four games in the first round.

In 1972-1973, Rutherford enjoyed his best season, with an average of 2.91 in 49 games. After being traded to the Red Wings in January 1974 for defencemen Jack Lynch and Ron

Jim Rutherford uses his pads to make a save on Jacques Lemaire of the Canadiens.

Stackhouse, the goalie played the next six seasons with the team, making it to the playoffs only once, in 1977-1978.

In 1976-1977, Detroit lived through its worst season since 1939-1940, winning only 16 of 80 games and earning 41 points. Rutherford (48 games) and veteran Ed Giacomin (33 games) tried in vain to limit the damage. The next season Detroit won 32 games, ending the season with 78 points, in second place in the Norris Division, taking part in the playoffs for the first time since 1970. Rutherford (43 games and an average of 3.26) shared his job with Ron Low, acquired from the Washington Capitals. Detroit eliminated the Flames in two games, but were easy prey for the Canadiens in the quarter finals. Montreal got rid of their opponents in five games. Rutherford played three games and maintained an average of 4.00.

In 1980-1981, the Red Wings acquired goalie Gilles Gilbert from the Boston Bruins and Rutherford had the opportunity to travel. In fact, he would play with four different teams in all during that particularly tumultuous season, including the Detroit Red Wings, the Toronto Maple Leafs and the Los Angeles Kings; in this time, he goaltended only 31 games and maintained an average of 4.65.

In 1981-1982, Rutherford played only seven games with the Kings as backup to lead goalies Mario Lessard and Doug Keans. Rutherford returned to the Detroit Red Wings the next season, but played only one game, his last in the National League, in which he allowed seven goals.

# ROBERT SAUVÉ

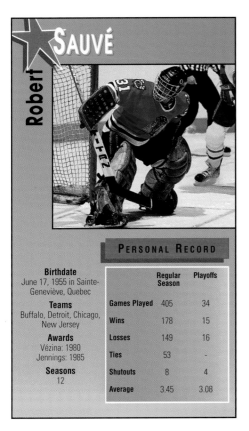

## PERSONAL RECORD

**Birthdate**
June 17, 1955 in Sainte-
Geneviève, Quebec

**Teams**
Buffalo, Detroit, Chicago,
New Jersey

**Awards**
Vézina: 1980
Jennings: 1985

**Seasons**
12

| | Regular Season | Playoffs |
|---|---|---|
| Games Played | 405 | 34 |
| Wins | 178 | 15 |
| Losses | 149 | 16 |
| Ties | 53 | - |
| Shutouts | 8 | 4 |
| Average | 3.45 | 3.08 |

The former star goalie of the Laval National team in the Quebec Major Junior Hockey League, Robert Sauvé was a first-round pick in the 1975 draft, going to the 17th place Buffalo Sabres. Buffalo was where he spent most of his career, which started in 1976. In 1979-1980, when he was sharing goaltending duties with Don Edwards, he maintained an average of 2.36 in 32 games, the best record in the League; he and Edwards allowed only 201 goals in 80 games and the duo was awarded the Vézina Trophy. Their performance helped the Sabres win the Adams

When he was with the Buffalo Sabres, Robert Sauvé had the chance to play on the same team as his younger brother, Jean-François, a centre who played three seasons with the Sabres in the early 80s.

Division championship for the first time since 1974-1975.

In 1985, Sauvé won the Jennings Trophy, this time in tandem with Tom Barrasso; he maintained an average of 3.22 in 27 games. In 1985-1986, he went to Chicago, where he played for two seasons. He ended his career with the New Jersey Devils in 1987-1988.

Since his retirement, he has been active in the business sector and has

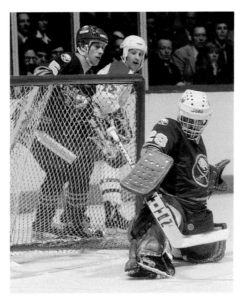

Robert Sauvé managed eight shutouts in his career, four of which he won during the 1979-1980 season, his best in the NHL.

worked with Pierre Lacroix as a player's agent. When Lacroix was appointed general manager of the Quebec Nordiques, Robert Sauvé took over the business, which represents a number of National League players.

# BILLY SMITH

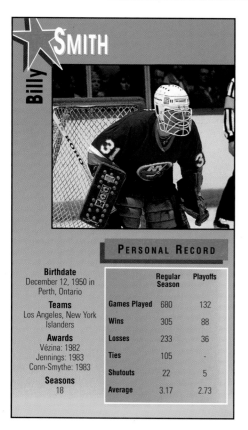

Billy Smith

SMITH

## PERSONAL RECORD

**Birthdate**
December 12, 1950 in
Perth, Ontario

**Teams**
Los Angeles, New York
Islanders

**Awards**
Vézina: 1982
Jennings: 1983
Conn-Smythe: 1983

**Seasons**
18

| | Regular Season | Playoffs |
|---|---|---|
| Games Played | 680 | 132 |
| Wins | 305 | 88 |
| Losses | 233 | 36 |
| Ties | 105 | - |
| Shutouts | 22 | 5 |
| Average | 3.17 | 2.73 |

When his 18-season career in the National League came to an end, Billy Smith could boast a very impressive record. He won the Stanley Cup four times with the New York Islanders and earned the Vézina, Jennings and Conn-Smythe Trophies as well. His induction into the Hockey Hall of Fame in 1993 was a given.

He made his debut in 1971-1972 with the Los Angeles Kings, but played only five games with the team. The next season, he joined a new expansion team, the New York Islanders, and stayed with that organization until 1988-1989.

Goaltender Billy Smith uses his stick to try to keep the puck out of his net.

On November 28, 1979, he became the first goalie to be credited with a goal: after Smith stopped a shot, a Colorado Rockies player got the puck and accidentally put it in his own net.

In 1980, he won the first of four consecutive Stanley Cups. During the 1981-1982 season, he maintained an average of 2.97 in 46 games, winning 32 of them and earning the Vézina Trophy. During the playoffs he proved that his reputation as a "money player" was fully justified, winning 15 of 18 games and maintaining an average of 2.52. That year he was chosen to play on the first All Star team.

He did even better in 1982-1983, with an average of 2.87 in 41 regular season games, a performance that earned him the Jennings Trophy along with teammate Roland Melanson. During the playoffs he once again led the Islanders all the way to the Stanley Cup, winning 13 of 16 games and maintaining an average of 2.68. He was particularly astounding during the finals, allowing only six goals in four games against the powerful Edmonton Oilers. He became the fourth consecutive Islanders player to win the Conn-Smythe Trophy, after Brian Trottier (1980), Butch Goring (1981) and Mike Bossy (1982).

Smith was renowned as a player who wasn't afraid to use his stick to clear opponents out of his crease. He holds the League record for most playoff games played, with a total of 132. During the 1993-1994 and 1994-1995 seasons, he was goaltending coach for the Florida Panthers.

Billy Smith was known as a player who wasn't easily intimidated around his own net. On this play, Guy Carbonneau of the Canadiens gets a taste of the goaltender's medicine.

Four years after hanging up his skates after 17 seasons with the New York Islanders, in 1993 Billy Smith was inducted into the Hockey Hall of Fame.

# DOUG SOETAERT

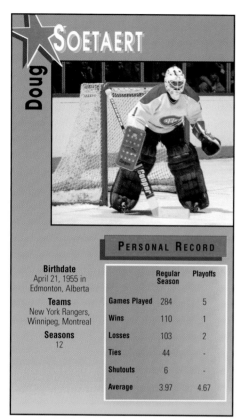

Doug Soetaert

## PERSONAL RECORD

**Birthdate**
April 21, 1955 in
Edmonton, Alberta

**Teams**
New York Rangers,
Winnipeg, Montreal

**Seasons**
12

| | Regular Season | Playoffs |
|---|---|---|
| Games Played | 284 | 5 |
| Wins | 110 | 1 |
| Losses | 103 | 2 |
| Ties | 44 | - |
| Shutouts | 6 | - |
| Average | 3.97 | 4.67 |

When Doug Soetaert started with the New York Rangers during the 1975-1976 season, John Davidson was the team's lead goalie; in 1977-1978, the Rangers chose Wayne Thomas as their Number 1 goaltender. In six seasons with the Rangers, Soetaert had to play second fiddle, playing only 90 games.

The Rangers' second pick in the 1975 draft, he was traded to the Winnipeg Jets before the start of the 1981-1982 season. Soetaert stayed with the Jets for three seasons, playing 39, 44 and 47 games respectively. Backed by experienced defencemen, Soetaert maintained averages of 4.31, 4.12 and 4.30.

On October 9, 1984, Soetaert was traded to the Montreal Canadiens for goalie Mark Holden. He played two seasons with the Canadiens and expe-

Doug Soetaert blocks the net with his skate as a Philadelphia Flyers player tries to slip the puck past him.

rienced the best year in his career in 1985-1986, maintaining an average of 2.77 in 23 games. This time Soetaert was matched with a rookie by the name of Patrick Roy, who led the Canadiens to the Stanley Cup in the spring of 1986, to the detriment of the Calgary Flames. Doug Soetaert ended his career in the National League the following season with the New York Rangers, after playing only 13 games with the team.

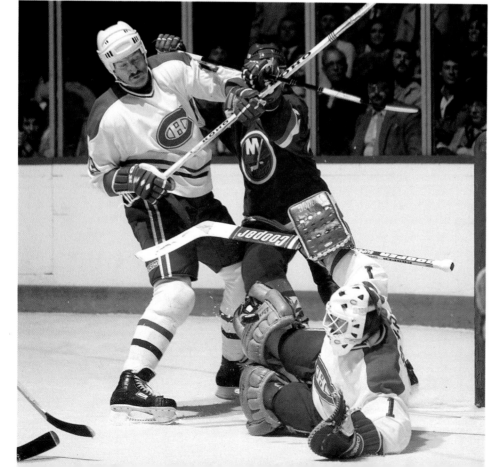

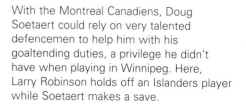

With the Montreal Canadiens, Doug Soetaert could rely on very talented defencemen to help him with his goaltending duties, a privilege he didn't have when playing in Winnipeg. Here, Larry Robinson holds off an Islanders player while Soetaert makes a save.

# RICK ST. CROIX

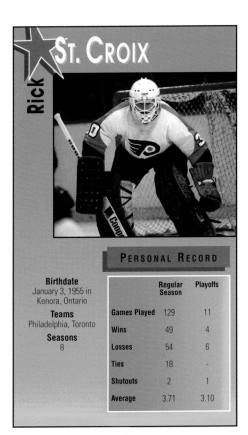

**ST. CROIX**
Rick

### PERSONAL RECORD

**Birthdate**
January 3, 1955 in
Kenora, Ontario

**Teams**
Philadelphia, Toronto

**Seasons**
8

| | Regular Season | Playoffs |
|---|---|---|
| Games Played | 129 | 11 |
| Wins | 49 | 4 |
| Losses | 54 | 6 |
| Ties | 18 | - |
| Shutouts | 2 | 1 |
| Average | 3.71 | 3.10 |

The goaltender for the Oshawa Generals in the Ontario Junior Hockey League, Rick St. Croix was the Philadelphia Flyers' third pick in the 1975 draft. With the Flint organization in the International League, he maintained an average of 3.63 in 53 games and led the League's other goalies with a total of three shutouts. In 1977-1978, he played in four games with the Flyers, but spent most of the season with the Maine Mariners in the American League, where he maintained an average of 3.07 in 40 games.

During the next two seasons St. Croix played only three games with the Flyers, but he joined the team for good in 1980-1981 as Pete Peeters's backup. St. Croix maintained an average of 2.49 in 27 games, including four shutouts, and this was the best season of his career. He didn't do as well the following year: he ended the season with a 3.89 average in 29 games. During the 1982-1983 season, St. Croix played 33 games and maintained an average of 3.61.

# WAYNE STEPHENSON

Wayne Stephenson played 10 years in the National League, including five with the Philadelphia Flyers. In 1974-1975, he was backup to Bernard Parent, and by virtue of playing 12 games, he saw his name engraved on the Stanley Cup for the one and only time in his career.

In 1975-1976, the Flyers, Stanley Cup champions, had to deal with very bad news: their excellent goalie, considered to be the best in the League, had to leave the game to receive treatment for an eye injury. The team's management decided to test Stephenson and he came through brilliantly for them. In 66 games, he maintained an average of 2.58, with 40 wins. Stephenson was in his team's net for nine games during the playoffs,

but the Flyers were unable to withstand the pressure of the Montreal Canadiens. The Habs put an end to the reign of the famous Broad Street Bullies.

At the end of the 1978-1979 season, Stephenson went to the Washington Capitals. The team's lead goalie from the outset, he played 56 games and maintained an average of 3.57. The team ended up in last place in the Patrick Division, with 27 wins and 67 points, failing to make the playoffs for the sixth consecutive year.

In 1980-1981 Mike Palmateer, newly arrived from Toronto, became the team's lead goalie and played 49 games. Stephenson played only 20 games in what was to be his last season in the League.

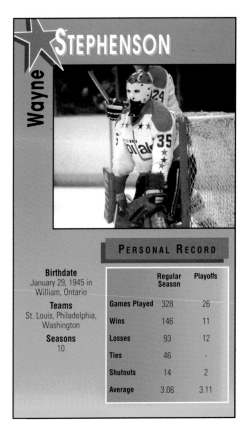

**STEPHENSON**
Wayne

### PERSONAL RECORD

**Birthdate**
January 29, 1945 in
William, Ontario

**Teams**
St. Louis, Philadelphia,
Washington

**Seasons**
10

| | Regular Season | Playoffs |
|---|---|---|
| Games Played | 328 | 26 |
| Wins | 146 | 11 |
| Losses | 93 | 12 |
| Ties | 46 | - |
| Shutouts | 14 | 2 |
| Average | 3.06 | 3.11 |

# WAYNE THOMAS

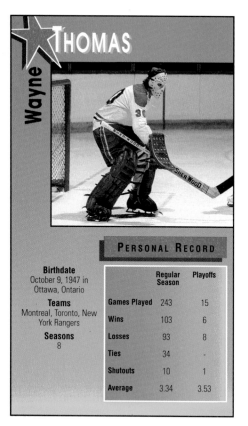

Wayne Thomas

**PERSONAL RECORD**

| Birthdate | | |
|---|---|---|
| October 9, 1947 in Ottawa, Ontario | | |

| | Regular Season | Playoffs |
|---|---|---|
| Games Played | 243 | 15 |
| Wins | 103 | 6 |
| Losses | 93 | 8 |
| Ties | 34 | - |
| Shutouts | 10 | 1 |
| Average | 3.34 | 3.53 |

**Teams**
Montreal, Toronto, New York Rangers

**Seasons**
8

Wayne Thomas played three seasons in the American League with the Montreal Canadiens' farm team (1970-1971 with the Montreal Voyagers and the next two years with Nova Scotia) before graduating to the team. The situation wasn't in Thomas's favour, because in front of the net was the 1972 Calder Trophy winner, Ken Dryden, the very same goalie who had led the Canadiens to their sixteenth Stanley Cup in 1971. Dryden played 54 games, Michel Plasse played 17 and Thomas was on the ice for 10. He maintained an average of 2.37 and managed one shutout. With Dryden in the net, the Canadiens won the Stanley Cup by eliminating the Chicago Black Hawks in six games.

The next season, Dryden decided to retire from competition to study law, which paved the way for Thomas to become the team's lead goalie. He played 42 games, with rookie Michel Larocque playing 27 (with an average of 2.89). Thomas did well, with an average of 2.76, but head coach Scotty Bowman decided to go with Michel Larocque to start the playoffs. The Canadiens were eliminated in six games by the New York Rangers.

Wayne Thomas was traded to the Toronto Maple Leafs in June 1975. He played 64 games in 1975-1976 with his new team and maintained an average of 3.19. Just as they had done in the previous two seasons, Toronto lost in the quarter finals, this time against the Philadelphia Flyers, who took the series in seven games. Thomas played all of his team's playoff games. He played another season with the Leafs before going to the New York Rangers. In 1977-1978, he

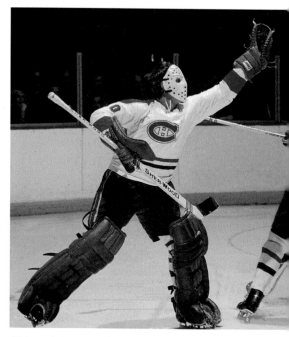

Although he experienced the thrill of winning the Stanley Cup with the Canadiens in 1973, Wayne Thomas's name doesn't appear on the trophy because he only played 10 games in 1972-1973, none of them in the playoffs.

managed four shutouts and maintained an average of 3.60 in 41 games. The next season Thomas played 31 games and the Rangers made it to the Stanley Cup finals against the Canadiens, who won in five games. During the following two seasons (1979-1980 and 1980-1981), Thomas played only 22 games with the Rangers, eventually deciding to retire. Since 1993, he has been assistant coach with the San Jose Sharks.

Early in his career Wayne Thomas played 52 games in two seasons with the Canadiens.

# VLADISLAV TRETIAK

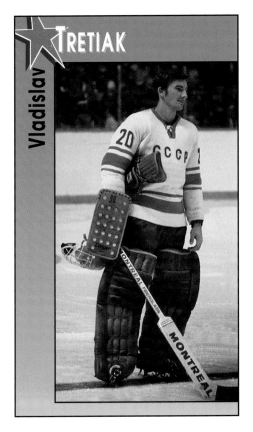

The year 1972 was determinant in the history of professional hockey. Every hockey fan remembers the Super Series, which pitted the biggest Canadian stars of the National League against the Soviet Union's national team. Ken Dryden and Tony Esposito were in the nets for Team Canada, and at the opposite end of the ice was a 20-year-old named Vladislav Tretiak—a name that is indelible in the minds of hockey lovers.

Tretiak was his team's hero and a major source of frustration for the Canadian players. He maintained an average of 3.87 for the eight games in the series. In the end, Canada scraped through to win the series, but a new star had been born. The young Russian had earned the admiration of North American hockey fans.

Tretiak enjoyed a brilliant career in the USSR. He won 10 world championships and three gold medals at the Olympic Games. Recognized as a national hero in his country, he was part of the prestigious Red Army team and the Soviet Union's national team from 1969 to 1984.

In 1976 and 1979, he came to America to play against the professionals, notably in the Canada Cup tournament. Each time, hockey fans greeted him with open arms, acclaiming his amazing talent.

Tretiak was drafted by the Canadiens in 1983, but was unable to fulfill his dream of playing in the National League. He retired in 1985 and in 1989, became the first Russian player to be inducted into the Hockey Hall of Fame. Today, he is a special consultant for Chicago Black Hawks goaltenders.

Vladislav Tretiak is considered to be the greatest goaltender in the history of the USSR, a national hero who was an excellent ambassador for his country throughout his career. On this play, the goaltender watches the play while Canadiens Ryan Walter tries to distract him.

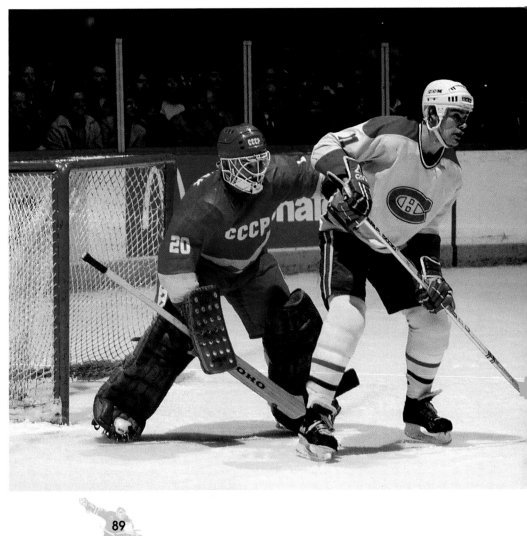

In this series of photos taken at the Philadelphia Spectrum by Denis Brodeur, Vladislav Tretiak makes a save with his pads and then, diving with his stick extended, manages to push the puck out of the Flyers' reach.

(Opposite page) During a match involving the Canadiens and Tretiak's team, the goaltender stops a shot that rightwinger Guy Lafleur has tried to deflect into the net.

Throughout his career, Vladislav Tretiak was intent on keeping fit. Agile, quick and an excellent technician, he was a great goaltender who, for political reasons, was unable to fulfill a cherished dream of playing with the Canadiens.

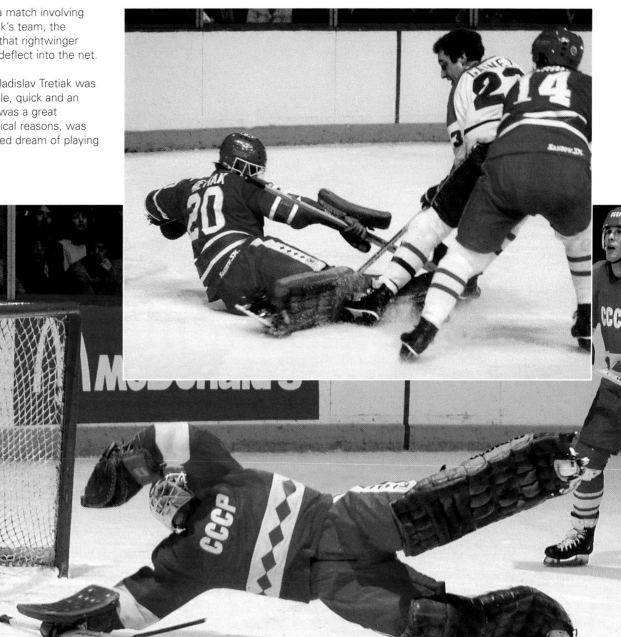

Tretiak in the net during a game between the USSR team and the Canadiens. At the heart of the action is rightwinger Mark Napier.

Vladislav Tretiak was only 20 years old when he came to Canada in 1972 for the series between the USSR and Canada.

# MIKE VEISOR

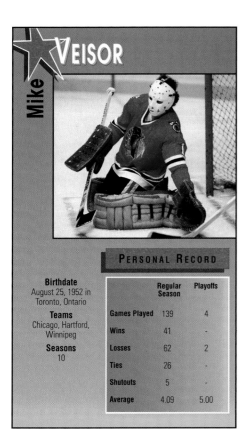

**PERSONAL RECORD**

**Birthdate**
August 25, 1952 in
Toronto, Ontario

**Teams**
Chicago, Hartford,
Winnipeg

**Seasons**
10

|  | Regular Season | Playoffs |
|---|---|---|
| Games Played | 139 | 4 |
| Wins | 41 | - |
| Losses | 62 | 2 |
| Ties | 26 | - |
| Shutouts | 5 | - |
| Average | 4.09 | 5.00 |

Mike Veisor played junior hockey with the Peterborough Petes in the Ontario Hockey League before becoming the Chicago Black Hawks' third pick in the 1972 draft. In 1972-1973, he was sensational in the Central Hockey League with the Dallas organization, proving to the Black Hawks management that they had been right to gamble on him. He was named rookie of the year based on his 2.75 average in 39 games, the best record in the League.

Veisor was called to Chicago the next season and played 10 games with the team. Tony Esposito was the team's lead goalie at the time and in six seasons with the team, Veisor played a total of 62 games. Veisor travelled between Chicago and Dallas a number of times and continued to do brilliantly for the Texas team, particularly in 1975-1976 when in 62 games he maintained the best average in the semi-pro circuit, with 2.93.

Before the start of the 1980-1981 season, Mike Veisor was sent to the Hartford Whalers, where he was finally given the chance to play more than 20 games. But with a 4.46 average over 29 games, his performance was less than impressive.

During his last season in the National League, Veisor played a total of 12 games with the Whalers and the Winnipeg Jets, and recorded an average of 4.18.

# GILLES VILLEMURE

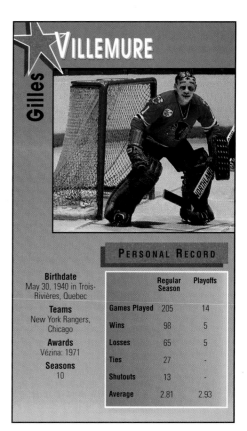

**PERSONAL RECORD**

**Birthdate**
May 30, 1940 in Trois-Rivières, Quebec

**Teams**
New York Rangers,
Chicago

**Awards**
Vézina: 1971

**Seasons**
10

|  | Regular Season | Playoffs |
|---|---|---|
| Games Played | 205 | 14 |
| Wins | 98 | 5 |
| Losses | 65 | 5 |
| Ties | 27 | - |
| Shutouts | 13 | - |
| Average | 2.81 | 2.93 |

Gilles Villemure played eight seasons with the New York Rangers, the team which had given him his first chance in 1963-1964; at the time he played five games. During the next two seasons he played only eight games, but in 1970-1971, he shared goaltending duties with Ed Giacomin. That year proved to be a memorable one for the two goalies since they allowed only 177 goals in 78 games, the best record in the League, earning them the Vézina Trophy; Villemure maintained an average of 2.30 in 34 games.

The Rangers had finished fourth in the Eastern Division in 1969-1970 and they climbed two positions further in 1970-1971, thanks to 109 points in 78 games.

The best season in Villemure's career came the next year, with an average of 2.09 in 37 games. The Rangers made it to the Stanley Cup finals for the first time since 1950, but they lost in six games against the Boston Bruins.

After playing 45 games in 1974-1975, a career high for a single season, and maintaining an average of 3.16, Villemure went to the Chicago Black Hawks. In 1976-1977, Villemure played only six games with the Black Hawks and with an average of 2.81 to his credit, he decided to retire.

The 8s

Several extremely talented young goalies made remarkable debuts in the 80s, while a few veterans, such as Billy Smith with the New York Islanders and Pete Peeters with the Boston Bruins, finally enjoyed some well-deserved glory.

In September 1981, a 19-year-old goalie named Grant Fuhr joined the Edmonton Oilers; his name appears on the Stanley Cup five times. In 1984 Tom Barrasso won the Calder and Vézina Trophies during his first season with the Buffalo Sabres. Another 19-year-old rookie, Patrick Roy, led the Canadiens to the Stanley Cup in 1986, winning 15 of his 20 playoff games.

A new award, the William M. Jennings Trophy, was created in 1982 to recognize the team goalies with the fewest goals-against in a season. Rick Wamsley and Denis Herron of the Canadiens were its first winners. Patrick Roy and Brian Hayward won the Jennings Trophy for three consecutive years during the decade.

The 80s also witnessed the debuts of Ron Hextall with the Philadelphia Flyers; Hextall took over from Pelle Lindbergh, a Swede who held great promise but was the victim of a tragic accident in November 1985. Hextall, winner of the 1987 Vézina and Conn-Smythe Trophies, became the first goalie to score a goal in the National League, a feat he accomplished in Boston during a game against the Bruins.

Ron Hextall played only one season with the New York Islanders, in 1993-1994. Here he faces forward John Leclair of the Canadiens; the two became teammates the following season.

# TOM BARRASSO

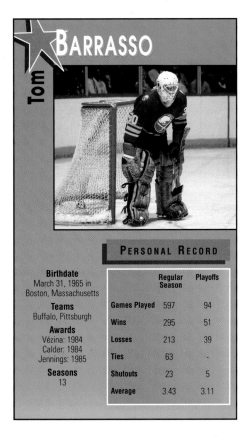

Tom BARRASSO

## PERSONAL RECORD

**Birthdate**
March 31, 1965 in
Boston, Massachusetts

**Teams**
Buffalo, Pittsburgh

**Awards**
Vézina: 1984
Calder: 1984
Jennings: 1985

**Seasons**
13

|  | Regular Season | Playoffs |
|---|---|---|
| Games Played | 597 | 94 |
| Wins | 295 | 51 |
| Losses | 213 | 39 |
| Ties | 63 | - |
| Shutouts | 23 | 5 |
| Average | 3.43 | 3.11 |

his teammate, veteran Robert Sauvé, he won the Jennings Trophy.

On November 12, 1988, the Sabres decided to gamble on a duo composed of Daren Puppa and Jacques Cloutier; so they traded Barrasso to the Pittsburgh Penguins for defenceman Doug Bodger and leftwinger Darrin Shannon. Barrasso was a driving force behind two Stanley Cup wins for the Penguins.

During the 1991 playoffs, he maintained the best average in the League (2.60) and won 12 of his 20 games. The following season, during the playoffs once again, he won 16 of 21 games, maintaining an average of 2.82. The two goalies who duelled during the finals, Ed Belfour of the Black Hawks and Barrasso of the Penguins, set a National League record by each winning 11 consecutive games during the playoffs.

Barrasso had another excellent season in 1992-1993, playing 63 of the Penguins' 84 games and leading the League's other goaltenders with 43 wins. The following season, however, he suffered a few injuries, played only 44 games and saw his average go from 3.01 to 3.36.

Although he played only two games in 1994-1995 because of elbow and wrist injuries, Barrasso made an impressive comeback in 1995-1996, playing 49 games for an average of 3.43. He shared goaltending duties with Ken Wregget, but during the playoffs the Penguins were eliminated in seven games by the unpredictable Florida Panthers.

Tom Barrasso was the Buffalo Sabres' first pick and one of the three American players who were among the top five selected during the 1983 draft. At age 18, he made a spectacular start in the National League. He won 26 of 42 games in the 1983-1984 season and maintained an average of 2.84, earning both the Calder and Vézina Trophies. He was the first goalie since Tony Esposito (in 1970) to receive both awards the same year.

The following season, he led the League in shutouts, with five, and maintained the best average in the circuit, with 2.66 in 54 games. With

Tom Barrasso uses his stick to stop a shot from winger Stephan Lebeau of the Montreal Canadiens, alone in front of the Penguins net.

# DON BEAUPRE

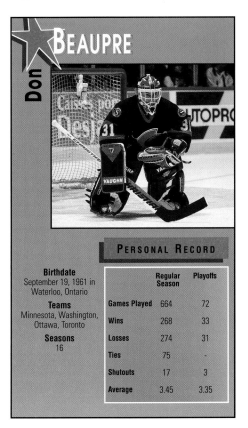

**BEAUPRE**

Don

### PERSONAL RECORD

**Birthdate**
September 19, 1961 in
Waterloo, Ontario

**Teams**
Minnesota, Washington,
Ottawa, Toronto

**Seasons**
16

| | Regular Season | Playoffs |
|---|---|---|
| Games Played | 664 | 72 |
| Wins | 268 | 33 |
| Losses | 274 | 31 |
| Ties | 75 | - |
| Shutouts | 17 | 3 |
| Average | 3.45 | 3.35 |

The Minnesota North Stars' second pick in the 1980 draft, Don Beaupre made his debut the following season and played 44 games. He returned to the minors sporadically over the next seasons, sharing goaltending duties for the North Stars with Gilles Meloche and Kari Takko. In 1983-1984, the North Stars finished in first place in the Norris Division but lost the conference finals to the Edmonton Oilers. Beaupre played 13 games, winning six and finishing with an average of 3.07.

Don Beaupre played nine seasons with Minnesota before going to the Washington Capitals on November 1, 1988. His best season with the team came in 1990-1991, when he maintained an average of 2.64 in 45 games and dominated the League for most shutouts, with five. During the playoffs, Beaupre took part in 11 games, winning five and maintaining an average of 2.79.

After the second best season of his career in 1993-1994, when he posted an average of 2.84 in 53 games, Beaupre went to the Ottawa Senators. During the 1995-1996 season, after playing 33 games with Ottawa, Beaupre was traded to the Maple Leafs, where he served as backup to Félix Potvin, playing only eight games.

Don Beaupre played in the All Star games in 1981 and 1992. Here we see him in action on the Forum ice in Montreal, stopping a puck while Gilbert Dionne of the Canadiens tries to get the rebound.

# ED BELFOUR

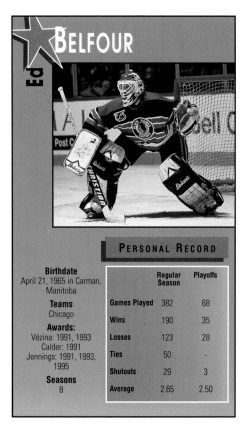

## BELFOUR

Ed

### PERSONAL RECORD

**Birthdate**
April 21, 1965 in Carman, Manitoba

**Teams**
Chicago

**Awards:**
Vézina: 1991, 1993
Calder: 1991
Jennings: 1991, 1993, 1995

**Seasons**
8

| | Regular Season | Playoffs |
|---|---|---|
| Games Played | 382 | 68 |
| Wins | 190 | 35 |
| Losses | 123 | 28 |
| Ties | 50 | - |
| Shutouts | 29 | 3 |
| Average | 2.65 | 2.50 |

The Chicago Black Hawks struck gold on September 25, 1987 when they signed Ed Belfour, a free agent who was tending goals for the Saginaw team in the International League. At the end of the 1987-1988 season in that league, Belfour was named rookie of the year. The following season, he played 23 games with Chicago and during the 1990 playoffs, he maintained an average of 2.49 and was credited with four wins in nine games.

In 1990-1991, he finally earned a permanent position as a goaltender and at age 25 became the first goalie in history to win the Calder, Vézina and Jennings Trophies all in the same year. That season he won 43 of 74 games, maintaining an average of 2.47, the best in the League. Since then, Belfour has won the Vézina Trophy a second time

and the Jennings a third. In 1994-1995, he ended the season with a record of 22 wins in 42 games and maintained an average of 2.28.

During the 1992 playoffs, Belfour set a record by winning 11 consecutive games, a milestone he shares with Tom Barrasso and Patrick Roy, who accomplished the same exploit in 1992 and 1993 respectively. For the first time in his career, Belfour participated in the Stanley Cup finals, but the Hawks went down in four games against the Pittsburgh Penguins. Nevertheless, his 2.47 average in 18 playoff games was the best in the League.

From 1992 to 1995, Belfour dominated the League for most shutouts and in 1994-1995, he recorded the best average of his career. In 1995-1996, Belfour won 22 of his 50 games and maintained an average of 2.74. Although he did well during the playoffs (with an average of 2.07 in nine games), he failed to prevent his team's elimination by the Colorado Avalanche.

Ed Belfour, in the old Chicago Black Hawks uniform, worn to commemorate the 75th anniversary of the National Hockey League. With Belfour in the net, Chicago played in the Stanley Cup finals in 1992 for the first time since 1973.

Ed Belfour won 22 games in 42 and maintained an average of 2.28 in 1994-1995, earning the Jennings Trophy for the third time in his career.

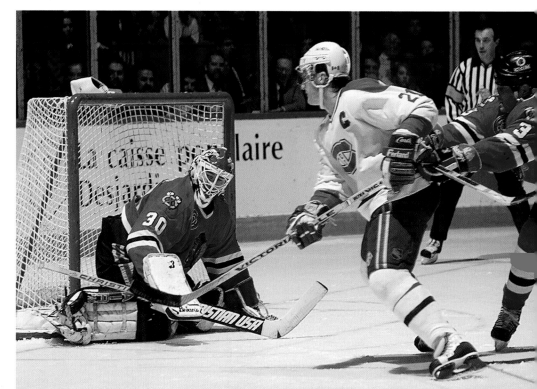

# TIM BERNHARDT

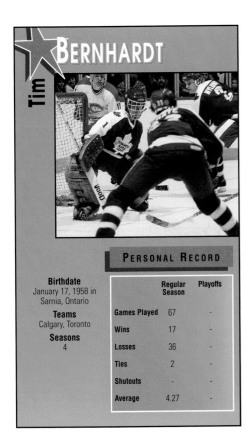

**PERSONAL RECORD**

**Birthdate**
January 17, 1958 in
Sarnia, Ontario

**Teams**
Calgary, Toronto

**Seasons**
4

| | Regular Season | Playoffs |
|---|---|---|
| Games Played | 67 | - |
| Wins | 17 | - |
| Losses | 36 | - |
| Ties | 2 | - |
| Shutouts | - | - |
| Average | 4.27 | - |

Tim Bernhardt was 24 years old when he was given the chance to play his first games in the National League, with the Calgary Flames, in 1982-1983. He played only six games with the team and had to wait until the 1984-1985 season before playing with the professionals again, this time with the Toronto Maple Leafs.

In 1984-1985 Bernhardt played 37 games, maintaining an average of 3.74 and sharing duties with Ken Wregget. For a second consecutive year, Toronto finished last in the Norris Division, winning only 20 of its 80 games.

During the 1985-1986 season, Tim Bernhardt was relegated to being the team's backup goalie, as Toronto had acquired veteran Don Edwards from the Calgary Flames. Edwards played 38 games (with an average of 4.78) while Bernhardt played only 23 and maintained an unimpressive average of 5.07. Toronto won only five more games than they had the previous season and allowed 386 goals in 80 games, outdone only by two other teams, Los Angeles (389 goals) and Detroit (415 goals).

Tim Bernhardt played in only one game the following season, letting in three goals in a single period. That was his last game in the National League. Bernhardt is currently working as a scout for the Dallas Stars.

# DANIEL BERTHIAUME

Drafted by the Winnipeg Jets in 1985, Daniel Berthiaume, who also played with the Chicoutimi Saguenéens, earned a place on the team the following year. He played in 31 games, won 18 and maintained an average of 3.17, the best in his career.

In 1988-1989 Berthiaume became the Jets' lead goalie. He played 56 games, sustained an average of 3.51 and logged 22 wins, the highest total of his career. On January 22, 1990, Berthiaume went to the Minnesota North Stars, where he played only five games. In September of the same year, he was traded to the Los Angeles Kings, where he played 37 games in 1990-1991. In January 1992, Berthiaume packed his suitcases again, this time heading for Boston, where he played only eight games. In 1992-1993, Berthiaume decided to play in Europe and after 28 games with the Graz team, he signed a contract as a free agent with the Ottawa Senators, on December 15, 1992. Berthiaume played 25 games with Ottawa, winning only two of them. In 1993-1994, he played in only one of the Senators' games (letting in two goals in one minute!). In March 1994, the Detroit Red Wings retained his services. Berthiaume has not played in the National League for the past two seasons.

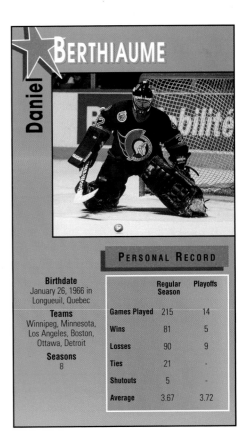

**PERSONAL RECORD**

**Birthdate**
January 26, 1966 in
Longueuil, Quebec

**Teams**
Winnipeg, Minnesota,
Los Angeles, Boston,
Ottawa, Detroit

**Seasons**
8

| | Regular Season | Playoffs |
|---|---|---|
| Games Played | 215 | 14 |
| Wins | 81 | 5 |
| Losses | 90 | 9 |
| Ties | 21 | - |
| Shutouts | 5 | - |
| Average | 3.67 | 3.72 |

# CRAIG BILLINGTON

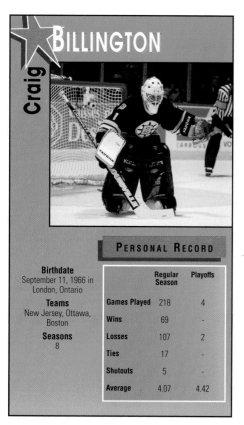

**Craig BILLINGTON**

### PERSONAL RECORD

**Birthdate**
September 11, 1966 in
London, Ontario

**Teams**
New Jersey, Ottawa,
Boston

**Seasons**
8

| | Regular Season | Playoffs |
|---|---|---|
| Games Played | 218 | 4 |
| Wins | 69 | - |
| Losses | 107 | 2 |
| Ties | 17 | - |
| Shutouts | 5 | - |
| Average | 4.07 | 4.42 |

Craig Billington took a while to carve out a place for himself in the National League. The New Jersey Devils' second pick in the 1984 draft played only 43 games with the Devils between 1985 and 1989, but did play 158 games in the American League during that same period.

Billington played 59 games with the Utica Devils in the American League, the most of any goalie that season. He chalked up 22 wins and maintained an average of 3.67. Billington also played with Canada's national team in 1990-1991, winning 17 of 34 games and maintaining an average of 3.51.

After playing 26 games with the Devils in 1991-1992, he had the chance to play in 42 games in 1992-1993, sharing goaltending duties with Chris Terreri. Billington won 21 games and ended the season with an average of 3.67. However, in June 1993 he was traded to the Ottawa Senators for goalie Peter Sidorkiewicz. The Devils' transaction was motivated by goalie Chris Terreri's performance and by the imminent arrival of young Martin Brodeur, who had also honed his skills with the Utica Devils and who earned the title of rookie of the year in 1993-1994.

In 1993-1994 Billington played 63 games with Ottawa, winning 11 and maintaining an average of 4.59. Traded to the Bruins in April 1995, Billington played 27 games in 1995-1996 and maintained an average of 3.43.

Craig Billington played two seasons with the Ottawa Senators and holds the team record for most wins in one season: 11 in 63 games in 1993-1994.

# SEAN BURKE

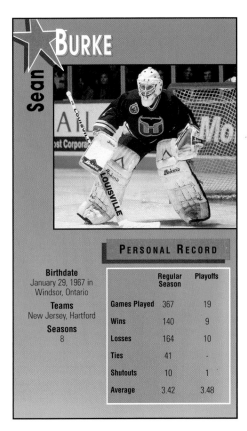

Sean BURKE

## PERSONAL RECORD

**Birthdate**
January 29, 1967 in
Windsor, Ontario

**Teams**
New Jersey, Hartford

**Seasons**
8

| | Regular Season | Playoffs |
|---|---|---|
| Games Played | 367 | 19 |
| Wins | 140 | 9 |
| Losses | 164 | 10 |
| Ties | 41 | - |
| Shutouts | 10 | 1 |
| Average | 3.42 | 3.48 |

Sean Burke first made his mark with Canada's national junior team, playing three seasons (1986-1987, 1987-1988, 1991-1992). He also played with Canada's Olympic team in 1987-1988 and 1991-1992.

Although he was the New Jersey Devils' second pick in the 1985 draft, he joined the team only in 1987-1988, playing 13 regular season games and 17 games in the playoffs. He was one of the Devils' star players during the playoffs, which the team made for the first time since 1978. To everyone's surprise, the Devils beat the New York Islanders in six games and eliminated the Capitals in seven games

The Devils traded Sean Burke to the Whalers in the summer of 1992 following a brilliant showing by rookie Chris Terreri, who maintained an average of 2.91 in 53 games in 1990-1991 with New Jersey.

before going down to defeat in seven games at the hands of the Boston Bruins in the conference finals.

Burke stayed with New Jersey for three seasons. He was traded to the Hartford Whalers in August 1992, along with defenceman Eric Weinrich, for Bobby Holik. After a disappointing season in 1992-1993 (with an average of 4.16 in 50 games), he shone in 1993-1994 with an average of 2.99 in 47 games. He did even better the next season, bringing his average down to 2.68 in 42 games and recording 17 wins. Despite his efforts, the Whalers missed the playoffs for the third consecutive season.

Sean Burke hasn't been involved in the playoffs since the spring of 1990, when he was with the New Jersey Devils. In 1996, for the fourth consecutive season, the Whalers failed to make it to the playoffs.

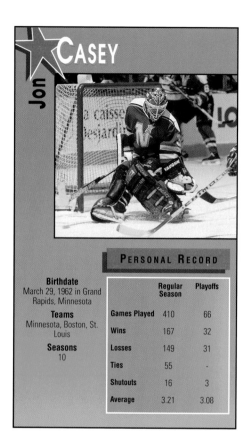

# JON CASEY

**Jon Casey**

## PERSONAL RECORD

**Birthdate**
March 29, 1962 in Grand
Rapids, Minnesota

**Teams**
Minnesota, Boston, St.
Louis

**Seasons**
10

| | Regular Season | Playoffs |
|---|---|---|
| Games Played | 410 | 66 |
| Wins | 167 | 32 |
| Losses | 149 | 31 |
| Ties | 55 | - |
| Shutouts | 16 | 3 |
| Average | 3.21 | 3.08 |

Signed by the Minnesota North Stars in April 1984 when he was a free agent, Jon Casey played eight seasons with the team, interspersed by several stints in the American League. He joined the team for good in 1988-1989. In 1989-1990 Casey led the League in wins, with 31 in 61 games. But his best times with the team came during the following season. He maintained an average of 2.98 in 55 games, but he was at his peak during the playoffs. He played 23 games and won 14 of them, a high for the 1991 playoffs. He maintained an average of 3.04 and was one of the artisans of the success enjoyed by the North Stars, who made it to the finals against the Pittsburgh Penguins but lost in six games.

In June 1993, Casey was traded to the Boston Bruins for goalie Andy Moog. In 1993-1994 he played the best season of his career, maintaining an average of 2.88 in 57 games and managing four shutouts, a personal best.

Casey has played only 28 games since he joined the Blues for 1994-1995, including nine games in 1995-1996. Although he was brilliant during the playoffs when he stood in for injured Grant Fuhr, the Blues were eliminated by Detroit in a seven-game series.

# JACQUES CLOUTIER

In 1979, Jacques Cloutier was selected to play on the Quebec Major Junior Hockey League's first All Star team, having dominated the League's other goalies with an average of 3.14 in 72 games. A little over one year later, he joined the Buffalo Sabres, where he stayed for most of his career. In eight seasons with the team, from 1981 to 1989, he played 144 games. In 1988-1989, when he played 36 games, he enjoyed his glory days and maintained an average of 3.63.

In September 1989, he was traded to the Chicago Black Hawks, where he played one and a half seasons. The 1989-1990 season was the best of his career. He played 43 games and lowered his average to 3.09. In January 1991, he was traded to the Quebec Nordiques for left-winger Tony McKegney. He played only 26 games in the 1991-1992 season before retiring.

Since deciding to hang up his skates, Jacques Cloutier has worked as a goaltending coach with the Halifax Citadels in the American League, with the Quebec Nordiques, and with the Colorado Avalanche. His experience is a valuable asset for the team's young goalies.

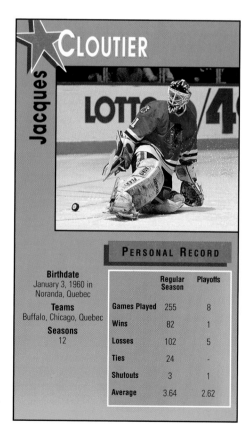

**Jacques Cloutier**

## PERSONAL RECORD

**Birthdate**
January 3, 1960 in
Noranda, Quebec

**Teams**
Buffalo, Chicago, Quebec

**Seasons**
12

| | Regular Season | Playoffs |
|---|---|---|
| Games Played | 255 | 8 |
| Wins | 82 | 1 |
| Losses | 102 | 5 |
| Ties | 24 | - |
| Shutouts | 3 | 1 |
| Average | 3.64 | 2.62 |

# BOB FROESE

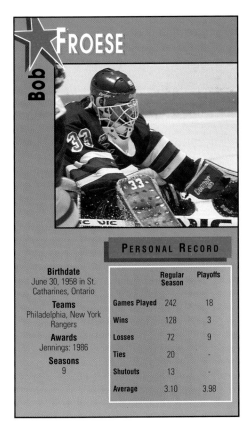

**Bob FROESE**

### PERSONAL RECORD

**Birthdate**
June 30, 1958 in St. Catharines, Ontario

**Teams**
Philadelphia, New York Rangers

**Awards**
Jennings: 1986

**Seasons**
9

| | Regular Season | Playoffs |
|---|---|---|
| Games Played | 242 | 18 |
| Wins | 128 | 3 |
| Losses | 72 | 9 |
| Ties | 20 | - |
| Shutouts | 13 | - |
| Average | 3.10 | 3.98 |

Bob Froese began his career with the Philadelphia Flyers in 1982-1983. He played 25 games, managed four shutouts and maintained an average of 2.52. At the time the team's lead goalie was rookie Pelle Lindbergh, who played 40 games and maintained an average of 2.98. During the next seasons Froese played 48 and 17 games. When teammate Pelle Lindbergh was killed in a car accident on November 19, 1985, Froese took over the Number 1 spot in the team's net. He made the most of his opportunity: he led the League with a 2.55 average in 51 games in addition to managing five shutouts. With teammate Darren Jensen, he won the Jennings Trophy, awarded to the team goaltenders with the fewest goals-against in the season.

Despite their goalies' accomplishments, the Flyers lost in the division semifinals against the New York Rangers. The following season, rookie Ron Hextall took over as the team's lead goalie and Froese was traded to the New York Rangers. In 1986-1987, with the Flyers and the Rangers, he played a total of 31 games and maintained an average of 3.63.

John Vanbiesbrouck was the Rangers' lead goalie at the time and Froese played 25, 30 and 15 games in the next three seasons. He ended his career with the team in 1990, with a career average of 3.10.

Stretched out on the ice, Bob Froese intends to abort an attack launched by Canadiens players, taking aim at the puck as Guy Carbonneau shoots it.

# GRANT FUHR

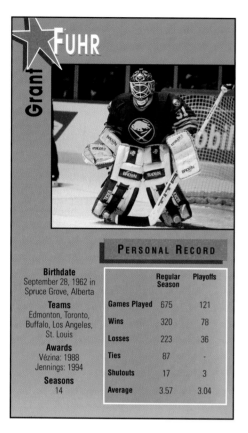

**Grant FUHR**

### PERSONAL RECORD

**Birthdate**
September 28, 1962 in
Spruce Grove, Alberta

**Teams**
Edmonton, Toronto,
Buffalo, Los Angeles,
St. Louis

**Awards**
Vézina: 1988
Jennings: 1994

**Seasons**
14

| | Regular Season | Playoffs |
|---|---|---|
| Games Played | 675 | 121 |
| Wins | 320 | 78 |
| Losses | 223 | 36 |
| Ties | 87 | - |
| Shutouts | 17 | 3 |
| Average | 3.57 | 3.04 |

League's president, John Ziegler; this was the heaviest penalty imposed on a player in NHL history.

Fuhr played only 13 games with the Oilers in 1990-1991; on September 19, 1991, he was traded to the Maple Leafs with Craig Berube and Glenn Anderson in exchange for Vincent Damphousse, Luke Richardson, Scott Thornton and Peter Ing. After one and a half seasons with the Leafs, Fuhr headed for Buffalo, where he shared the Jennings Trophy with Dominik Hasek in 1994. After a brief stint in Los Angeles, Fuhr went to the Blues last season and played 79 games in 1995-1996, a League high for goalies. His average of 2.87 was the best of his career.

Grant Fuhr made an astounding comeback under Mike Keenan in St. Louis, but injuries limited him to just two playoff games. He is pictured here in a Buffalo Sabres uniform.

There can be no question that Grant Fuhr was one of the top goaltenders of the 80s, performing magnificently with the Edmonton Oilers. The Oilers' first pick in the 1981 draft, he made his debut in Edmonton immediately and played 10 seasons there before being traded to Toronto. He was involved in five Stanley Cup victories for the Oilers (1984, 1985, 1987, 1988 and 1990) and won the Vézina Trophy in 1988; that year he won 40 of 75 games, a League high.

On March 31, 1990, Fuhr dropped a bombshell on the hockey world when he admitted to having used drugs in previous years. He was suspended for 60 games by the

Grant Fuhr played one and a half seasons with the Toronto Maple Leafs. On this play, he robs Canadiens Kirk Muller of a goal.

Grant Fuhr makes a save as Canadiens centre Jesse Bélanger watches. Taking it all in is Dale Hawerchuk of the Sabres.

Grant Fuhr screens his net to deflect incoming Canadiens Brent Gilchrist.

Grant Fuhr in an Edmonton Oilers uniform. He won the Stanley Cup five times with the Oilers. Fuhr played a vital role in ensuring Edmonton's success in the 80s. He was awarded the Vézina Trophy once, in 1988.

# MARIO GOSSELIN

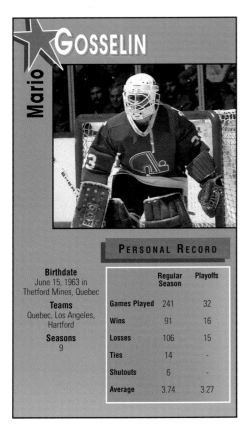

Mario GOSSELIN

### PERSONAL RECORD

**Birthdate**
June 15, 1963 in
Thetford Mines, Quebec

**Teams**
Quebec, Los Angeles,
Hartford

**Seasons**
9

| | Regular Season | Playoffs |
|---|---|---|
| Games Played | 241 | 32 |
| Wins | 91 | 16 |
| Losses | 106 | 15 |
| Ties | 14 | - |
| Shutouts | 6 | - |
| Average | 3.74 | 3.27 |

In 1988-1989 he played 39 games with the Nordiques. Then, as a free agent, he was signed by Los Angeles. He played only 26 games in California before signing a new contract with the Hartford Whalers in September 1991. He was limited to 23 games in two seasons and skated for the last time in the National League in the 1993-1994 season.

Mario Gosselin won 91 games in his career in the National Hockey League and played six of his nine seasons with the Quebec Nordiques.

**M**ario Gosselin sparked the interest of the hockey world in 1982-1983 when he was only 19 and playing with the Shawinigan Cataractes in the Quebec Major Junior Hockey League. In 46 games he had recorded 32 wins, maintaining an average of 3.12. Signed by Quebec in 1982, he played with Canada's Olympic team the next season and joined the Nordiques later.

In 1984-1985, he helped the team make it to the conference finals against the Philadelphia Flyers but lost in six games. Gosselin played 17 games during the playoffs, with an average of 3.06.

Mario Gosselin tries to immobilize the puck before Canadiens Bob Gainey has a chance to slide it into the net.

# BRIAN HAYWARD

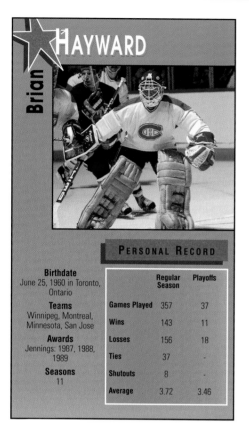

**PERSONAL RECORD**

**Birthdate**
June 25, 1960 in Toronto, Ontario

**Teams**
Winnipeg, Montreal, Minnesota, San Jose

**Awards**
Jennings: 1987, 1988, 1989

**Seasons**
11

| | Regular Season | Playoffs |
|---|---|---|
| Games Played | 357 | 37 |
| Wins | 143 | 11 |
| Losses | 156 | 18 |
| Ties | 37 | - |
| Shutouts | 8 | - |
| Average | 3.72 | 3.46 |

After goaltending for Cornell University in Boston for four years, Brian Hayward was signed by the Winnipeg Jets in May 1982 and joined the team early the following season. He played four years with the Jets before being traded to the Montreal Canadiens for goaltender Steve Penney in August 1986. The highlights of his career came in Montreal, even if he played in the shadow of the League's best goaltender, Patrick Roy.

In the spring the Canadiens had won the Stanley Cup for the 22nd time in their history and Hayward

finally had the opportunity to play with a winning team. During his first season with Montreal, the goalie played 37 games and maintained the best average in the League: 2.81. For his part, Roy played 46 games and ended the season with an average of 2.93. Roy and Hayward were awarded the Jennings Trophy, an honour they received the two following seasons as well. During the 1987 playoffs, Hayward became the team's lead goalie. He played 13 games, but after eliminating Boston in four games and the Nordiques in seven, the Canadiens went down in six games against the Philadelphia Flyers. However, Hayward maintained an excellent average of 2.71.

Even if Patrick Roy was a crowd pleaser, Hayward never played fewer than 29 games in any of his seasons

with the team and maintained averages of under 3.00 three times in four seasons.

In November 1990, Brian Hayward was traded to the Minnesota North Stars, leaving the way free for young goaltender André Racicot to play as Patrick Roy's new backup. Hayward played 26 games in the North Stars uniform in 1990-1991 before going to the San Jose Sharks in May 1991. The 1992-1993 season, during which he played only 18 games and chalked up only two wins, was his last in the National League.

Brian Hayward spent glorious years with the Canadiens despite the remarkable performance of rookie Patrick Roy. Hayward and Roy won the Jennings Trophy three years running.

# GLENN HEALY

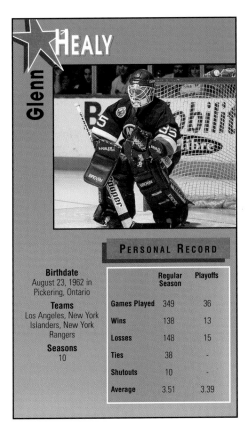

**Glenn Healy**

## PERSONAL RECORD

**Birthdate**
August 23, 1962 in
Pickering, Ontario

**Teams**
Los Angeles, New York
Islanders, New York
Rangers

**Seasons**
10

| | Regular Season | Playoffs |
|---|---|---|
| Games Played | 349 | 36 |
| Wins | 138 | 13 |
| Losses | 148 | 15 |
| Ties | 38 | - |
| Shutouts | 10 | - |
| Average | 3.51 | 3.39 |

Glenn Healy, a goaltender who played college hockey in the United States, was signed as a free agent on June 13, 1985 by the Los Angeles Kings. Healy played two seasons with New Haven in the American League before playing regularly with the Kings. In his two seasons with Los Angeles, Healy maintained averages of 4.33 and 4.27 before going to the New York Islanders in August 1989. During this first season with his new team, Healy played 39 games and maintained an average of 3.50. The next season, in

Glenn Healy played four seasons with the New York Islanders before joining the New York Rangers. On this play, during a game between the Islanders and the Canadiens, Healy fails to stop the puck.

53 games, he lowered his average to 3.32. In 1992-1993 he enjoyed his finest hours in hockey, when he won 22 out of his 47 games and maintained an average of 3.30. During the playoffs, the Islanders eliminated Washington, then surprised the Stanley Cup champions, the Pittsburgh Penguins, by taking a seven-game series. The Montreal Canadiens finally ended the Islanders' dream by eliminating them in five games. Healy played 18 of his team's games and maintained an average of 3.19.

The Los Angeles Kings signed Glenn Healy as a free agent on June 13, 1985. He played three seasons with the team before going to the New York Islanders, in August 1989. He played four seasons with the Islanders, reaching his peak in 1992-1993: in 47 games, he recorded 22 wins and maintained an average of 3.30.

A member of the New York Rangers since June 1993, he played

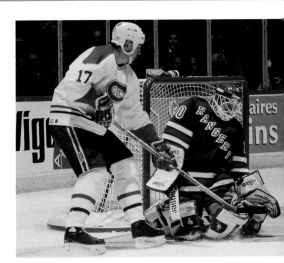

John Leclair of the Canadiens tries to retrieve the puck that Glenn Healy has just stopped.

as Mike Richter's backup for two seasons. The Rangers won the Stanley Cup in 1994, but Healy was involved in only two games and played only 68 minutes during the playoffs. In 1995-1996 he played 44 games, maintaining an average of 2.90.

# RON HEXTALL

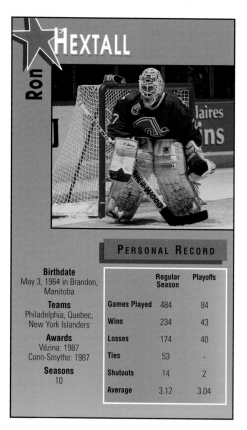

**Ron Hextall**

### PERSONAL RECORD

**Birthdate**
May 3, 1964 in Brandon, Manitoba

**Teams**
Philadelphia, Quebec, New York Islanders

**Awards**
Vézina: 1987
Conn-Smythe: 1987

**Seasons**
10

|  | Regular Season | Playoffs |
|---|---|---|
| Games Played | 484 | 84 |
| Wins | 234 | 43 |
| Losses | 174 | 40 |
| Ties | 53 | - |
| Shutouts | 14 | 2 |
| Average | 3.12 | 3.04 |

Ron Hextall has a temper, just ask anyone who has ever played against him. During the 1989 playoffs, the Flyers goaltender literally attacked defenceman Chris Chelios, who was playing with the Canadiens at the time. Since his debut in 1986, Hextall has attracted attention because of his aggressive behaviour (in 1987-1988, he was given 104 minutes of penalties), his excellent work in the net and ... his talent as a goal scorer!

On December 8, 1987, in a game against the Boston Bruins, he became the first goaltender in the history of the National Hockey League to score a goal; as he cleared the puck out of his own zone at the end of the game, it strayed into the opposing team's empty net. Hextall repeated the performance on April 11, 1989, in a playoffs game against Washington.

During his first season with the Flyers, Hextall led the League for most games played (66) and most wins (37); with an average of 3.00, he was awarded the Vézina Trophy. During the playoffs he did better still, winning 15 of 26 games and maintaining an average of 2.77, which earned him the Conn-Smythe Trophy although the Flyers were beaten in seven games by the Edmonton Oilers in the finals. He finished second behind Luc Robitaille in the bid for title of rookie of the year, but certainly found some consolation in becoming the first goaltender since Bernie Parent in 1974 to win the Vézina and Conn-Smythe Trophies in the same year, in addition to being selected to play on the first All Star team.

The grandson of Bryan Hextall, a Hockey Hall of Famer who played 11 seasons with the New York Rangers, Ron Hextall played six seasons in Philadelphia before going to the Quebec Nordiques on June 30, 1992; the transaction made it possible for the Flyers to get their hands on the Nordiques' first pick in the draft, the most promising player of the hour, Eric Lindros, who refused to play in Quebec City.

Hextall played one season with the Nordiques, another in Long Island with the Islanders and in 1994-1995, he came back to the Flyers.

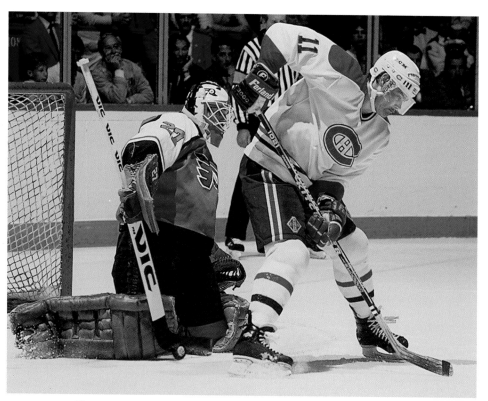

During the 1995 playoffs, Ron Hextall was one of his team's dominant players, leading the Flyers to the Eastern Conference finals. But the New Jersey Devils were too powerful for Hextall and his team. In this photo taken during Hextall's first stay with the Flyers, he takes on Ryan Walter of the Canadiens.

In 1995-1996, Hextall dominated the League's goaltenders with an average of 2.17 in 53 games, a career best. During the playoffs, Hextall played 12 games (with an average of 2.13), but the Flyers were eliminated in six games in the semifinals by the Florida Panthers. In this photo, Hextall keeps an eye on action behind his net.

Ron Hextall played only one season with the New York Islanders, in 1993-1994, maintaining an average of 3.08 in 65 games, his best since his first season in the League.

Traded to the Quebec Nordiques in the mammoth transaction that sent Eric Lindros to the Flyers, Hextall spent only one season with the team.

The Flyers' Number 27 takes a break while play is stopped.

Ron Hextall has always liked to wander out of his net and tried time and time again to score a goal, a feat he accomplished in 1987.

# KELLY HRUDEY

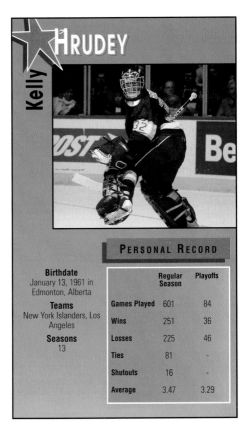

**Kelly HRUDEY**

### PERSONAL RECORD

**Birthdate**
January 13, 1961 in
Edmonton, Alberta

**Teams**
New York Islanders, Los
Angeles

**Seasons**
13

| | Regular Season | Playoffs |
|---|---|---|
| Games Played | 601 | 84 |
| Wins | 251 | 36 |
| Losses | 225 | 46 |
| Ties | 81 | - |
| Shutouts | 16 | - |
| Average | 3.47 | 3.29 |

In 1992-1993 he played 50 games for an average of 3.86, and the Kings went into the playoffs for the seventh consecutive year. Surprisingly, the Kings defeated the Calgary Flames in six games and their dream stayed alive while Gretzky's gang disposed of the Toronto Maple Leafs in seven games. Los Angeles lost in five games in the Stanley Cup finals against the Canadiens, while Hrudey's record showed 10 wins in 20 games and an average of 3.52.

In 1995-1996, Hrudey shared goaltending duties with Byron Dafoe, acquired from the Washington Capitals. In 36 games, he maintained a 3.26 average with Larry Robinson's team.

Kelly Hrudey uses his pads to stop a shot by a Canadiens forward.

Kelly Hrudey came to the New York Islanders during the 1983-1984 season, playing 12 games and recording seven wins. The following season, he became the team's lead goalie. In 1987, he played 14 games during the playoffs, when the Islanders reached the Patrick Division finals.

Traded to the Los Angeles Kings on February 22, 1989 for goaltender Mark Fitzpatrick and defenceman Wayne McBean, Hrudey experienced his best season in 1990-1991: that year he maintained an average of 2.90 in 47 games.

Kelly Hrudey foils leftwinger Vincent Damphousse of the Canadiens, alone in front of the net during a game at the Forum in Montreal.

# PETER ING

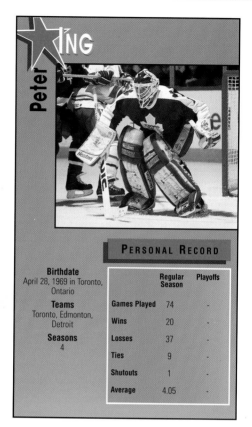

## PERSONAL RECORD

**Birthdate**
April 28, 1969 in Toronto,
Ontario

**Teams**
Toronto, Edmonton,
Detroit

**Seasons**
4

| | Regular Season | Playoffs |
|---|---|---|
| Games Played | 74 | - |
| Wins | 20 | - |
| Losses | 37 | - |
| Ties | 9 | - |
| Shutouts | 1 | - |
| Average | 4.05 | - |

Peter Ing, the Maple Leafs' third pick in the 1988 draft, made his debut in the National League in 1989-1990, but played only three games with the team. His was an entirely different story the following season, when he became the lead goaltender for the Maple Leafs. Ing played 56 games and maintained an average of 3.84, with only 16 wins. The Toronto team ended the season with only 23 wins in 80 games and allowed 318 goals; only the Nordiques managed to do worse, letting in a total of 354 goals.

Traded to the Edmonton Oilers in 1991 in a transaction notable for sending Grant Fuhr to Toronto, Ing played only 12 games with his new team. In 1993-1994 he went to Detroit, but played only three games there, spending the better part of the season with the Las Vegas team in the International League.

In 1995-1996, Peter Ing played 32 games with the Cincinnati Cyclones in the International League, maintaining an average of 4.05.

Peter Ing, playing for the Toronto Maple Leafs, the team that picked him in the 1988 draft.

# AL JENSEN

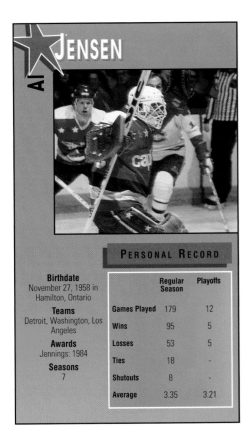

**PERSONAL RECORD**

**Birthdate**
November 27, 1958 in
Hamilton, Ontario

**Teams**
Detroit, Washington, Los
Angeles

**Awards**
Jennings: 1984

**Seasons**
7

| | Regular Season | Playoffs |
|---|---|---|
| Games Played | 179 | 12 |
| Wins | 95 | 5 |
| Losses | 53 | 5 |
| Ties | 18 | - |
| Shutouts | 8 | - |
| Average | 3.35 | 3.21 |

After playing only one game with the Detroit Red Wings in the 1980-1981 season and allowing seven goals, Al Jensen was traded to the Washington Capitals. He spent the better part of his career with the team.

In 1982-1983 he maintained an average of 3.44 in 40 games, but the following season, he improved on his performance by managing four shutouts and achieving an average of 2.91 in 43 games. That average, combined with his teammate's, Pat Riggin (2.66 in 41 games), earned the duo the Jennings Trophy.

The Capitals finished in second place in the Patrick Division and broke the 100-point mark (101 points in 80 games) for the first time in the team's history. After eliminating the Flyers, the Capitals suffered the same fate in the Patrick Division finals, going down to defeat at the hands of the Islanders in five games.

During the 1986-1987 season, Jensen went to the Los Angeles Kings and played only 11 games that year, his swan song in the National League.

# DOUG KEANS

Doug Keans played four seasons with the Los Angeles Kings, but he played only 56 games with the team. The Kings, who had earned 99 points in 1980-1981 and finished second in the Norris Division, stumbled the following season, amassing only 63 points and dropping to fourth place in the Smythe Division. Worse: goaltenders Keans and Mario Lessard allowed 369 goals, barely ahead of the Toronto Maple Leafs, a team that let in 380 goals.

Before the start of the 1983-1984 season, Keans headed for Boston. Backed by more experienced Bruins defencemen, Keans had a chance to prove himself. In 33 games, he maintained an average of 3.10, the best of his career. In five seasons in Boston, Doug Keans never recorded an average higher than 3.65 and he played approximately 30 games each year.

In 1987-1988, Keans played 30 games while Réjean Lemelin played 49, and the team made it to the Stanley Cup finals. The Bruins lost in four games against the Edmonton Oilers, who won the Stanley Cup for the fourth time in five seasons. During the playoffs, Lemelin was backed by Andy Moog, who had been acquired from the Edmonton Oilers in March 1988 and who played seven games. By then Keans's days with the Bruins were numbered and 1987-1988 proved to be his last year in the National League.

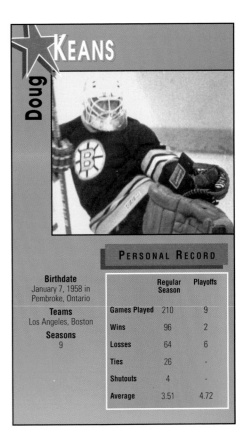

**PERSONAL RECORD**

**Birthdate**
January 7, 1958 in
Pembroke, Ontario

**Teams**
Los Angeles, Boston

**Seasons**
9

| | Regular Season | Playoffs |
|---|---|---|
| Games Played | 210 | 9 |
| Wins | 96 | 2 |
| Losses | 64 | 6 |
| Ties | 26 | - |
| Shutouts | 4 | - |
| Average | 3.51 | 4.72 |

# RÉJEAN LEMELIN

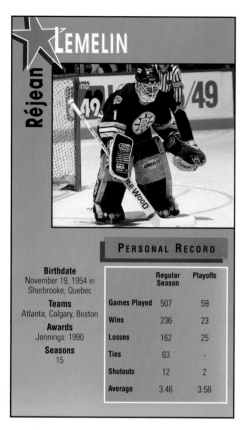

**LEMELIN**

Réjean

### PERSONAL RECORD

**Birthdate**
November 19, 1954 in
Sherbrooke, Quebec

**Teams**
Atlanta, Calgary, Boston

**Awards**
Jennings: 1990

**Seasons**
15

| | Regular Season | Playoffs |
|---|---|---|
| Games Played | 507 | 59 |
| Wins | 236 | 23 |
| Losses | 162 | 25 |
| Ties | 63 | - |
| Shutouts | 12 | 2 |
| Average | 3.46 | 3.58 |

Réjean Lemelin played 15 years in the National League, experiencing his best times with the Boston Bruins in 1989-1990. That year, he maintained an average of 2.81 in 43 games and along with teammate Andy Moog (2.89 in 46 games), he won the Jennings Trophy.

He had begun his career in 1978-1979 with the Atlanta Flames, who moved to Calgary in 1980. He was the lead goaltender for the Flames until the spring of 1987, when he became a free agent and signed with the Boston Bruins. In 1987-1988, he achieved his best average during the playoffs, 2.63 in 17 games, but the Bruins lost in the finals to the Edmonton Oilers.

Lemelin ended his career in 1993 after playing only 18 games in his last two seasons.

Réjean Lemelin tries to snag the puck after making a save.

The goaltender played 15 seasons in the National League, including five with the Boston Bruins late in his career, without ever winning the Stanley Cup. However, in 1990 his performance earned him the Jennings Trophy. On this play, he makes a stop while Mats Naslund and Mike Keane of the Canadiens and defenceman Greg Hawgood keep their eyes glued to the puck.

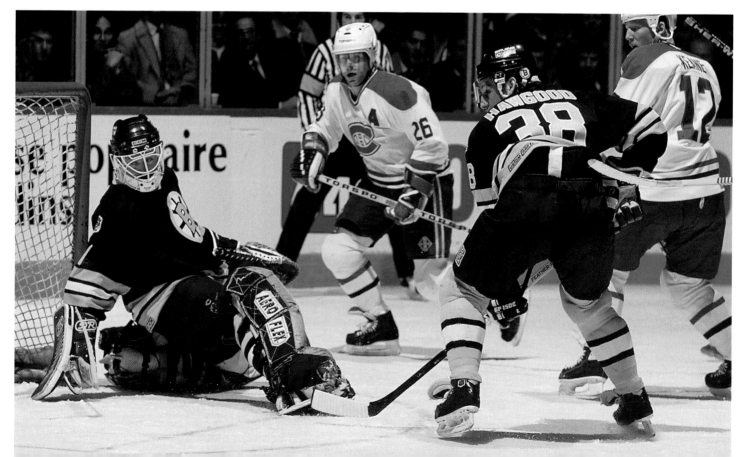

# PELLE LINDBERG

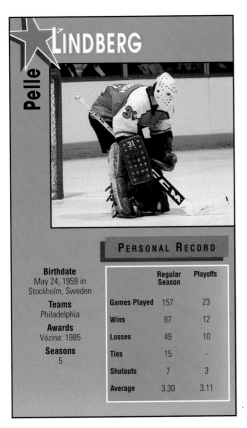

### PERSONAL RECORD

**Birthdate**
May 24, 1959 in
Stockholm, Sweden

**Teams**
Philadelphia

**Awards**
Vézina: 1985

**Seasons**
5

| | Regular Season | Playoffs |
|---|---|---|
| Games Played | 157 | 23 |
| Wins | 87 | 12 |
| Losses | 49 | 10 |
| Ties | 15 | - |
| Shutouts | 7 | 3 |
| Average | 3.30 | 3.11 |

Picked by the Philadelphia Flyers in the second round of the 1979 draft, Swedish goaltender Pelle Lindbergh was 22 when he began his career in the National League in 1981-1982. He played only eight games, since Pete Peeters was the Flyers' Number 1 goalie. However, when Peeters was traded to the Boston Bruins at the end of the season, Lindbergh took over as the Flyers' lead goalie, with Bob Froese as his backup.

In 1982-1983 Lindbergh played 40 games, winning 23 of them and maintaining an average of 2.98. In 1984-1985, he proved that he was one of the best by recording 40 wins in 65 games, the best performance in the League, and maintaining a 3.02 average. The Flyers were proclaimed champions of their division and Lindbergh helped them make it to the Stanley Cup finals for the first time since 1980. In the semifinals, he surpassed himself, allowing only 12 goals to the Quebec Nordiques, who were eliminated in six games. In the finals the Edmonton Oilers, the previous year's champions, got the better of Lindbergh and the Flyers in five games. Lindbergh was awarded the Vézina Trophy at the end of the season, becoming the first Flyers goalie to receive the honour since Bernard Parent in 1975.

The following season, Lindbergh played eight games only. On November 19, 1985, he lost control of his Porsche and crashed into a wall. One of professional hockey's most promising stars, the first European goaltender to win the Vézina Trophy, he died tragically at the age of 26.

The Swedish goaltender, out of his net to stop Bobby Smith of the Canadiens, stares as the play goes on behind him.

# CLINT MALARCHUK

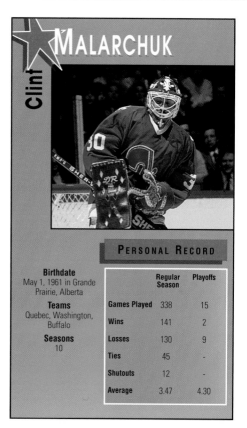

### Clint MALARCHUK

**PERSONAL RECORD**

**Birthdate**
May 1, 1961 in Grande Prairie, Alberta

**Teams**
Quebec, Washington, Buffalo

**Seasons**
10

| | Regular Season | Playoffs |
|---|---|---|
| Games Played | 338 | 15 |
| Wins | 141 | 2 |
| Losses | 130 | 9 |
| Ties | 45 | - |
| Shutouts | 12 | - |
| Average | 3.47 | 4.30 |

On March 7, 1989, Clint Malarchuk went from the Washington Capitals to the Buffalo Sabres. Two weeks later, he was the victim of a serious accident that could have cost him his life. He showed a great deal of courage in returning to play in the 1989-1990 season.

Clint Malarchuk was the Nordiques' third pick in the 1981 draft and he played his first games with the team during the 1981-1982 season. His first big chance came in 1985-1986, when he became the team's lead goalie, a privilege he enjoyed for two seasons. On June 13, 1987, he was traded to the Washington Capitals along with Dale Hunter, for Alan Haworth and Gaétan Duchesne. The best season of his career was in Washington in 1987-1988, when he maintained an average of 3.16 in 54 games and dominated the League by managing four shutouts.

In March 1989 he was traded again, this time to the Buffalo Sabres, but he was the victim of a very serious accident: on March 22, his jugular vein was cut by St. Louis Blues rightwinger Steve Tuttle's skate blade. He was rushed to hospital by ambulance, where surgeons saved his life. The following season, he was back in the Sabres' net.

Malarchuk played four other seasons with the Buffalo Sabres before going to the International League in 1992-1993 to play for San Diego. In 1993-1994, he led the International League for most wins (34 in 55 games) and maintained an average of 3.35 with the Las Vegas Thunder. In 1994-1995, Clint Malarchuk played in 38 games with Las Vegas and ended the season with an average of 3.74.

Malarchuk began his career in the National League with the Quebec Nordiques, playing only two games during the 1981-1982 season.

# KIRK MCLEAN

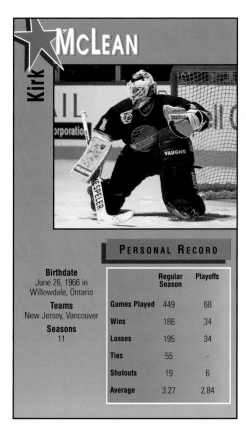

Kirk McLEAN

**PERSONAL RECORD**

**Birthdate**
June 26, 1966 in
Willowdale, Ontario

**Teams**
New Jersey, Vancouver

**Seasons**
11

| | Regular Season | Playoffs |
|---|---|---|
| Games Played | 449 | 68 |
| Wins | 186 | 34 |
| Losses | 195 | 34 |
| Ties | 55 | - |
| Shutouts | 19 | 6 |
| Average | 3.27 | 2.84 |

Kirk McLean harpoons a puck with his stick, preventing the rival team from making a rebound shot.

In 1991-1992 he set the League's best record, with 38 wins and five shutouts in 65 games. That year he also recorded the best average in his career, 2.74, helping the Canucks win the Smythe Division championship for the first time since 1974-1975.

In 1995-1996, he maintained an average of 3.54 in 45 games.

In 1994 Kirk McLean came close to leading the Vancouver Canucks to their first-ever Stanley Cup win. Under coach Pat Quinn, the team lost in seven games in the finals against the New York Rangers. During the playoffs, McLean dominated the League in number of games played, with 24, and in shutouts, with four; he maintained the remarkable average of 2.29.

He had made his debut with the New Jersey Devils in 1985-1986, but over two seasons had played only six games. He went to the Canucks in September 1987 and immediately became the team's lead goalie. In 1989-1990 he played 63 games, a League high, recording 21 wins and ending the season with an average of 3.47.

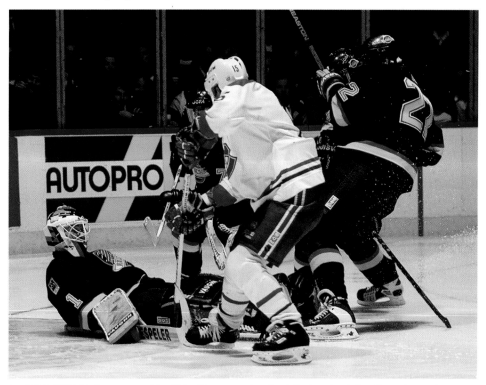

In 1994-1995 McLean won 18 of his 40 games, but he failed to lead the Canucks to the Stanley Cup; for the second consecutive year, the team lost in the conference semifinals to the Chicago Black Hawks.

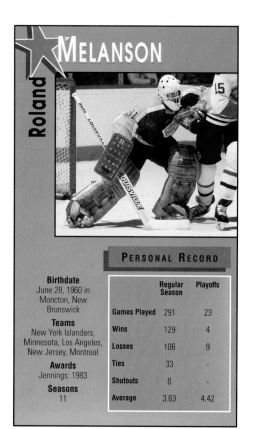

# ROLAND MELANSON

The first goaltender from New Brunswick to play in the National League, Roland Melanson saw his name engraved on the Stanley Cup three times, in 1981, 1982 and 1983, each time with the New York Islanders. His best season came in his third year with the team, in 1982-1983, when he maintained an average of 2.66 in 44 games. Billy Smith and he won the Jennings Trophy, awarded to team goalies with the fewest goals-against in the season.

The next year Melanson was traded to the Minnesota North Stars and in 1985-1986, he went to the Los Angeles Kings. In 1986-1987 he played 46 games, recorded 18 wins and maintained a 3.69 average.

During the 1988-1989 season, Melanson played only four games with the Kings. He was sent to New Haven in the American League, where he played 29 games. Acquired as a free agent by the New Jersey Devils on August 10, 1989, Melanson played only one game with the team before going to the Canadiens along with Kirk Muller, for Stéphane Richer and Tom Chorske, on September 20, 1991. He ended his career at the end of the 1991-1992 season after playing nine games with the Canadiens.

### PERSONAL RECORD

**Birthdate**
June 28, 1960 in Moncton, New Brunswick

**Teams**
New York Islanders, Minnesota, Los Angeles, New Jersey, Montreal

**Awards**
Jennings: 1983

**Seasons**
11

| | Regular Season | Playoffs |
|---|---|---|
| Games Played | 291 | 23 |
| Wins | 129 | 4 |
| Losses | 106 | 9 |
| Ties | 33 | - |
| Shutouts | 6 | - |
| Average | 3.63 | 4.42 |

# CORRADO MICALEF

A native of Montreal, goalie Corrado Micalef played junior hockey with the Sherbrooke Castors in the Quebec Major Junior Hockey League from 1978 to 1981. He made his debut in the National League with the Detroit Red Wings in 1981-1982, playing 18 games. The next season, head coach Nick Polano decided to gamble on the young goaltender and Micalef played 34 games, maintaining an average of 3.62, the best of his career.

After playing only 14 games in 1983-1984, Micalef had a second chance the following season when he played 36. He maintained an average of 4.40 and for the second consecutive year, the Detroit Red Wings won a playoffs berth. But like the previous season, the team lost in the first round.

In 1985-1986, Micalef played only 11 games with the Red Wings, his last games in the National League. From 1987 to 1994, he went to Europe, where he played for various teams in Switzerland, France and Italy. He also converted to roller hockey. Micalef spent the 1995-1996 season with the San Francisco Spiders in the International League, playing 18 games.

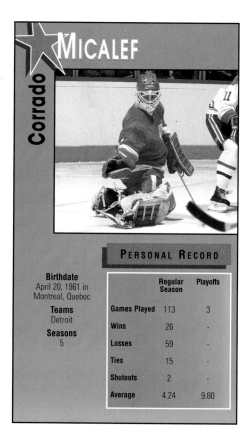

### PERSONAL RECORD

**Birthdate**
April 20, 1961 in Montreal, Quebec

**Teams**
Detroit

**Seasons**
5

| | Regular Season | Playoffs |
|---|---|---|
| Games Played | 113 | 3 |
| Wins | 26 | - |
| Losses | 59 | - |
| Ties | 15 | - |
| Shutouts | 2 | - |
| Average | 4.24 | 9.80 |

# GREG MILLEN

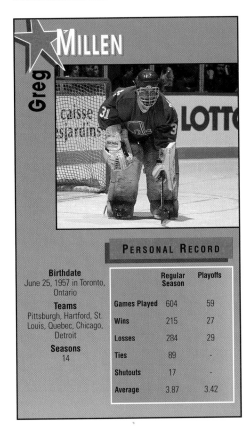

Greg Millen

## PERSONAL RECORD

**Birthdate**
June 25, 1957 in Toronto, Ontario

**Teams**
Pittsburgh, Hartford, St. Louis, Quebec, Chicago, Detroit

**Seasons**
14

|  | Regular Season | Playoffs |
|---|---|---|
| Games Played | 604 | 59 |
| Wins | 215 | 27 |
| Losses | 284 | 29 |
| Ties | 89 | - |
| Shutouts | 17 | - |
| Average | 3.87 | 3.42 |

Greg Millen played 14 seasons and more than 600 games in the National League, with six teams. He started his career with the Pittsburgh Penguins in 1978-1979, where he played for three years.

The Penguins' fourth pick in the 1977 draft, he signed as a free agent with the Hartford Whalers in June 1981. Millen stayed four seasons with the team, playing two consecutive 60-game seasons (1982-1983 and 1983-1984) in his team's net. In February 1985, he headed for St. Louis along with Mark Johnson, in exchange for Mike Liut and Jorgen Pettersson. Millen experienced the best season of his career with his new team; he played 52 games in 1988-1989, managing a League high of six shutouts and maintaining an average of 3.38.

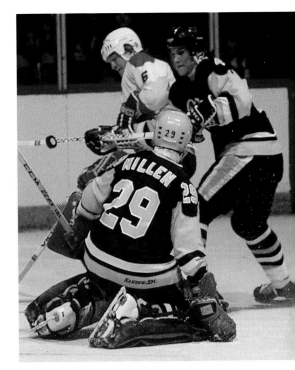

Greg Millen spent three seasons with the Pittsburgh Penguins. His 63 games in 1980-1981 were a career high.

On December 13, 1989, he was traded to the Quebec Nordiques with Tony Hrkac in exchange for Jeff Brown. Millen played only 18 games with Quebec, including three wins, before being sent to the Chicago Black Hawks along with star winger Michel Goulet. The following season, 1990-1991, Millen played only three games with Chicago while rookie Ed Belfour played 74 (the highest number of games in the League) and recorded 43 wins. In September 1991, Millen was traded to the New York Rangers, but he never played a single game with the team. Three months later, he went to the Detroit Red Wings where he worked the net a total of 10 times.

With the St. Louis Blues, Millen took part in the playoffs for five consecutive years, playing a total of 35 games and logging 17 wins.

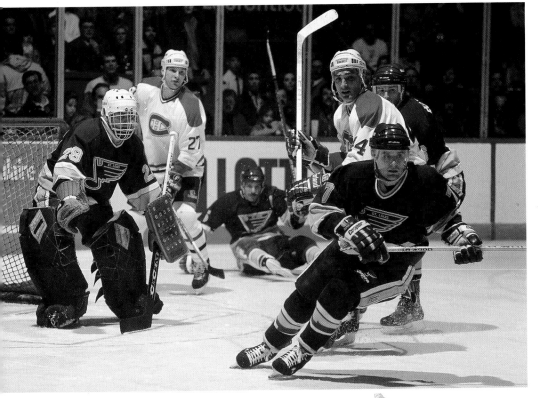

# ANDY MOOG

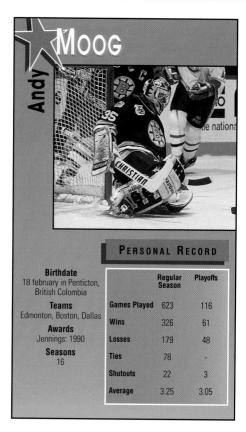

Andy MOOG

## PERSONAL RECORD

**Birthdate**
18 february in Penticton, British Colombia

**Teams**
Edmonton, Boston, Dallas

**Awards**
Jennings: 1990

**Seasons**
16

| | Regular Season | Playoffs |
|---|---|---|
| Games Played | 623 | 116 |
| Wins | 326 | 61 |
| Losses | 179 | 48 |
| Ties | 78 | - |
| Shutouts | 22 | 3 |
| Average | 3.25 | 3.05 |

In 1994-1995 Andy Moog was in his fifteenth season with the National Hockey League. Although the season was cut short because of the conflict between players and owners, it was the best of Moog's career. As the goaltender for the Dallas Stars, he maintained an average of 2.44 in 31 games.

Moog had started out with the Edmonton Oilers in 1980-1981. In seven seasons with the team, he won the Stanley Cup three times, in 1984, 1985 and 1987. At the time he was backup to Grant Fuhr, the Oilers' star goaltender.

On March 8, 1988, the Boston Bruins and Edmonton Oilers made a trade that was very positive for both

Alone in front of Andy Moog, leftwinger Mark Pederson of the Canadiens is frustrated by the Bruins goalie.

teams: Andy Moog went to the Bruins in exchange for Geoff Courtnall and goalie Bill Ranford, who had made his debut with Boston in 1985-1986. In the spring of 1988, the Bruins made it to the Stanley Cup finals, but lost in four games against the Oilers. Moog played in only seven games during the playoffs.

The 1989-1990 season was a dream come true for Moog and along with Réjean Lemelin, he won the Jennings Trophy. Moog played 46 games and maintained an average of 2.89. During the post-season playoffs, he was the team's lead goalie, playing 20 games and maintaining an average of 2.21, the best of the playoffs. Once again, the Bruins met the Oilers in the finals and Moog was unable to prevent his opponents from winning the fifth Stanley Cup in their history.

Andy Moog played three other seasons with Boston, becoming the team's official Number 1 goalie. On

June 20, 1993, he was traded to Dallas for goaltender Jon Casey.

In 1992-1993 with Boston, Andy Moog won 37 of his 55 games, a career high.

# DARREN PANG

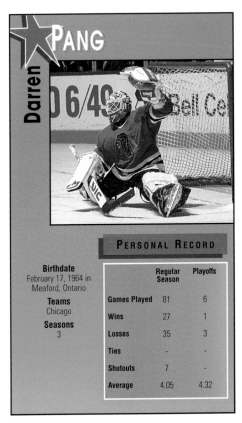

Darren PANG

## PERSONAL RECORD

**Birthdate**
February 17, 1964 in
Meaford, Ontario

**Teams**
Chicago

**Seasons**
3

|  | Regular Season | Playoffs |
|---|---|---|
| Games Played | 81 | 6 |
| Wins | 27 | 1 |
| Losses | 35 | 3 |
| Ties | - | - |
| Shutouts | 7 | - |
| Average | 4.05 | 4.32 |

Darren Pang played his first game in the National Hockey League during the 1984-1985 season. That year, he played only one game with the Chicago Black Hawks. At the time the team's Number 1 goalie was Murray Bannerman, who had been with Chicago since the 1980-1981 season. Bannerman played 60 games in 1984-1985, a career high.

The following season Darren Pang was sent to the minors and in 1987-1988, with Bannerman in retirement, he had the chance to play 45 games, maintaining an average of 3.84. Like the previous season, the Black Hawks finished third in the Norris Division and lost the first round of the playoffs.

The next season, Pang played 35 games and maintained an average of 4.38 while a rookie by the name of Ed Belfour played 23 games and recorded an average of 3.87. That was Pang's last season in the National League and since the fall of 1994, he has been a television commentator for Black Hawks games.

Darren Pang gets help from defenceman Dave Manson as he stops Shayne Corson of the Canadiens, who has spotted the unprotected puck near the crease.

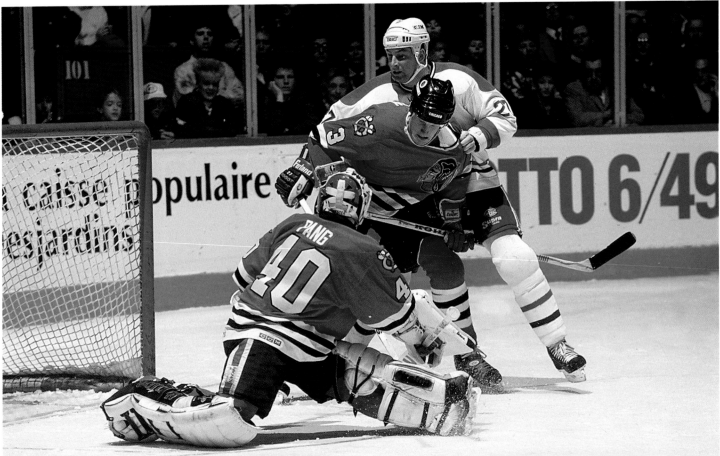

# PETE PEETERS

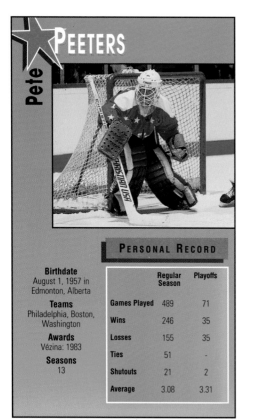

Pete **PEETERS**

## PERSONAL RECORD

**Birthdate**
August 1, 1957 in
Edmonton, Alberta

**Teams**
Philadelphia, Boston,
Washington

**Awards**
Vézina: 1983

**Seasons**
13

|  | Regular Season | Playoffs |
|---|---|---|
| Games Played | 489 | 71 |
| Wins | 246 | 35 |
| Losses | 155 | 35 |
| Ties | 51 | - |
| Shutouts | 21 | 2 |
| Average | 3.08 | 3.31 |

Pete Peeters made his debut in the National League with the Philadelphia Flyers in 1978-1979, playing six games. The next season, he had more opportunity to make his mark since Bernard Parent had retired; he played 40 games, recording 29 wins and maintaining an average of 2.73.

He was the Flyers' Number 1 goalie for the next two seasons, after which he was traded to the Boston Bruins. His best season was in 1982-1983, when the Bruins won the championship; he maintained an average of 2.36 in 62 games, recording 40 wins and managing eight shutouts, a performance that earned him the Vézina Trophy. He became the first Boston Bruins goalie to win the trophy since Frank Brimsek in 1942.

After being traded to the Washington Capitals during the 1985-1986 season, Peeters excelled with the team, dominating the League with the best average in 1987-1988: 2.78. At the end of the 1988-1989 season, he went back to Philadelphia, where he played two seasons before hanging up his skates in 1993. In the past two seasons, Peeters has been the goaltending coach for the Winnipeg Jets.

With the Washington Capitals in 1987-1988, Peeters played in 12 games in the playoffs, recording seven wins and maintaining an average of 3.12. The Capitals were eliminated in the Patrick Division finals by the New Jersey Devils. In this shot, Pete Peeters makes a save on Mats Naslund of the Canadiens.

# STEVE PENNEY

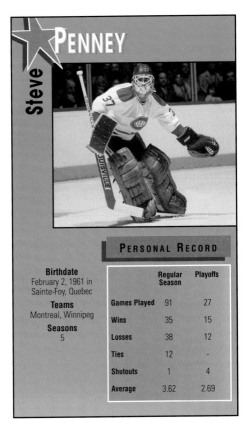

## PENNEY
### Steve

### PERSONAL RECORD

**Birthdate**
February 2, 1961 in
Sainte-Foy, Quebec

**Teams**
Montreal, Winnipeg

**Seasons**
5

| | Regular Season | Playoffs |
|---|---|---|
| Games Played | 91 | 27 |
| Wins | 35 | 15 |
| Losses | 38 | 12 |
| Ties | 12 | - |
| Shutouts | 1 | 4 |
| Average | 3.62 | 2.69 |

Steve Penney made his debut in the National League in 1983-1984, playing four regular season games with the Montreal Canadiens. At the time the team's goaltenders were Richard Sévigny and Rick Wamsley; Penney never thought he would get a chance to play during the playoffs. "It's an unforgettable memory," recounts Steve Penney. "I was practising in the morning, on the ice in Boston Garden since we were playing the Bruins in the first round. Head coach Jacques Lemaire came up to me and asked straight out, 'Would you like to play tonight?' I said yes, of course, and he answered, "Fine, you'll play!' That night we won the

Steve Penny watches the puck come towards him after a brilliant manoeuvre by leftwinger Anton Stastny of the Nordiques.

game." Penney allowed only two goals in three games and the Canadiens eliminated the Bruins in three games and went on to face the Nordiques. "It was exciting because I'm a native of Quebec City and I had the chance to play against the Nordiques, with the Canadiens, in the Adams Division finals. We won the series in six games and it's one of the highlights of my career since the Montreal-Quebec City rivalry was at its peak then."

Montreal won the series, which included the infamous "Good Friday" game, and Penney allowed only 13 goals. The Canadiens later lost a six-game series against the New York Islanders.

The next season, Penney played 54 games and maintained an average of 3.08. His backup, Doug Soetaert, played 28 games. Penny won the Molson Cup thanks to his steady performance in the goals and the Canadiens finished in first place in the Adams Division with 94 points, 19 more than the previous season. However, the Nordiques had their revenge during the playoffs, eliminating the Canadiens in seven games in the Adams Division finals.

The next season, 1985-1986, a brilliant rookie named Patrick Roy stepped into the spotlight and Penney played only 18 games. Penney was traded to the Winnipeg Jets on August 15, 1986 for goaltender Brian Hayward. He played only 15 games in two years before deciding to retire.

Steve Penney blocks his crease with his pad while a Sabres forward handles the puck. Although his name does not appear on the 1986 Stanley Cup when he was the team's third goalie, playing with Patrick Roy and Doug Soetaert, Steve Penney can nonetheless claim to have been a member of a champion team during his time in the National League.

The Canadiens' goalie, who played only 91 games in the National League, including 76 with Montreal, makes a nice stop on Kevin McClelland of the Edmonton Oilers.

# FRANK PIETRANGELO

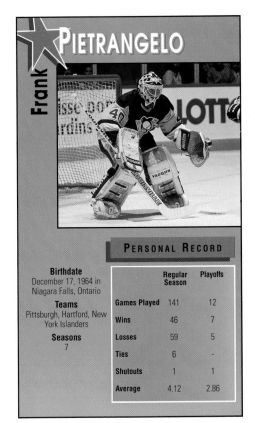

### PERSONAL RECORD

**Birthdate**
December 17, 1964 in
Niagara Falls, Ontario

**Teams**
Pittsburgh, Hartford, New
York Islanders

**Seasons**
7

| | Regular Season | Playoffs |
|---|---|---|
| Games Played | 141 | 12 |
| Wins | 46 | 7 |
| Losses | 59 | 5 |
| Ties | 6 | - |
| Shutouts | 1 | 1 |
| Average | 4.12 | 2.86 |

Frank Pietrangelo had the luck of seeing his name engraved on the Stanley Cup in 1991 with the Pittsburgh Penguins. That was his fourth season in the National League; he had played 25 regular season games, maintaining an average of 3.94 and recording 10 wins. During the playoffs, he played five games, winning four and even managing one shutout.

Pietrangelo, the Penguins' fourth pick in the 1983 draft, had played junior hockey with the University of Minnesota, where he won 15 of his 23 games in 1985-1986. With the Penguins, however, Pietrangelo played only 25 games in four seasons. On March 10, 1992, he was traded to the Hartford Whalers and played only 10 games that season, five with Pittsburgh and five with Hartford. In

Frank Pietrangelo, in the Hartford Whalers uniform, which he wore from 1992 to 1994. He uses his pads to make a save in this shot.

1992-1993, he played 30 games with the Whalers, maintaining an average of 4.85, while Sean Burke played 50 games and ended the season with an average of 4.16. In 1993-1994, he played 19 games with the Whalers and 23 with the Springfield Falcons in the American League. As a free agent, he signed a contract with the New York Islanders in July 1994. However, he failed to start in a single game for the team in the curtailed 1994-1995 season.

In close to five seasons with the Pittsburgh Penguins, Pietrangelo was sent to the International League three times, winning 30 of his 40 games with the Muskegon team.

# DAREN PUPPA

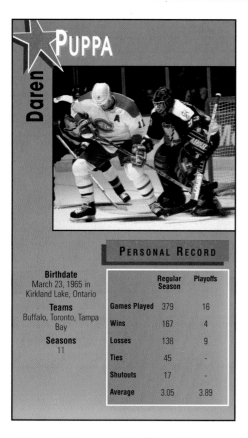

**Daren Puppa**

## PERSONAL RECORD

**Birthdate**
March 23, 1965 in
Kirkland Lake, Ontario
**Teams**
Buffalo, Toronto, Tampa
Bay
**Seasons**
11

|  | Regular Season | Playoffs |
|---|---|---|
| Games Played | 379 | 16 |
| Wins | 167 | 4 |
| Losses | 138 | 9 |
| Ties | 45 | - |
| Shutouts | 17 | - |
| Average | 3.05 | 3.89 |

Daren Puppa played a little over seven seasons with the Buffalo Sabres, but was involved in only eight playoff games with the team. Puppa played in one All Star game, in 1990.

Signed by the Buffalo Sabres in 1983, Daren Puppa made his mark with the Rochester Americans in the American League in 1986-1987. He won 33 games and maintained an average of 2.80 in 57 games that year.

Although he had played some 20 games with Buffalo as of 1985, he only became a regular player with the Sabres in 1988-1989. His best season came in 1989-1990, when he won 31 of his 56 games, a League high. He was selected to play on the second All Star team in 1990.

On February 2, 1993, he went to the Toronto Maple Leafs with Dave Andreychuk, in exchange for goaltender Grant Fuhr. He played only eight games with Pat Burns's team since all eyes were on a formidable rookie goaltender, Félix Potvin.

On June 24, 1993, he was picked up by the Florida Panthers and went to the Tampa Bay Lightning the next day. In 1995-1996, he had the best season of his career; he won 29 of his 57 games, maintained an average of 2.46 with the Lightning, and helped the team secure a spot in the playoffs for the first time in its history.

Number 93 of the Tampa Bay Lightning had never won a trophy since his debut in the National League, but in 1990, he came in second for the Vézina Trophy. The honour went to Canadiens goalie Patrick Roy for the second consecutive year.

# BILL RANFORD

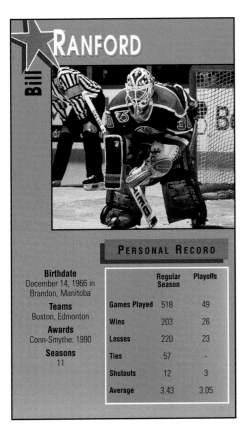

RANFORD
Bill

### PERSONAL RECORD

| Birthdate | | Regular Season | Playoffs |
|---|---|---|---|
| December 14, 1966 in Brandon, Manitoba | | | |
| **Teams** Boston, Edmonton | Games Played | 518 | 49 |
| **Awards** Conn-Smythe: 1990 | Wins | 203 | 26 |
| | Losses | 220 | 23 |
| **Seasons** 11 | Ties | 57 | - |
| | Shutouts | 12 | 3 |
| | Average | 3.43 | 3.05 |

The Boston Bruins' second pick in the 1985 draft, Bill Ranford had his first real chance to shine when he played with another team. He played four games with the Bruins in 1985-1986, and 41 the following season, before going to the Edmonton Oilers—Stanley Cup victors the previous season—on March 8, 1988. The same transaction sent Andy Moog to the Bruins and in addition to Ranford, brought winger Geoff Courtnall to Edmonton.

So Ranford joined a winning team and soon saw his name added to the Stanley Cup, which the Oilers won again that season. However, he didn't have much to do with the win, as Grant Fuhr, the team's Number 1 goaltender, played every single play-off game against the Oilers.

In 1989-1990, Fuhr injured a shoulder and was able to play only 21 games. This cleared the way for Ranford to prove himself. And he did, playing his best season ever. In 56 games, he maintained an average of 3.19. During the playoffs, he led the Oilers to another Stanley Cup, winning 16 of his 22 games, a high for that year, ending up with an average of 2.53; he was the unanimous choice for the Conn-Smythe Trophy.

Ranford was also Team Canada's hero in 1991, helping his team win the Canada Cup for the third consecutive time. He was named most valuable player of the series.

Ranford's performance in the Oilers' net led general manager Glen Sather to trade Grant Fuhr, who was four years older than Ranford, to the Toronto Maple Leafs along with Glenn Anderson and Craig Berube, in exchange for Vincent Damphousse, Peter Ing, Scott Thornton and Luke Richardson. In 1990-1991, Ranford had maintained an average of 3.20 in 60 games, including 27 wins, but Fuhr was the team's lead goalie during the playoffs, winning 17 games.

In 1995-1996, Ranford played 37 games with the Oilers before being brought back to Boston by Harry Sinden. In 40 games with the Bruins, he maintained an average of 2.83. In the playoffs, Ranford and the Bruins fell in the first round to the Panthers.

The Bruins' second draft pick in 1985, Ranford played a little more than eight seasons with the Edmonton Oilers before Harry Sinden brought him back to Boston during the 1995-1996 season.

# ELDON REDDICK

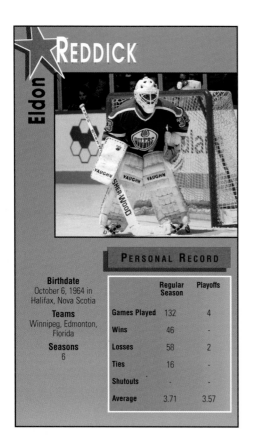

Eldon

REDDICK

## PERSONAL RECORD

**Birthdate**
October 6, 1964 in
Halifax, Nova Scotia

**Teams**
Winnipeg, Edmonton,
Florida

**Seasons**
6

| | Regular Season | Playoffs |
|---|---|---|
| Games Played | 132 | 4 |
| Wins | 46 | - |
| Losses | 58 | 2 |
| Ties | 16 | - |
| Shutouts | - | - |
| Average | 3.71 | 3.57 |

Eldon Reddick, nicknamed "Pokey," made his debut in the NHL with Winnipeg in 1986-1987. Previously, he had played with no fewer than three teams in the Western Hockey League: Nanaimo, New Westminster and Brandon. The Jets signed him in September 1985, when he was a free agent.

During his first season with the team he played 48 games, maintaining an average of 3.24, his best to date.

In September 1989, after playing 41 games with the Jets the previous season, recording 11 wins and maintaining an average of 4.10, he was traded to the Edmonton Oilers, where he played 13 games. Since then, Reddick has played in the American League and the International League for a variety of teams. In 1992-1993, when he was with the Fort Wayne Komets, Reddick won 33 of his 54 games and maintained a 3.08 average. During the playoffs, he played 12 games and chalked up a high of 12 wins, maintaining the brilliant average of 1.49. He was awarded the Bud Poilé Trophy, presented to the most valuable player in the playoffs. On July 12, 1993, he signed as a free agent with the Florida Panthers, but played only two games with the team in 1993-1994. The Panthers already had John Vanbiesbrouck and Mark Fitzpatrick to tend their goals. In 1995-1996, Reddick was the Number 1 goalie for the Las Vegas Thunder. In 47 games, he posted an excellent average of 2.94.

# VINCENT RIENDEAU

Signed by the Montreal Canadiens in 1985 when he was a free agent, Vincent Riendeau played only one game with the team, in 1987-1988, a victim of Patrick Roy's success in the Habs' net. In 1985-1986, Riendeau won 33 of his 57 games with Drummondville in the Quebec Major Junior Hockey League (with an average of 3.87) and he did even better the next season with Sherbrooke in the American League. That year he won 25 of 41 games, maintaining an average of 2.87 and winning the Harry "Hap" Holmes Trophy as the goalie with the best goals-against record.

In 1987-1988, while still with Sherbrooke, he achieved the best average in the circuit (2.67) and managed a high of four shutouts in 44 games. This time he shared the Harry "Hap" Holmes Trophy with Jocelyn Perreault. But there just wasn't enough room for Riendeau in Montreal and on August 9, 1988, he was traded to St. Louis along with Sergio Momesso, in return for Jocelyn Lemieux and goaltender Darrell May.

His best season came in 1990-1991, when he maintained an average of 3.01 in 44 games. He played three full seasons with the Blues before leaving for Detroit in October 1991. He played almost no games with Detroit and in January 1994, he went to the Boston Bruins. During the 1994-1995 season, he played only 11 games with the team.

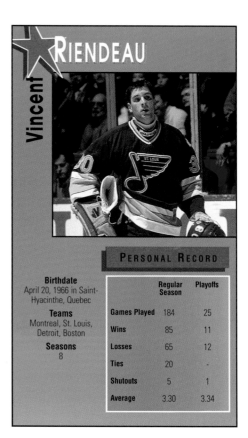

Vincent

RIENDEAU

## PERSONAL RECORD

**Birthdate**
April 20, 1966 in Saint-Hyacinthe, Quebec

**Teams**
Montreal, St. Louis, Detroit, Boston

**Seasons**
8

| | Regular Season | Playoffs |
|---|---|---|
| Games Played | 184 | 25 |
| Wins | 85 | 11 |
| Losses | 65 | 12 |
| Ties | 20 | - |
| Shutouts | 5 | 1 |
| Average | 3.30 | 3.34 |

# PATRICK ROY

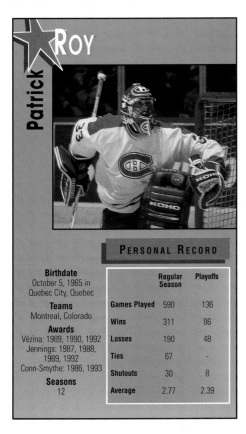

ROY

Patrick

### PERSONAL RECORD

**Birthdate**
October 5, 1965 in
Quebec City, Quebec

**Teams**
Montreal, Colorado

**Awards**
Vézina: 1989, 1990, 1992
Jennings: 1987, 1988,
1989, 1992
Conn-Smythe: 1986, 1993

**Seasons**
12

|  | Regular Season | Playoffs |
|---|---|---|
| Games Played | 590 | 136 |
| Wins | 311 | 86 |
| Losses | 190 | 48 |
| Ties | 67 | - |
| Shutouts | 30 | 8 |
| Average | 2.77 | 2.39 |

When the Montreal Canadiens made Patrick Roy their fourth pick in the 1984 draft, the young goaltender was playing with the Granby Bisons in the Quebec Major Junior Hockey League. The Bisons weren't very strong and night after night, Roy was bombarded from all sides. During the 1983-1984 season, he won 29 of his 61 games and maintained an average of 4.44. The following season, he played one game in the American League. Who could have predicted that he would become one of the best—if not the best—goaltenders in the National League, and the Canadiens' mainstay for the next 10 seasons?

It was during the 1986 playoffs that Roy's star really began to shine. He recorded 15 wins and maintained an average of 1.92 in 20 games, contributing significantly to the Canadiens' fabulous and unexpected win in the Stanley Cup finals. He won the Conn-Smythe Trophy, an exploit he repeated in 1993. He and Bernard Parent are the only goaltenders to have won the trophy twice.

Roy attained the League's best average twice (2.47 in 1988-1989 and 2.36 in 1992-1993) and won the Vézina Trophy three times. Since his debut with the Canadiens, he has maintained an average under 3.00 for eight seasons.

A specialist in the butterfly style, he is recognized as one of the best technicians of his profession. And it is mainly because of the advice of François Allaire, the Canadiens' goaltending coach, that he has been able to reach such a high level of technical expertise.

Roy was the hero of the 1993 playoffs once again, when the Canadiens snatched the Stanley Cup from the Los Angeles Kings. During the playoffs, he won 16 of his 20 games, maintaining an average of 2.13. A highlight of the playoffs, and a record as well: the Canadiens won 10 games in overtime.

In December 1995, a bombshell fell on the hockey world: general manager Réjean Houle traded Roy to the Colorado Avalanche, where the star goalie maintained an average of 2.68 in 39 games. During the playoffs, Roy proved that he is still at the very top of his form, taking his team all the way to the Stanley Cup and finishing with an average of 2.10 in 22 games.

Patrick Roy was undoubtedly the Canadiens' most popular player for close to 10 years and he has inspired many young hockey players who dream of goaltending in the National League.

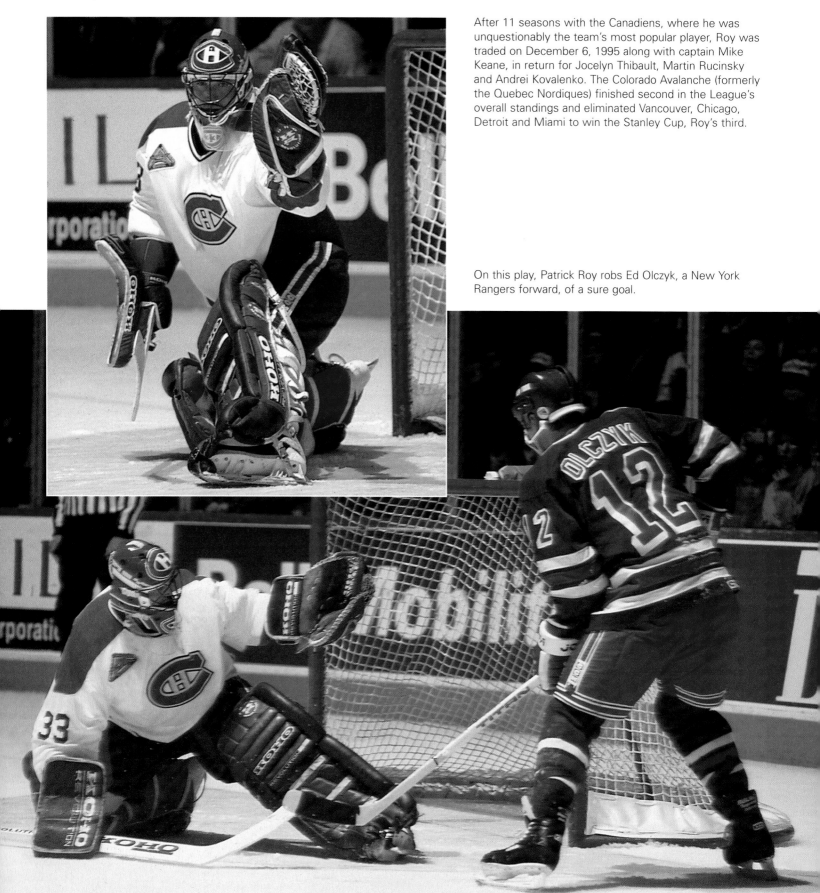

After 11 seasons with the Canadiens, where he was unquestionably the team's most popular player, Roy was traded on December 6, 1995 along with captain Mike Keane, in return for Jocelyn Thibault, Martin Rucinsky and Andrei Kovalenko. The Colorado Avalanche (formerly the Quebec Nordiques) finished second in the League's overall standings and eliminated Vancouver, Chicago, Detroit and Miami to win the Stanley Cup, Roy's third.

On this play, Patrick Roy robs Ed Olczyk, a New York Rangers forward, of a sure goal.

# RICHARD SÉVIGNY

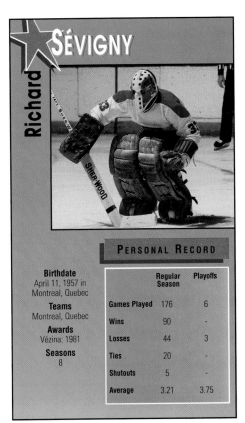

**Richard SÉVIGNY**

### PERSONAL RECORD

**Birthdate**
April 11, 1957 in
Montreal, Quebec

**Teams**
Montreal, Quebec

**Awards**
Vézina: 1981

**Seasons**
8

| | Regular Season | Playoffs |
|---|---|---|
| Games Played | 176 | 6 |
| Wins | 90 | - |
| Losses | 44 | 3 |
| Ties | 20 | - |
| Shutouts | 5 | - |
| Average | 3.21 | 3.75 |

Richard Sévigny began his career in the National League in 1979-1980 with the Canadiens, after Ken Dryden announced his retirement at the end of the previous season. He played only 11 games since the 1979 Stanley Cup champions were very well defended by Denis Herron and Michel Larocque in the net. However, Sévigny got a chance to prove his worth the following season. In 33 games, he recorded 20 wins and maintained an average of 2.40. His brilliant showing, along with solid performances from Herron and Larocque, earned the trio the Vézina Trophy.

In 1981-1982 Rick Wamsley was the team's Number 1 goalie, playing 38 games to Sévigny's 19. The next season, Wamsley worked 46 games, while Sévigny played 38 and maintained an average of 3.44. The duo shared goaltending functions once again in 1983-1984 and Sévigny, a Montreal native, played 40 games and lowered his average to 3.38.

In 1984-1985, Sévigny went to the Quebec Nordiques. With the Nordiques, Sévigny played 20 games and maintained an average of 3.37. The team's two regular goaltenders at the time were Mario Gosselin and veteran Daniel Bouchard. In 1985-1986, Clint Malarchuk became the Nordiques' lead goalie, backed by Gosselin, and Sévigny played only 11 games. In 1986-1987, at age 30, Sévigny played only four games and decided to end his hockey career.

Richard Sévigny makes a save with his glove while a Hartford Whalers player tries to get in his way.

On this play, Richard Sévigny doesn't leave an opening for Boston Bruins defenceman Raymond Bourque.

Only three players have worn Number 33 in the history of the Montreal Canadiens: centre Jack Riley in 1934-1935, Richard Sévigny from 1979 to 1984 and, beginning in 1985, Patrick Roy.

# PETER SIDORKIEWICZ

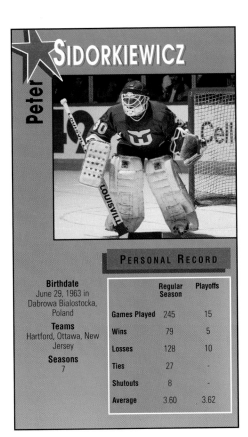

**PERSONAL RECORD**

**Birthdate**
June 29, 1963 in
Dabrowa Bialostocka,
Poland

**Teams**
Hartford, Ottawa, New
Jersey

**Seasons**
7

|  | Regular Season | Playoffs |
|---|---|---|
| Games Played | 245 | 15 |
| Wins | 79 | 5 |
| Losses | 128 | 10 |
| Ties | 27 | - |
| Shutouts | 8 | - |
| Average | 3.60 | 3.62 |

To date, Peter Sidorkiewicz is the only Polish-born goaltender ever to play in the National League. In 1981, at the age of 18, he was signed by the Washington Capitals. From 1980 to 1984, the goalie played for the Oshawa Generals in the Ontario Junior League and later, in the American League. On March 12, 1985, without ever having played a single game with Washington, he was traded to the Hartford Whalers along with Dean Evanson, in exchange for centre David Jensen. In 1988-1989, Sidorkiewicz played 44 games with the Whalers, recording 22 wins, managing four shutouts and maintaining an average of 3.03, the best of his career in the NHL. His performance earned him a spot on the rookie All Star team. Sidorkiewicz played three additional seasons with the Whalers before packing his bags.

He was traded to Ottawa for the 1992-1993 season and changed teams the following year, this time taking the plane to New Jersey in exchange for goaltender Craig Billington and leftwinger Troy Mallette.

Sidorkiewicz played only three games with the Devils, who were already very well defended by goaltenders Martin Brodeur and Chris Terreri. In 1995-1996, he played 32 games with the Albany River Rats in the American League, maintaining an average of 2.95.

# KARI TAKKO

Finnish goaltender Kari Takko played his first game in the National League in 1985-1986 with the Minnesota North Stars. The next season, he shared goaltending duties with Don Beaupre, a veteran with six years of experience with the North Stars. Takko played 38 games, a career high for one season, and maintained a goals-against average of 3.44, the best in the National League. That season was disastrous for the team; it was excluded from the playoffs for the first time since 1979 and finished in fifth place in the Norris Division, compared to a second-place finish the previous year.

The following season, in 1987-1988, Takko was a disappointment, maintaining a 4.47 average in 37 games, and the North Stars missed the playoffs for a second consecutive year.

Takko got back on track in 1988-1989, maintaining an average of 3.48 in 32 games. Don Beaupre was traded to the Washington Capitals and Jon Casey played 55 games. The North Stars finished in third place in their division, but were eliminated quickly in the division semifinals. The next season, Takko played only 21 games.

During his last season in the National League, Takko played only two games with Minnesota and was traded to the Edmonton Oilers, where he ended his career at age 28.

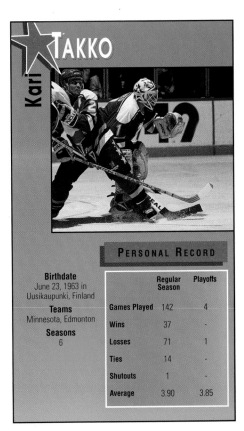

**PERSONAL RECORD**

**Birthdate**
June 23, 1963 in
Uusikaupunki, Finland

**Teams**
Minnesota, Edmonton

**Seasons**
6

|  | Regular Season | Playoffs |
|---|---|---|
| Games Played | 142 | 4 |
| Wins | 37 | - |
| Losses | 71 | 1 |
| Ties | 14 | - |
| Shutouts | 1 | - |
| Average | 3.90 | 3.85 |

# CHRIS TERRERI

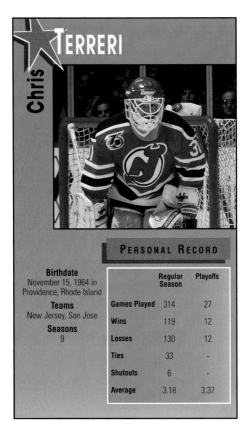

**Chris TERRERI**

### PERSONAL RECORD

**Birthdate**
November 15, 1964 in
Providence, Rhode Island

**Teams**
New Jersey, San Jose

**Seasons**
9

| | Regular Season | Playoffs |
|---|---|---|
| Games Played | 314 | 27 |
| Wins | 119 | 12 |
| Losses | 130 | 12 |
| Ties | 33 | - |
| Shutouts | 6 | - |
| Average | 3.18 | 3.37 |

The Devils' third pick in the 1983 draft, Chris Terreri played his first games with the team in 1986-1987, taking part in seven games. He played the next season with the American national team, then returned to the Devils, playing only eight games with the team in 1988-1989.

He became the team's regular goaltender the following season and enjoyed good times in 1990-1991 when he played 53 games, recorded 24 wins and maintained an average of 2.91. During the playoffs, Terreri and the Devils faced the Pittsburgh Penguins, who had a very hard time

eliminating the New Jersey team in seven games. Terreri maintained an average of 2.94 during the first round and the Penguins went on to win the Stanley Cup for the first time by eliminating the Bruins, then the North Stars.

In 1993-1994, when head coach Jacques Lemaire was in his first season behind the Devils' bench, Terreri had his best season. He played 44 games, bagged 20 wins and ended the season with an average of 2.72. That season also marked the debut of Martin Brodeur, who beat Edmonton Oilers centre Jason Arnott in the vote for rookie of the year. The Terreri-Brodeur duo came in second behind

Dominik Hasek and Grant Fuhr of the Buffalo Sabres in the race for the Jennings Trophy; the Devils' goalies allowed only two goals more than the Sabres.

In 1994-1995 Terreri played only 15 games, compared to Brodeur's 40, but he maintained an excellent average of 2.53. Terreri played only eight minutes of one game during the 1995 playoffs, while Martin Brodeur excelled and led the team to its first Stanley Cup.

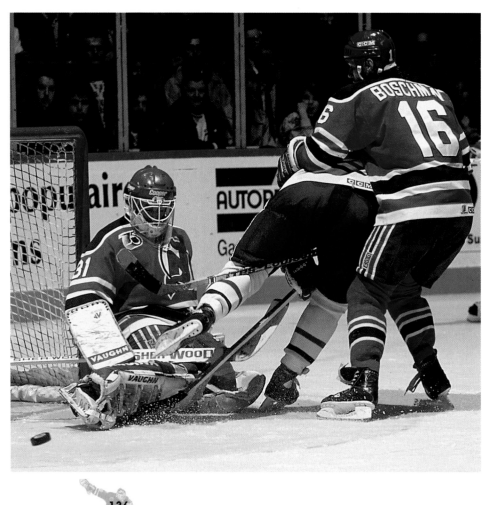

After playing only four games with the Devils, Terreri was traded to the San Jose Sharks during the 1995-1996 season.

# RON TUGNUTT

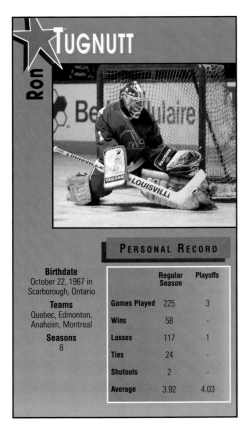

| PERSONAL RECORD | | |
| --- | --- | --- |

**Birthdate**
October 22, 1967 in
Scarborough, Ontario

**Teams**
Quebec, Edmonton,
Anaheim, Montreal

**Seasons**
8

| | Regular Season | Playoffs |
| --- | --- | --- |
| Games Played | 225 | 3 |
| Wins | 58 | - |
| Losses | 117 | 1 |
| Ties | 24 | - |
| Shutouts | 2 | - |
| Average | 3.92 | 4.03 |

The Quebec Nordiques' fourth pick in the 1986 draft, Ron Tugnutt first made his mark in 1986-1987 with the Peterborough Petes in the Ontario Junior Hockey League. In 31 games, he recorded 21 wins and maintained an average of 2.79, the best in the league. The next season, he played six games with the Nordiques and won 20 of his 34 games with the Fredericton farm team in the American League. Tugnutt played five seasons with the Nordiques. His best season was in 1988-1989, when he played 26 games, recorded 10 wins and ended with a 3.60 average.

On March 10, 1992 Tugnutt was traded to the Edmonton Oilers in return for forward Martin Rucinsky. In 1992-1993, he played only 26 games while the team's star goalie,

In five seasons with the Nordiques, Ron Tugnutt never played a playoff game, since the Nordiques failed to make it to the post-season finals from 1988 to 1992.

Bill Ranford, played 67. After being picked by the Anaheim Mighty Ducks in the June 1993 draft, Tugnutt maintained the best average of his career with that team: in 28 games, he recorded 10 wins and achieved an average of 3.00. His stay in California was short and in February 1994, he went to the Montreal Canadiens in exchange for Stephan Lebeau. Over two seasons with Montreal, Tugnutt had to settle for watching Patrick Roy from the bench, and played only 15 games.

Tugnutt hasn't played in the National League since he joined the Montreal Canadiens. In 1995-1996, he played with the Portland Pirates in the American League.

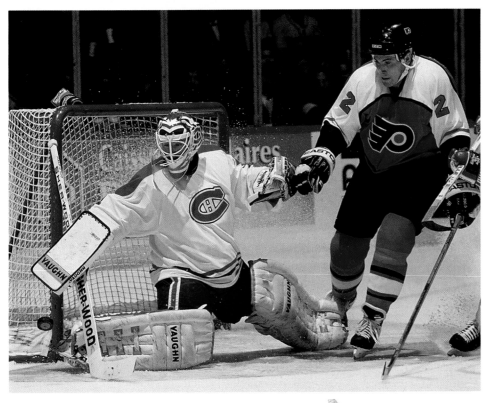

# JOHN VANBIESBROUCK

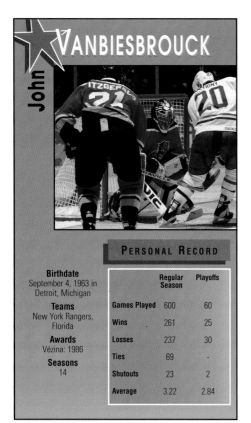

## PERSONAL RECORD

**Birthdate**
September 4, 1963 in
Detroit, Michigan

**Teams**
New York Rangers,
Florida

**Awards**
Vézina: 1986

**Seasons**
14

|  | Regular Season | Playoffs |
|---|---|---|
| Games Played | 600 | 60 |
| Wins | 261 | 25 |
| Losses | 237 | 30 |
| Ties | 69 | - |
| Shutouts | 23 | 2 |
| Average | 3.22 | 2.84 |

Veteran John Vanbiesbrouck got a new lease on life with the Florida Panthers, the team that picked him in June 1993. In a career that had begun with the New York Rangers in 1981, his best year was 1993-1994, when he recorded a 2.53 average in 57 games. As a result, the Panthers came very close to being in the playoffs in their first season in the NHL.

In 1994-1995 Vanbiesbrouck maintained an average of 2.47 in 37 games while his backup, Mark Fitzpatrick, ended the season with an average of 2.64 in 15 games. The two goalies had a combined average of 2.61, the sixth best in the League.

Vanbiesbrouck played 11 seasons with the Rangers, a team that had selected him as their fifth pick in the 1981 draft. During the 1985-1986 season, he recorded 31 wins, a high, playing in 61 games and maintaining an average of 3.32. The Rangers' goaltenders (Vanbiesbrouck and Glen Hanlon) allowed 276 goals, 69 less than the previous season, and Vanbiesbrouck won the Vézina Trophy, beating out Bob Froese of the Philadelphia Flyers. He was also chosen to be on the first All Star team. During the 1986 playoffs, the Rangers got the better of Philadelphia and Washington before losing a five-game series to the Canadiens. In 16 games, Vanbiesbrouck recorded eight wins and maintained an average of 3.27.

In 1987-1988 and 1988-1989, Vanbiesbrouck won 27 and 28 games respectively with the Rangers, playing 56 games in both seasons.

Vanbiesbrouck played 449 games with the Rangers and recorded 200 wins before being traded to the Vancouver Canucks on June 20, 1993. Four days later, he was signed by the Florida Panthers during the expansion draft.

In 1995-1996, Vanbiesbrouck and the Panthers enjoyed a dream season (fourth place in the Eastern Conference), taking part in the playoffs and reaching the finals against Colorado. Vanbiesbrouck was his team's hero, maintaining an average of 2.25 in 22 games and helping the Panthers eliminate Boston, Philadelphia and Pittsburgh.

John Vanbiesbrouck makes a tough save on a deflected shot by rightwinger Mike Keane of the Canadiens.

# MIKE VERNON

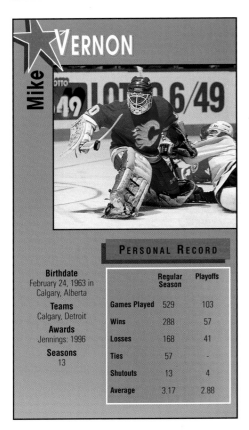

### PERSONAL RECORD

**Birthdate**
February 24, 1963 in
Calgary, Alberta

**Teams**
Calgary, Detroit

**Awards**
Jennings: 1996

**Seasons**
13

| | Regular Season | Playoffs |
|---|---|---|
| Games Played | 529 | 103 |
| Wins | 288 | 57 |
| Losses | 168 | 41 |
| Ties | 57 | - |
| Shutouts | 13 | 4 |
| Average | 3.17 | 2.88 |

Calgary native Mike Vernon got his break when he was signed by the Flames in 1981, and he spent most of his career with that team. In 1986 he played his first games in the playoffs, helping the team advance to the Stanley Cup finals for the first time in its history. He played 21 games, maintaining an average of 2.93, but he was unable to withstand the onslaught by the Habs' forwards during the playoffs and was clearly outplayed by the 20-year-old rookie, Patrick Roy, at the other end of the ice.

In 1989 he got his revenge. After leading the League in regular season wins (37 in 52 games), he won 16 games, managed three shutouts and posted an average of 2.26 in 22 play-off games. The Flames won the Stanley Cup in six games against the Canadiens, becoming the first visiting team to win the Cup in the Forum.

Vernon shares the record for most wins (16) in a playoff series with five other goaltenders: Grant Fuhr, Tom Barrasso, Bill Ranford, Patrick Roy and Mike Richter.

Vernon and the Flames have met with little success during the playoffs since 1989. In 1990, the Flames were eliminated in the first round by Los Angeles; the same fate awaited them in 1991, this time at the hands of the Vancouver Canucks. In 1992, the team failed to secure a spot in the playoffs and in 1993, it failed to go further than the first round, losing to Los Angeles. Then in 1994, the Flames lost in a seven-game series against the Canucks. Over the course of those years Vernon played 24 playoff games and recorded only nine wins.

Acquired by Detroit in June 1994, Vernon and Chris Osgood placed second among the League's goalies, with a combined average of 2.42 for the 1994-1995 season. The team finished first, but lost to New Jersey in the Stanley Cup finals. In 1995-1996, Vernon and Osgood won the Jennings Trophy (best combined average: 2.19) and Detroit set a record for the most wins in one season, with 62 in 82 games (the previous record of 60 wins in 80 games was set by the Canadiens in 1976-1977). Detroit was a favourite to win the Stanley Cup, but was eliminated by Colorado in a six-game series in the finals.

After playing 11 seasons with Calgary, Mike Vernon went to the Red Wings and won his first award in the NHL in 1996, with help from teammate Chris Osgood. In 1995-1996, Vernon maintained an average of 2.26 in 32 games.

139

# RICK WAMSLEY

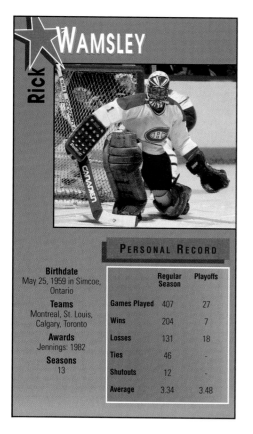

In 1981-1982, his first season with the Canadiens, Wamsley ended the season with 23 wins and seven losses in 38 games while Montreal took first place in the Adams Division, accumulating 109 points, six more than the previous season.

## PERSONAL RECORD

**Birthdate**
May 25, 1959 in Simcoe, Ontario

**Teams**
Montreal, St. Louis, Calgary, Toronto

**Awards**
Jennings: 1982

**Seasons**
13

| | Regular Season | Playoffs |
|---|---|---|
| Games Played | 407 | 27 |
| Wins | 204 | 7 |
| Losses | 131 | 18 |
| Ties | 46 | - |
| Shutouts | 12 | - |
| Average | 3.34 | 3.48 |

Rick Wamsley played 13 years in the National League with four teams. After a five-game tryout with the Canadiens during the 1980-1981 season, he played 38 games the next season, maintaining an average of 2.75. His teammate Denis Herron won 27 games and maintained an average of 2.64, which earned the duo the Jennings Trophy.

Wamsley played a total of four seasons with the Canadiens before being traded to the St. Louis Blues in June 1984 when Montreal found another very promising young goaltender, namely Steve Penney. Wamsley was the Blues' Number 1 goalie as soon as he joined the team and his first season in St. Louis was excellent: in 40 games, he maintained an average of 3.26. In 1986, he led the Blues to the Campbell Conference finals against the Calgary Flames, who won in seven games. In March 1988, he was traded to the Calgary Flames along with Rob Ramage, in exchange for Brett Hull and Steve Bozek, no doubt one of the better deals made by Blues general manager Ron Caron. With the Flames, in 1989, he had the pleasure of seeing his name added to the Stanley Cup when Calgary eliminated the Canadiens, his former team, in six games. However, he had played in only one game during the playoffs, as Mike Vernon was the team's star goaltender.

On January 2, 1992, he was involved in the biggest trade in the League's history as he went to the Maple Leafs with Doug Gilmour, Ric Nattress, Jamie Macoun and Kent Manderville in exchange for Alexander Godynyuk, Jeff Reese, Michel Petit, Gary Leeman and Craig Berube. But with Grant Fuhr and especially rookie Félix Potvin on the same team, Wamsley played only 11 games in Toronto; he hung up his skates to become an assistant coach with the Leafs.

Apart from the 1981-1982 season with the Canadiens, when he maintained an average of 2.75, Rick Wamsley's best regular season performance was with the Calgary Flames in 1988-1989, when he maintained a 2.96 average in 35 games. Wamsley and Vernon finished second behind Patrick Roy and Brian Hayward in the competition for the Jennings Trophy.

# KEN WREGGET

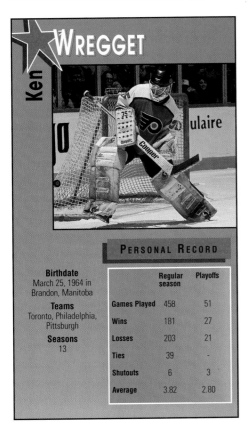

**WREGGET**
Ken

## PERSONAL RECORD

**Birthdate**
March 25, 1964 in
Brandon, Manitoba

**Teams**
Toronto, Philadelphia,
Pittsburgh

**Seasons**
13

|  | Regular season | Playoffs |
|---|---|---|
| Games Played | 458 | 51 |
| Wins | 181 | 27 |
| Losses | 203 | 21 |
| Ties | 39 | - |
| Shutouts | 6 | 3 |
| Average | 3.82 | 2.80 |

Picked in the 1982 draft by the Toronto Maple Leafs, Ken Wregget first made his mark with the Lethbridge team in the Western Hockey League in 1983-1984. In 53 games, he recorded 32 wins and maintained an average of 3.16, the best in the circuit. He was selected to play on the first All Star team.

Wregget played five full seasons with Toronto. They weren't all smooth, and the Leafs were not very strong on defence. In 1986-1987, Wregget experienced his best season with the team, winning 22 of his 56 games, for an average of 3.97. During the playoffs, he won seven of his 13 games before the Maple Leafs were eliminated in seven games by Detroit in the Norris Division finals. Traded to the Philadelphia Flyers in March 1989, Wregget switched teams again in February 1992, this time joining the Pittsburgh Penguins.

In 1991-1992, Wregget won five of his nine games and had the thrill of contributing to the Penguins' second Stanley Cup victory. In 1993-1994, he maintained an average of 3.37 in 42 games, and bettered that in 1994-1995, leading the League's goaltenders with 25 wins. However, the Penguins didn't last very long in the playoffs, losing in a five-game series against the New Jersey Devils in the conference semifinals. In 1995-1996, Wregget played 37 games (with an average of 3.24) and shared goaltending duties with Tom Barrasso during the playoffs (for an average of 2.30 in nine games). However, the two goalies were unable to prevent the Panthers from eliminating their team in seven games, in the Eastern Conference finals.

Ken Wregget, wearing Philadelphia colours, during a game between the Flyers and the Montreal Canadiens.

# The 90s

**E**veryone knows it for a fact: Quebec, and more specifically the Quebec Major Junior Hockey League, has become the spawning ground for goaltenders. This is the first place National League managers look for the best players.

Of course, a name that comes immediately to mind is Patrick Roy, who began playing with the Canadiens in 1986 and continues to be one of the greatest of his profession. But the same could be said for Brodeur, Potvin, Fiset, Thibault, Roussel, Fichaud and others. Not to mention several Quebec goaltenders who haven't yet had the chance to skate on National League ice; one excellent example is José Théodore, who was picked by the Canadiens in 1994.

The 90s are also marked by the astounding performance of Ed Belfour, goaltender for the Chicago Black Hawks and three-time winner of the Vézina Trophy. There is also Dominik Hasek who, at the age of 29, was awarded both the Vézina and the Jennings Trophies while wearing the Buffalo Sabres uniform in 1994. His average of 1.95 in 58 games in 1993-1994 was the best since the 1973-1974 season, when Bernard Parent finished with 1.89 in 73 games. Hasek went on to win the Vézina Trophy again in 1995.

Since the early 90s, two goaltenders have been chosen as rookie of the year: Ed Belfour in 1991 and Martin Brodeur in 1994. Brodeur, son of photographer Denis Brodeur, saw his name added to the Stanley Cup in 1995, in only his third season in the National League.

While French-speaking goaltenders do extremely well in the National League, several foreign goalies have matched their performances. Kolzig, Trefilov, Khabibulin, Irbe and Soderstrom—not to mention Dominik Hasek—have proved that they can excel in the NHL, and a number of younger goalies are on the verge of showing the scouts who first spotted them that they were well worth a second look.

Goaltender Martin Brodeur, a sensational player signed by the New Jersey Devils, makes a save against forward Oleg Petrov of the Canadiens.

# STÉPHANE BEAUREGARD

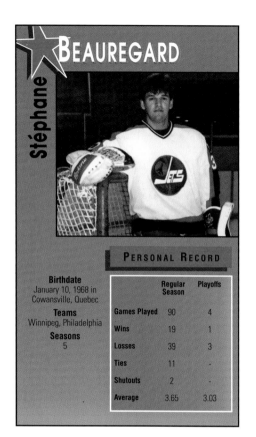

Stéphane Beauregard, the Winnipeg Jets' third pick in the 1988 draft, made his National League debut in 1989-1990. He had been named best junior goalie in Canada in 1988 while playing with Saint-Jean in the Quebec Major Junior Hockey League. In his three seasons with the Jets, he played only 61 games. In October 1992 he was traded to the Philadelphia Flyers, where he played 16 games before heading back to Winnipeg in June 1993.

Over the years, Beauregard played many more games in the International League (Fort Wayne) and in the American League (Hershey and Moncton) than he did in the NHL. He was most active with the Jets in 1991-1992, when he played 26 games, winning six of them.

During the 1995-1996 season, Beauregard played with the San Francisco Spiders in the International League. In 69 games, he recorded 36 wins and maintained an average of 3.09.

## PERSONAL RECORD

**Birthdate**
January 10, 1968 in
Cowansville, Quebec

**Teams**
Winnipeg, Philadelphia

**Seasons**
5

| | Regular Season | Playoffs |
|---|---|---|
| Games Played | 90 | 4 |
| Wins | 19 | 1 |
| Losses | 39 | 3 |
| Ties | 11 | - |
| Shutouts | 2 | - |
| Average | 3.65 | 3.03 |

# JEAN-CLAUDE BERGERON

The fifth draft pick by the Canadiens in 1988, Jean-Claude Bergeron first made his mark in the American League, with Sherbrooke. In 1989-1990 he maintained the best average in the League (2.74 in 40 games) and was awarded the Baz Bastien Trophy as best goalie. But since the Canadiens could count on star goaltender Patrick Roy and his solid backup, André Racicot, Bergeron played only 18 games in Montreal the following season before being traded to Tampa Bay on June 19, 1992, in exchange for Frédéric Chabot.

In 1993-1994 he played only three games in the National League, spending most of the season with the Atlanta Knights in the International League. During the 1994-1995 season he played 17 games, backing Daren Puppa; in 1995-1996, he played 12 games with the Tampa Bay Lightning. Bergeron also played 25 games with the Atlanta Knights.

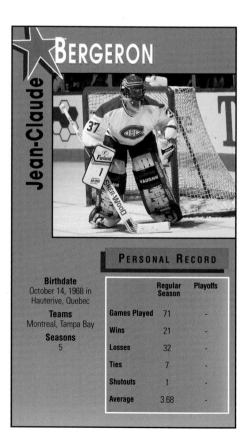

## PERSONAL RECORD

**Birthdate**
October 14, 1968 in
Hauterive, Quebec

**Teams**
Montreal, Tampa Bay

**Seasons**
5

| | Regular Season | Playoffs |
|---|---|---|
| Games Played | 71 | - |
| Wins | 21 | - |
| Losses | 32 | - |
| Ties | 7 | - |
| Shutouts | 1 | - |
| Average | 3.68 | - |

# JOHN BLUE

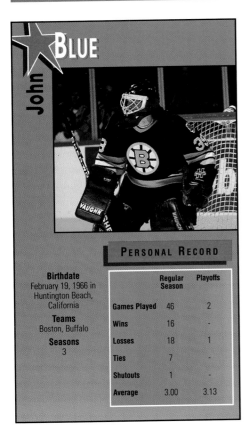

### BLUE
John

**PERSONAL RECORD**

**Birthdate**
February 19, 1966 in
Huntington Beach,
California

**Teams**
Boston, Buffalo

**Seasons**
3

| | Regular Season | Playoffs |
|---|---|---|
| Games Played | 46 | 2 |
| Wins | 16 | - |
| Losses | 18 | 1 |
| Ties | 7 | - |
| Shutouts | 1 | - |
| Average | 3.00 | 3.13 |

**B**efore getting his chance to play with the Boston Bruins, goaltender John Blue had belonged to two teams in the National League, Winnipeg and Minnesota, without ever playing a single game for either organization. Selected 197th overall by the Winnipeg Jets, who made him their seventh choice in the 1986 draft, John Blue was chosen to be on the first All Star team in the Western Collegial Hockey League in 1985-1986. He had won 20 of his 29 games and had maintained an average of 3.02 with the University of Minnesota team. Blue was traded to the Minnesota North Stars in March

During his career with the Bruins, John Blue played only 41 games, recording 14 wins.

1988, and later he signed as a free agent with the Boston Bruins, in August 1991.

Beginning in the 1987-1988 season, Blue played with a number of teams in the International League and the American League. He played the most games in the 1991-1992 season: 43 with the Maine Mariners in the American League. That year he won 11 games and maintained an average of 4.57. In 1992-1993, after Boston goaltender Réjean Lemelin retired, he graduated to the National League as a backup for Andy Moog with the Bruins. Blue played 23 games and maintained an average of 2.90, but also played with the Providence Bruins that same season,

winning 14 of 19 games. The following season, he maintained an average of 2.99 in 18 games with Boston and played 24 games with Providence, for an average of 3.51. In 1994-1995, Blue was not asked to play a single game with Boston, while rookie Blaine Lacher played 35 games with the team and Vincent Riendeau (11 games) and Craig Billington (eight games) played as his backups. After being signed by the Buffalo Sabres, Blue played five games with the team in 1995-1996, spending most of the season with the Rochester Americans in the American League.

# MARTIN BROCHU

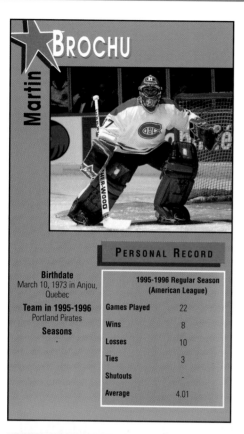

**Martin BROCHU**

## PERSONAL RECORD

**Birthdate**
March 10, 1973 in Anjou, Quebec

**Team in 1995-1996**
Portland Pirates

**Seasons**
-

| 1995-1996 Regular Season (American League) | |
|---|---|
| Games Played | 22 |
| Wins | 8 |
| Losses | 10 |
| Ties | 3 |
| Shutouts | - |
| Average | 4.01 |

A native of Anjou, Quebec, like Félix Potvin of the Toronto Maple Leafs, Martin Brochu learned his trade in the Quebec Major Junior Hockey League over two seasons, with Granby and Hull. After the first 1991-1992 season with Granby, a team that his role model Patrick Roy had played with in the early 80s, Brochu, with an average of 4.72 in 52 games, signed a contract with the Habs on September 22, 1992 as a free agent. He played the next season with Hull and in 1993-1994, was sent to the Fredericton Canadiens, the Canadiens farm team in the American League. He maintained an average of 3.03 in 32 games.

In 1994-1995 he became Fredericton's Number 1 goalie. In 44 games, he won 18 and maintained an average of 3.51. Brochu was called up to Montreal a few times when Patrick Roy was injured, but did not have a chance to actually take to the ice with his dream team.

Since the Canadiens could rely on another excellent goalie, José Théodore, Brochu was traded to the Washington Capitals and spent the 1995-1996 season with the Portland Pirates, the organization's farm team in the American League.

When his career in the juniors came to an end, Martin Brochu was not picked in the National League draft. The Canadiens decided to gamble on him, however, by signing him as a free agent.

# MARTIN BRODEUR

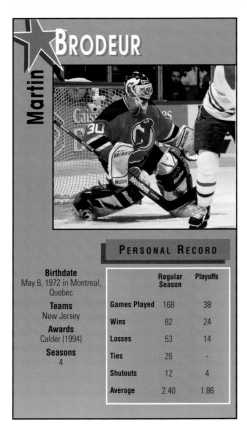

### PERSONAL RECORD

**Birthdate**
May 6, 1972 in Montreal, Quebec

**Teams**
New Jersey

**Awards**
Calder (1994)

**Seasons**
4

| | Regular Season | Playoffs |
|---|---|---|
| Games Played | 168 | 38 |
| Wins | 82 | 24 |
| Losses | 53 | 14 |
| Ties | 26 | - |
| Shutouts | 12 | 4 |
| Average | 2.40 | 1.86 |

Seated in his basement and surrounded by family members, photographer Denis Brodeur has his eyes riveted on the huge television set that dominates the room. He is intently watching the performance of his son, Martin, who is working the net for the New Jersey Devils. This father has every reason to be proud. In a very short time, Martin Brodeur has come to be recognized as one of the National League's biggest stars.

The Devils surely had a good idea of his talent when they made him their first pick in the 1990 draft. They gave him his first chance in 1991-1992, when he played in four games, but Martin really proved that he could live up to the Devils' expectations two seasons

later, when he won the Calder Trophy. With 27 wins in 47 games and an average of 2.40, he had carved out a very impressive place among the League's best goaltenders. He also became the first Montreal-born goalie, after Lorne Worsley in 1953, to win the trophy for rookie of the year.

During the 1994 playoffs, Martin Brodeur came very close to bringing the Devils to the Stanley Cup finals. In the conference finals against the New York Rangers, the Devils won three games but lost a crucial one when Stéphane Matteau scored a lucky goal in the second period of overtime. In 17 playoff games, Brodeur recorded eight victories and maintained an average of 1.95.

In 1994-1995, the young goaltender confirmed his extraordinary talent by maintaining an average of 2.45 in 40 games. Calm and able to remain consistently and remarkably cool, he was a significant factor in helping the Devils move beyond the stage where they had been stopped the previous year when, under Jacques Lemaire, the team made it to the Stanley Cup finals against the Detroit Red Wings. To everyone's surprise, the Devils beat the Red Wings in four consecutive games, winning the first Stanley Cup in their history. The Devils' defencemen were extraordinary, keeping the rival team's powerful forwards to less than 20 shots on goal per game; Brodeur made every save he was expected to make and allowed only seven goals. Throughout the playoffs, he maintained the remarkable

average of 1.67 in 20 games, winning 16 and managing three shutouts.

In 1995-1996 Martin Brodeur played 77 games with the Devils, a new record for the most games played in a single season by a goaltender. Despite his average of 2.34, the Devils failed to make the playoffs.

After the 1995-1996 season, Martin joined Team Canada, which won a silver medal in the World Championship series. In this shot, Brodeur makes a nice save against Kirk Muller of the Canadiens as defenceman Ken Daneyko checks the forward.

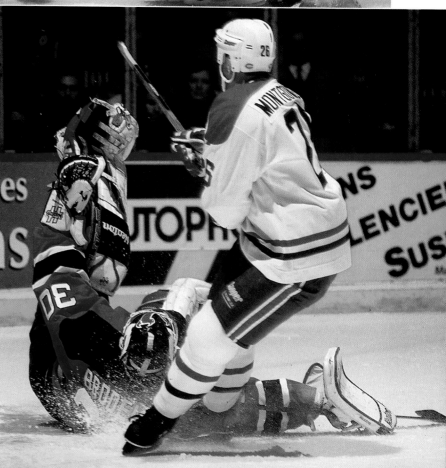

The son of photographer Denis Brodeur, Martin is considered one of the five best goaltenders in the National League. In this photo, he makes a spectacular save on Jim Montgomery of the Canadiens.

# JIM CAREY

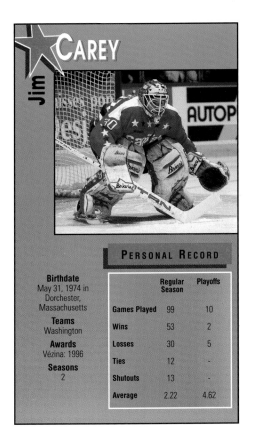

## PERSONAL RECORD

**Birthdate**
May 31, 1974 in
Dorchester,
Massachusetts

**Teams**
Washington

**Awards**
Vézina: 1996

**Seasons**
2

| | Regular Season | Playoffs |
|---|---|---|
| Games Played | 99 | 10 |
| Wins | 53 | 2 |
| Losses | 30 | 5 |
| Ties | 12 | - |
| Shutouts | 13 | - |
| Average | 2.22 | 4.62 |

At 20 years of age, Jim Carey was one of the most promising new players in the National League in the 1994-1995 season. The Washington Capitals' second pick in the 1992 draft had been the best goaltender for the University of Wisconsin in the Western Collegial League in 1993-1994, winning 24 of his 40 games and maintaining an average of 3.04.

After a bad start in 1994-1995, the Capitals called on Carey, who was playing with the Portland Pirates in the American League. The young goalie was a real saviour, leading the Capitals to the playoffs for the thirteenth consecutive season. In 28 games, he recorded 18 wins and maintained an average of 2.13, managing four shutouts. He ended the season in third place for best goals-against average, behind Dominik Hasek (2.11 in 41 games) and Rick Tabaracci (2.11 in 13 games).

In 1995-1996, Carey maintained an excellent average of 2.26 in 71 games with the Capitals and managed nine shutouts, an NHL high for the season. His solid performance earned him the Vézina Trophy for the first time in his career. Carey and teammate Olaf Kolzig ranked third among the circuit's best goalies, behind their counterparts in Detroit and New Jersey. However, Washington was eliminated in the first round of the playoffs, losing in six games to the Pittsburgh Penguins.

# TIM CHEVELDAE

Tim Cheveldae played almost six seasons with the Detroit Red Wings before being traded to the Winnipeg Jets on March 8, 1994, along with Dallas Drake, in exchange for Sergei Bautin and goaltender Bob Essensa. The Red Wings' fourth pick in 1986, Cheveldae was brilliant in 1987-1988 with Saskatoon in the Western Hockey League, winning 44 of 66 games; he was also selected to play on the circuit's All Star team. Cheveldae played his first games with Detroit in 1988-1989, but it took until 1990-1991 for him to become the team's lead goalie. In 65 games, he recorded 30 wins and maintained an average of 3.55. The next season he led the League's goalies for number of wins and number of games played (38 wins in 72 games), and maintained an average of 3.20, the best of his career. However, he never succeeded in leading the Red Wings further than the division finals during the playoffs, which proved to be the scenario for 1992. During the next two seasons, Cheveldae recorded 34 and 16 wins, in 67 and 30 games respectively, before going to the Jets. With Winnipeg, Cheveldae played 30 games in the 1995-1996 season—the same number as the previous season—sharing goaltending duties with Russian Nikolai Khabibulin, who played 53 games. Cheveldae recorded only eight wins and finished with an average of 3.93.

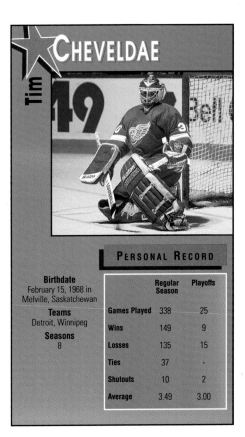

## PERSONAL RECORD

**Birthdate**
February 15, 1968 in
Melville, Saskatchewan

**Teams**
Detroit, Winnipeg

**Seasons**
8

| | Regular Season | Playoffs |
|---|---|---|
| Games Played | 338 | 25 |
| Wins | 149 | 9 |
| Losses | 135 | 15 |
| Ties | 37 | - |
| Shutouts | 10 | 2 |
| Average | 3.49 | 3.00 |

# PHILIPPE DEROUVILLE

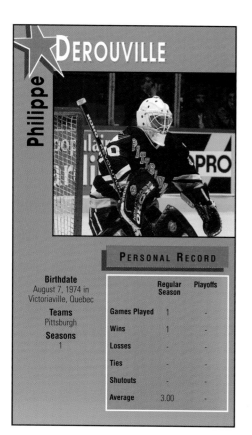

**DEROUVILLE**

Philippe

### PERSONAL RECORD

**Birthdate**
August 7, 1974 in
Victoriaville, Quebec

**Teams**
Pittsburgh

**Seasons**
1

| | Regular Season | Playoffs |
|---|---|---|
| Games Played | 1 | - |
| Wins | 1 | - |
| Losses | - | - |
| Ties | - | - |
| Shutouts | - | - |
| Average | 3.00 | - |

Philippe Derouville won his first and only game in the National League in the 1994-1995 season, with the Pittsburgh Penguins. As he waited for his first real chance, he wore a Cleveland Lumberjacks uniform in the International League, where he played 41 games, recording 24 wins and maintaining an average of 3.32.

Previously, he had played in the Quebec Major Junior Hockey League, first with Longueuil (1990-1991), then with Verdun for the next three seasons. He maintained the best average in the League in 1993-1994, with 3.06 in 51 games. In 1993 and 1994, he was selected to play on the second All Star team in the Quebec Major Junior Hockey League.

The Penguins' fifth pick in the 1992 draft, Derouville spent the 1995-1996 season with the Cleveland Lumberjacks. In 38 games, he maintained an average of 3.86, sharing duties with another goaltender from Quebec, Patrick Lalime (3.86 in 41 games).

# BOB ESSENSA

A native of Toronto, Bob Essensa played junior hockey with Michigan State in the Central Collegial Hockey League from 1983 to 1987. Essensa was the Winnipeg Jets' fifth pick in the 1983 draft, but he joined the Jets' farm team in Moncton, in the American League, only in 1987-1988. The following season, he played his first games with Winnipeg, winning six of 20. In 1989-1990, Essensa won 18 of his 36 games and maintained an average of 3.15, earning a spot on the National League's rookie All Star team.

In 1991-1992 Essensa had the best season of his career, winning 21 of his 47 games, managing five shutouts and maintaining an average of 2.88. During the 1993-1994 season, Essensa was traded to the Detroit Red Wings along with defenceman Sergei Bautin, in exchange for goaltender Tim Cheveldae and centre Dallas Drake. Essensa played 13 games with Detroit, winning four and maintaining an average of 2.62.

In the past two seasons, Essensa played only one game with Detroit. In 1995-1996, he played 45 games with the Fort Wayne Komets in the International League, maintaining a good average (2.89) and ranking third among the circuit's best goalies.

On June 14, 1996, Essensa was acquired by the Edmonton Oilers as a backup for Curtis Joseph.

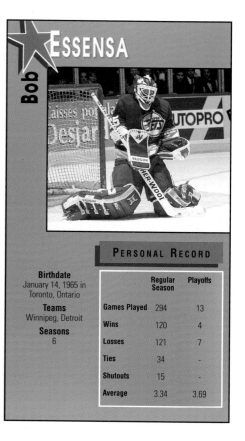

**ESSENSA**

Bob

### PERSONAL RECORD

**Birthdate**
January 14, 1965 in
Toronto, Ontario

**Teams**
Winnipeg, Detroit

**Seasons**
6

| | Regular Season | Playoffs |
|---|---|---|
| Games Played | 294 | 13 |
| Wins | 120 | 4 |
| Losses | 121 | 7 |
| Ties | 34 | - |
| Shutouts | 15 | - |
| Average | 3.34 | 3.69 |

# ÉRIC FICHAUD

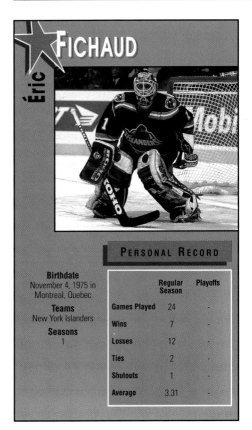

## PERSONAL RECORD

**Birthdate**
November 4, 1975 in
Montreal, Quebec

**Teams**
New York Islanders

**Seasons**
1

| | Regular Season | Playoffs |
|---|---|---|
| Games Played | 24 | - |
| Wins | 7 | - |
| Losses | 12 | - |
| Ties | 2 | - |
| Shutouts | 1 | - |
| Average | 3.31 | - |

Éric Fichaud is one of many young Quebec goaltenders who honed their skills in the Quebec Major Junior Hockey League and who are sure to become stars in the National League. Along with Martin Brodeur, Félix Potvin, Martin Brochu and Jocelyn Thibault, Fichaud is a name that has already begun to attract the attention of hockey experts.

Fichaud played junior hockey with the Chicoutimi Saguenéens. In 1993-1994, his second season with the team, he led the Quebec Major Junior Hockey League for most games played (63) and maintained an

average of 3.30. During the playoffs he won 16 of his 26 games, a high, and maintained an average of 3.31.

The Toronto Maple Leafs' first pick in the 1994 draft, Fichaud continued to demonstrate his talent with the Saguenéens in 1994-1995, recording 21 wins in 46 games and ending the season with an average of 3.44.

After being traded to the New York Islanders for Benoit Hogue in April 1995, Fichaud made his NHL debut in 1995-1996. He has a good chance of becoming the team's Number 1 goalie within the next few years.

Like Félix Potvin, Martin Brodeur and Jocelyn Thibault, to name but a few, Éric Fichaud will very likely have a brilliant career in the National League.

# STÉPHANE FISET

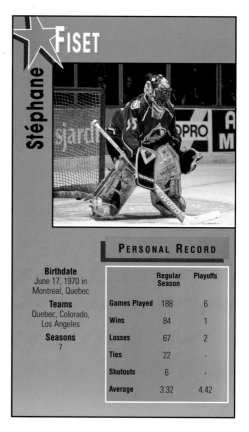

**FISET**

**Stéphane**

### PERSONAL RECORD

| **Birthdate**<br>June 17, 1970 in<br>Montreal, Quebec | | Regular<br>Season | Playoffs |
|---|---|---|---|
| **Teams**<br>Quebec, Colorado,<br>Los Angeles | **Games Played** | 188 | 6 |
| | **Wins** | 84 | 1 |
| **Seasons**<br>7 | **Losses** | 67 | 2 |
| | **Ties** | 22 | - |
| | **Shutouts** | 6 | - |
| | **Average** | 3.32 | 4.42 |

During the 1994-1995 season, Stéphane Fiset shared goaltending duties with teammate Jocelyn Thibault and had his best season with the Nordiques.

Although he was only 24 years old at the start of the 1994-1995 season, Stéphane Fiset was already in his sixth season with the Quebec Nordiques. He played junior hockey with Victoriaville and, during the 1988-1989 season, he maintained the best average in the league, with 3.45 in 43 games. The Nordiques' third pick in the 1988 draft, he played his first games in Quebec City in 1989-1990, suffering five losses in six games. The Nordiques were in a slump at the time and the team had not won a playoff berth since 1987.

Fiset was sent to the Halifax Citadels in the American League for the 1990-1991 season. He shuttled back and forth between Quebec and Halifax over the next two seasons, playing 23 games with the Nordiques in 1991-1992, then 37 in 1992-1993 for a season average of 3.40. When Ron Hextall was traded to the New York Islanders on June 20, 1993, Fiset was assured that he was the Nordiques starter.

In 1993-1994 he played 50 games, winning 20 and maintaining an average of 3.39. The Nordiques missed the playoffs for the seventh time in their history, but made up for it admirably in 1994-1995 when they finished first in their conference. Fiset won 17 of his 32 games, maintaining an average of 2.78, the best of his career.

Stéphane Fiset dives to stop the puck as Alexei Gusarov and Pierre Sévigny look on.

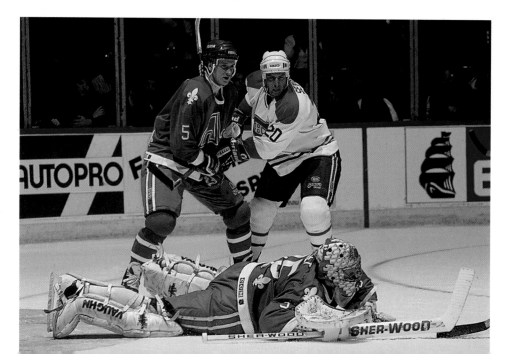

Stéphane Fiset uses his shoulder to stop a shot from Vincent Damphousse, robbing the Habs forward of a goal. In 1995-1996, with Patrick Roy's trade to the Avalanche, Fiset played 37 games compared to 39 for the former Number 33 Canadiens player, maintaining an average of 2.93. On June 20, 1996, he was traded to the Los Angeles Kings for leftwinger Éric Lacroix, son of Pierre Lacroix, head coach for the Avalanche.

During the 1995 playoffs, Stéphane Fiset was a bit of a disappointment. He played four games, winning only one, for an average of 4.59. Jocelyn Thibault played the other three games in the series between Quebec and the New York Rangers.

# MARK FITZPATRICK

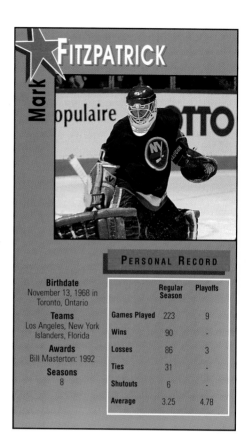

**Birthdate**
November 13, 1968 in
Toronto, Ontario

**Teams**
Los Angeles, New York
Islanders, Florida

**Awards**
Bill Masterton: 1992

**Seasons**
8

| PERSONAL RECORD | | |
| --- | --- | --- |
| | Regular Season | Playoffs |
| Games Played | 223 | 9 |
| Wins | 90 | - |
| Losses | 86 | 3 |
| Ties | 31 | - |
| Shutouts | 6 | - |
| Average | 3.25 | 4.78 |

In 1987 and 1988, Mark Fitzpatrick won the Hap Emms Trophy, which is awarded to the best goaltender in the Memorial Cup tournament; at the time, he was playing with the Medicine Hat team in the Western Hockey League. He came to the National League in 1988-1989 with the Los Angeles Kings, but was traded to the New York Islanders in February 1989. He played 47 games in 1989-1990, maintaining an average of 3.39.

The next season, he had played only two games when he was diagnosed with a very rare blood disease. He left the game to undergo various treatments and to rest, in the hope of controlling, if not curing, his illness.

In September 1991, he returned to play with the Islanders. He played 30 games during the season, maintaining an average of 3.20. His courage and determination earned him the Bill Masterton Trophy.

Fitzpatrick was acquired by the Panthers in June 1993 and in 1995-1996, after playing 28 and 15 games in the previous two seasons, he took part in 34 games. He maintained a good average of 2.96 and, along with teammate John Vanbiesbrouck, helped the Panthers reach the Stanley Cup finals.

# JEFF HACKETT

Jeff Hackett made his debut with the New York Islanders in 1988-1989, and played 13 games that season. Hackett had been the team's second pick in the 1987 draft and had learned his trade over two seasons with Springfield in the American League. In 1989-1990, he won 24 of his 54 games and maintained an average of 3.68. During the playoffs, he won 10 of his 17 games and earned the Jack Butterfield Trophy for the most valuable player in the playoffs.

In 1990-1991 Hackett played 30 games with the Islanders, maintaining an average of 3.62, before going to San Jose during the May 1991 expansion draft. In two seasons with the team, Hackett played only 78 games, recording only 13 wins and maintaining averages of 3.84 and 5.28. On July 13, 1993, he was traded to the Chicago Black Hawks.

In 1994-1995 he was Ed Belfour's backup, playing only seven games but maintaining a good average of 2.38. During the 1995-1996 season, Hackett really showed what he could do; he played 35 games, including 4 shutouts, and posted an excellent average of 2.40.

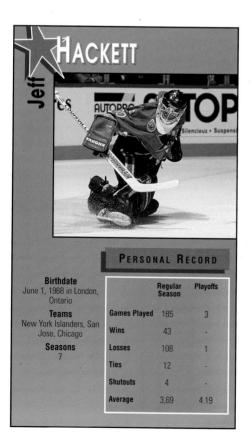

**Birthdate**
June 1, 1968 in London, Ontario

**Teams**
New York Islanders, San Jose, Chicago

**Seasons**
7

| PERSONAL RECORD | | |
| --- | --- | --- |
| | Regular Season | Playoffs |
| Games Played | 185 | 3 |
| Wins | 43 | - |
| Losses | 108 | 1 |
| Ties | 12 | - |
| Shutouts | 4 | - |
| Average | 3,69 | 4.19 |

# DOMINIK HASEK

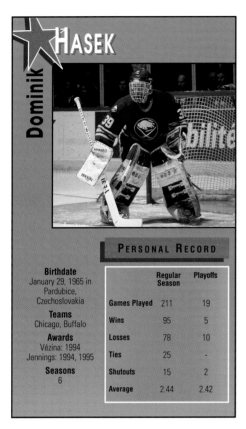

Dominik **HASEK**

## PERSONAL RECORD

**Birthdate**
January 29, 1965 in Pardubice, Czechoslovakia

**Teams**
Chicago, Buffalo

**Awards**
Vézina: 1994
Jennings: 1994, 1995

**Seasons**
6

| | Regular Season | Playoffs |
|---|---|---|
| Games Played | 211 | 19 |
| Wins | 95 | 5 |
| Losses | 78 | 10 |
| Ties | 25 | - |
| Shutouts | 15 | 2 |
| Average | 2.44 | 2.42 |

The patience shown by Czechoslovakian goaltender Dominik Hasek in recent years finally paid off. Named goaltender of the year in his country from 1986 to 1990, and best hockey player in 1987, 1989 and 1990, he decided to try his luck in North America in 1990.

The Chicago Black Hawks' eleventh pick in the 1983 draft, Hasek began by playing only 25 games with the team over two seasons (1990-1991 and 1991-1992). Chicago was relying on Ed Belfour, who was off to a sensational start. Hasek played with the Indianapolis Ice in the International League until the spring of 1992 before being traded to the Buffalo Sabres on August 7 for goaltender Stéphane Beauregard.

In 1992-1993 he played 28 games with the Sabres, maintaining an average of 3.15. He wasn't protected during the draft in June 1993, when it came time to fill the ranks of two new teams, the Anaheim Mighty Ducks and the Florida Panthers. Neither team thought it a good idea to test the 28-year-old Czech goalie.

That decision turned out to be lucky for the Sabres. In 1993-1994, Hasek became the first goalie since Bernard Parent (in 1973-1974) to maintain an average under 2.00, with 1.95 in 58 games. That performance earned him the Vézina Trophy. Hasek became the second European goaltender to win the trophy, after Pelle Lindbergh in 1985. With teammate Grant Fuhr, he also won the Jennings Trophy. He finished at the top of the League, on an equal footing with Ed Belfour and Patrick Roy, for the most shutouts, with seven.

Known for an unorthodox goaltending style, dropping to his knees often, Hasek had an excellent season in 1994-1995, winning 19 of 41 games and maintaining an average of 2.11. In 1995-1996, Hasek maintained an average of 2.83 in 59 games, but for the first time since 1987, the Sabres failed to make it to the playoffs.

During a game at the Forum against the Canadiens, the Sabres goaltender prepares to make a save despite the heavy traffic in front of his net. In 1994-1995, for the second consecutive year, he dominated the League's goalies with an average of 2.11, earning the Jennings Trophy for a second time.

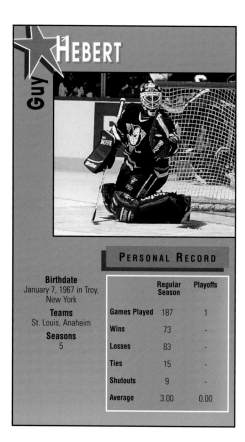

**Guy HEBERT**

### PERSONAL RECORD

**Birthdate**
January 7, 1967 in Troy, New York

**Teams**
St. Louis, Anaheim

**Seasons**
5

| | Regular Season | Playoffs |
|---|---|---|
| Games Played | 187 | 1 |
| Wins | 73 | - |
| Losses | 83 | - |
| Ties | 15 | - |
| Shutouts | 9 | - |
| Average | 3.00 | 0.00 |

# GUY HEBERT

Guy Hebert was signed by the St. Louis Blues in 1987 as their eighth pick. The young goaltender had caught the eye of the team's scouts for his performance with the Hamilton College team in 1986-1987. He won 12 of 18 games, managing three shutouts and maintaining an average of 2.19. In 1988-1989, with the same team, he won 18 of his 25 games and ended the season with an average of 2.56. Assigned to the Peoria Rivermen in the International League, Hebert earned a spot on the second All Star team in 1990-1991. At the time he had won 24 of his 36 games, for an average of 2.87.

Hebert played his first games in the NHL in 1991-1992, as a backup to Curtis Joseph. He won five of 13 games and maintained an average of 2.93. The next season, he played 24 games (eight wins, 3.67 average) before going to the Anaheim Mighty Ducks in the June 1993 expansion draft.

He became the team's Number 1 goalie in 1993-1994, playing 54 games and maintaining an average of 2.83. In 1995-1996, Hebert won 28 of his 59 games and ended the season with an average of 2.83.

# JIM HRIVNAK

Jim Hrivnak, a native of Montreal, played his first games in the National League during the 1989-1990 season. Signed by the Washington Capitals in 1986 when he was playing with the Merrimack team in the National Collegial Athletic Association, he had waited three years to join the NHL, but had very little chance to prove himself since he played only 32 games over three seasons.

He spent most of his time with the Baltimore Skipjacks in the American League. His best moments with the team came in 1989-1990 when he won 24 of his 47 games and ended the season with an average of 3.06.

After 27 games with the Capitals during the 1992-1993 season, he was traded to the Winnipeg Jets for goaltender Rick Tabaracci, on March 22, 1993. On July 29 of the same year, he went to the St. Louis Blues. In 1993-1994 he played 23 games with the Blues, winning only four and maintaining an average of 4.27.

Hrivnak has not played in the National League in the past two seasons. In 1995-1996, he played 17 games with the Kansas City Blades in the International League, recording 11 wins and maintaining an average of 3.12.

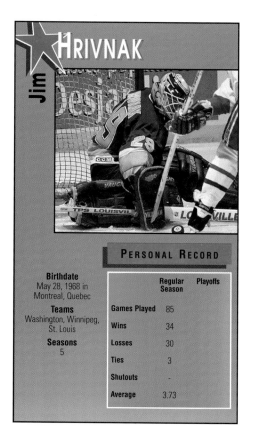

**Jim HRIVNAK**

### PERSONAL RECORD

**Birthdate**
May 28, 1968 in Montreal, Quebec

**Teams**
Washington, Winnipeg, St. Louis

**Seasons**
5

| | Regular Season | Playoffs |
|---|---|---|
| Games Played | 85 | |
| Wins | 34 | |
| Losses | 30 | |
| Ties | 3 | |
| Shutouts | - | |
| Average | 3.73 | |

# CURTIS JOSEPH

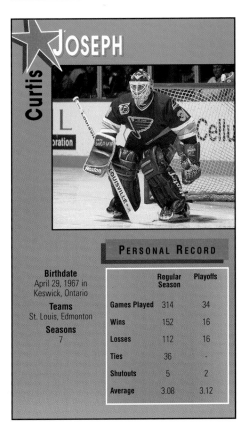

**Curtis JOSEPH**

### PERSONAL RECORD

**Birthdate**
April 29, 1967 in
Keswick, Ontario

**Teams**
St. Louis, Edmonton

**Seasons**
7

| | Regular Season | Playoffs |
|---|---|---|
| Games Played | 314 | 34 |
| Wins | 152 | 16 |
| Losses | 112 | 16 |
| Ties | 36 | - |
| Shutouts | 5 | 2 |
| Average | 3.08 | 3.12 |

an average of 3.01, his best before the start of the 1994-1995 season.

For the first time since his debut in the National League, Curtis Joseph successfully maintained an average of under 3.00. In 36 games with the St. Louis Blues, he recorded 20 wins and an average of 2.79. Placing fourth overall in 1994-1995, the team led by Mike Keenan was a favourite in the race for the Stanley Cup. However, the Blues disappointed their fans by losing in the first round, in a seven-game series against the Vancouver Canucks, who had finished in 13th place overall with 13 points less than the Blues. Joseph played all seven of his team's games, with three wins and an average of 3.67.

Signed by the Edmonton Oilers in the summer of 1995, Joseph Curtis played 34 games in 1995-1996, and maintained an average of 3.44. He was not able to keep his team from missing the playoffs for a fourth consecutive year.

Curtis Joseph, photographed when he was playing with the St. Louis Blues. On this play, he makes a nice save with his glove, spoiling forward Denis Savard's hope of earning more points.

In June 1989 the St. Louis Blues management signed goaltender Curtis Joseph, a free agent at the time. Joseph had just ended an excellent season with the University of Wisconsin team in the Western Collegial League. He had won 21 of 38 games for an average of 2.49, which earned him a spot on the circuit's first All Star team.

Joseph made his debut with St. Louis in 1989-1990, playing 15 games with the team, and 23 with the Peoria Rivermen, the Blues' affiliate in the International League. He became the Blues' starter in 1991-1992 when Vincent Riendeau was traded to the Detroit Red Wings on October 18, 1991 for defenceman Rick Zombo. In 1991-1992 Joseph played 60 games, recording 27 wins and maintaining

# TREVOR KIDD

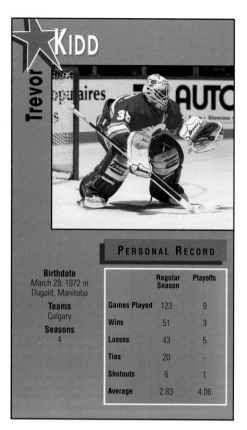

## PERSONAL RECORD

**Birthdate**
March 29, 1972 in
Dugald, Manitoba

**Teams**
Calgary

**Seasons**
4

| | Regular Season | Playoffs |
|---|---|---|
| Games Played | 123 | 9 |
| Wins | 51 | 3 |
| Losses | 43 | 5 |
| Ties | 20 | - |
| Shutouts | 6 | 1 |
| Average | 2.83 | 4.06 |

During his first full season in the National League in 1993-1994, Trevor Kidd showed the Calgary Flames management that he deserved a chance to prove his worth. In 31 games he maintained an average of 3.16, and came in third among rookie goalies for the most wins, with 13, after Martin Brodeur and Chris Osgood.

Thanks to a trade which sent veteran goalie Mike Vernon to the Detroit Red Wings, Kidd became the Flames' lead goalie in 1994-1995. He played 43 games, won 22 of them and maintained an average of 2.61. The Flames finished first in the Pacific

Division but were foiled in the playoffs once again, losing a seven-game series to the San Jose Sharks in the first round.

Kidd had been the Flames' first pick in the 1990 draft and the eleventh overall. He was chosen ahead of Martin Brodeur and Félix Potvin, that year's 20th and 31st picks respectively. With the Brandon team in the Western Hockey League in 1989-1990, Kidd had played 63 games, a league high, and had recorded 24 wins. He had been chosen to play on the first All Star team. Before joining the Flames, Trevor Kidd also played with the Canadian Olympic team and Canada's national team. With the national team in 1991-1992, he won 18 of 28 games and maintained an average of 3.51.

In 1995-1996, Kidd played 47 games and maintained an average of 2.78, sharing goaltending duties with Rick Tabaracci. The Flames didn't go far in the playoffs; they lost a four-game series in the first round against the Chicago Black Hawks.

Trevor Kidd manages to block a shot with his pads while his defencemen charge to the rescue. In the background is former Canadiens captain Guy Carbonneau.

# OLAF KOLZIG

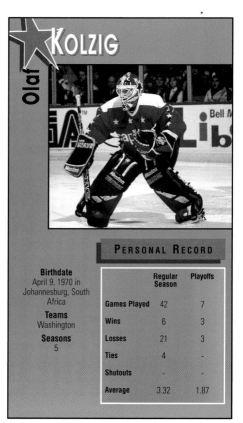

**Olaf Kolzig**

### PERSONAL RECORD

**Birthdate**
April 9, 1970 in
Johannesburg, South
Africa

**Teams**
Washington

**Seasons**
5

| | Regular Season | Playoffs |
|---|---|---|
| Games Played | 42 | 7 |
| Wins | 6 | 3 |
| Losses | 21 | 3 |
| Ties | 4 | - |
| Shutouts | - | - |
| Average | 3.32 | 1.87 |

he played only 18 games, backing up Jim Carey, who played 71.

The only National League player born in South Africa, Olaf Kolzig was Washington's first pick in the 1989 draft. In his first three seasons with the Capitals (1989-1990, 1992-1993 and 1993-1994) he played only 10 games. In 1993-1994, as a result of his excellent work with the Portland Pirates in the American League, he shared the Harry Holmes Trophy with teammate Byron Dafoe; the award goes to the goaltenders with the best goals-against average. Kolzig had maintained an average of 3.06 in 29 games. During the playoffs he won 12 of his 17 games, maintaining an average of 2.55.

In 1994-1995, Kolzig had more chances to prove his mettle, playing 14 games with the Capitals and ending with a 2.49 average. In 1995-1996

Olaf Kolzig played only 10 games with the Washington Capitals before the start of the 1994-1995 season. In the spring of 1994, he won the Jack Butterfield Trophy for the most valuable player in the playoffs in the American League, which led to a permanent spot with the Capitals.

# BLAINE LACHER

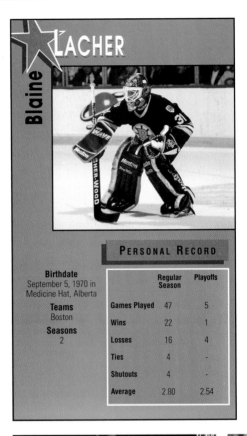

Blaine
LACHER

### PERSONAL RECORD

**Birthdate**
September 5, 1970 in
Medicine Hat, Alberta

**Teams**
Boston

**Seasons**
2

|  | Regular Season | Playoffs |
|---|---|---|
| Games Played | 47 | 5 |
| Wins | 22 | 1 |
| Losses | 16 | 4 |
| Ties | 4 | - |
| Shutouts | 4 | - |
| Average | 2.80 | 2.54 |

Blaine Lacher was undoubtedly one of the most exciting revelations of the 1994-1995 season and a very pleasant surprise for the Boston Bruins management. A free agent, Lacher signed a contract with the Bruins on June 2, 1994, after playing the previous three seasons with the Lake Superior team in the Central Collegial Hockey Association. In 1993-1994, he won 20 of 30 games and maintained an astounding average of 1.98, the best in the circuit. Jon Casey had been the Bruins' Number 1 goalie in 1993-1994, but when he signed with St. Louis as a free agent in June 1994, the road was clear for Lacher to prove himself to head coach Brian Sutter. He played 35 games, won 19 of them, and ended the year with an average of 2.41. During the playoffs, the Bruins were outplayed by the Devils and lost in five games. Lacher played all five of those games and finished with an average of 2.54, while his rival Martin Brodeur allowed only five goals and managed two shutouts. In 1995-1996, Lacher played only 12 games with the Bruins, while Bill Ranford, who had been acquired from the Edmonton Oilers, played 40.

At 24, Blaine Lacher demonstrated his ability with the Boston Bruins during his first season in the National League, in 1994-1995.

# DARRIN MADELEY

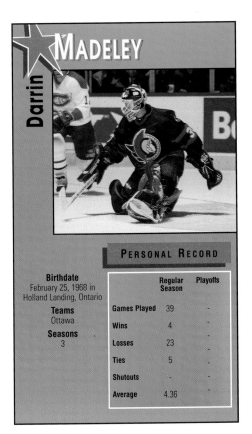

Darrin MADELEY

## PERSONAL RECORD

**Birthdate**
February 25, 1968 in
Holland Landing, Ontario

**Teams**
Ottawa

**Seasons**
3

| | Regular Season | Playoffs |
|---|---|---|
| Games Played | 39 | - |
| Wins | 4 | - |
| Losses | 23 | - |
| Ties | 5 | - |
| Shutouts | - | - |
| Average | 4.36 | - |

During the 1991-1992 season, goalie Darrin Madeley was brilliant with the Lake Superior team in the Central Collegial Hockey Association, winning 23 of 36 games and maintaining an average of 2.05, the best in the league. The following season, he dominated the league's other goalies with a record of 29 wins in 36 games. Once again, his was the best average in the league: 2.61. His statistics were impressive enough for the Ottawa Senators to sign him when he was a free agent in June 1992.

In 1992-1993, Madeley played two games with Ottawa and allowed 10 goals! He spent the season with the New Haven Nighthawks in the American League, where he played 41 games and maintained an average of 3.32. The next season, he played as backup to Craig Billington, the Senators' lead goalie. Madeley did his best for the team, which won only 14 of its 84 games. He played 32 games, winning three of them and ending the season with an average of 4.36.

After playing five games with Ottawa in 1994-1995, Madeley spent the following season with the Phoenix Roadrunners in the International League. In 40 games, he maintained an average of 3.17.

# CHRIS OSGOOD

The Red Wings' third pick in the 1991 draft, Chris Osgood made his debut in the 1993-1994 season. He was even appointed the team's lead goalie and played 41 games, while his teammate Tim Cheveldae played 30. He won 23 games and impressed everyone with an average of 2.86.

Unfortunately for him, the Red Wings acquired Mike Vernon in the summer of 1994. As a result, Osgood's outings on the ice were considerably fewer in number during the 1994-1995 season. Nonetheless, he did admirably, winning 14 of his 19 games and maintaining an average of 2.26. Osgood and Vernon ended in second place in the League with a combined average of 2.42.

In 1995-1996, Osgood finally had a chance to demonstrate his talent and he proved to be a very pleasant surprise for the Wings. In 50 games, he maintained an average of 2.17 and recorded 39 wins; with teammate Mike Vernon, he won the Jennings Trophy for the team with the best goals-against average (only 181 in 82 games, for a cumulative average of 2.19). During the playoffs Osgood was the starter for the Wings, but despite an average of 2.12, his team met with defeat at the hands of the Colorado Avalanche.

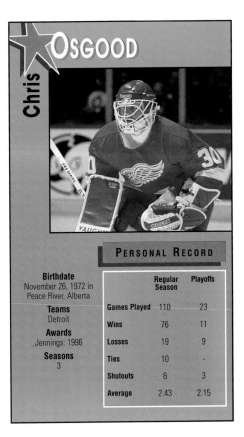

Chris OSGOOD

## PERSONAL RECORD

**Birthdate**
November 26, 1972 in
Peace River, Alberta

**Teams**
Detroit

**Awards**
Jennings: 1996

**Seasons**
3

| | Regular Season | Playoffs |
|---|---|---|
| Games Played | 110 | 23 |
| Wins | 76 | 11 |
| Losses | 19 | 9 |
| Ties | 10 | - |
| Shutouts | 8 | 3 |
| Average | 2.43 | 2.15 |

# FÉLIX POTVIN

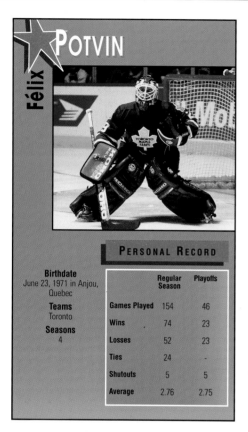

POTVIN

Félix

### PERSONAL RECORD

**Birthdate**
June 23, 1971 in Anjou, Quebec

**Teams**
Toronto

**Seasons**
4

| | Regular Season | Playoffs |
|---|---|---|
| Games Played | 154 | 46 |
| Wins | 74 | 23 |
| Losses | 52 | 23 |
| Ties | 24 | - |
| Shutouts | 5 | 5 |
| Average | 2.76 | 2.75 |

Named best goalie in the country when he played with the Chicoutimi Saguenéens in 1990-1991 (a 2.70 average in 54 games), and voted the best goalie in the Memorial Cup tournament that same year, Félix Potvin was amazing wherever he played. In 1991-1992, while with St. John's (the Toronto Maple Leafs' farm club) in the American League, he was named rookie of the year and best goaltender by virtue of 18 wins in 35 games and an average of 2.93.

The following season, he tended the Maple Leafs' net and dominated the League's other goalies with an average of 2.50 in 48 games. Stanley Cup fever gripped Toronto when Potvin's team made it to the Campbell Conference finals. In the end, Toronto lost in seven games against the Los Angeles Kings. Potvin maintained an average of 2.84 in 21 games.

In 1993-1994, he confirmed his first-class talent by maintaining an average of 2.89 in 66 games and by bringing his record down to 2.46 during the 18 playoff games. The Leafs were once again eliminated in the conference finals, this time by the Vancouver Canucks.

In 1994-1995, Potvin succeeded in keeping his average under 3.00 (2.91 in 36 games) and shared goaltending functions with rookie Damian Rhodes, who played 13 games and maintained an average of 2.68. In the first round of the playoffs, the Maple Leafs lost to the Chicago Black Hawks. Goalie Ed Belfour was astounding in his team's net, and Potvin stopped 42 shots for a shutout in the second game of the series (3-0). In seven games, Potvin maintained an average of 2.83.

In 1995-1996, Potvin played 69 games with Toronto and maintained an average of 2.87. The Leafs finished in 13th place in overall standings but were eliminated by St. Louis in the first round of the playoffs.

Félix Potvin, nicknamed "The Cat", had a brilliant career in junior hockey. In 1990-1991, with the Chicoutimi team, he maintained the best average in the Quebec Major Junior Hockey League (2.70 in 54 games) before moving up to the National League.

Félix Potvin and teammate Damian Rhodes maintained a combined average of 3.00 in 1994-1995, ending in 16th place overall.

The young Maple Leafs goaltender stops a shot on his stick while his defenceman prevents a Canadiens player from retrieving the puck.

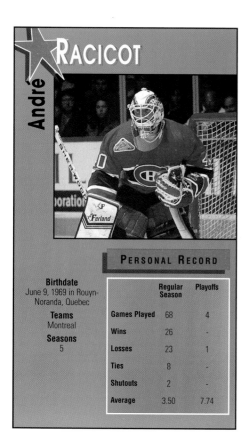

**Andre**
**RACICOT**

| PERSONAL RECORD | | |
| --- | --- | --- |

**Birthdate**
June 9, 1969 in Rouyn-Noranda, Quebec
**Teams**
Montreal
**Seasons**
5

| | Regular Season | Playoffs |
| --- | --- | --- |
| Games Played | 68 | 4 |
| Wins | 26 | - |
| Losses | 23 | 1 |
| Ties | 8 | - |
| Shutouts | 2 | - |
| Average | 3.50 | 7.74 |

# ANDRÉ RACICOT

André Racicot learned his trade with the Granby Bisons in the Quebec Major Junior Hockey League. In 1988-1989, Racicot maintained an average of 4.04 in 54 games and earned a place on the League's second All Star team.

Signed by the Canadiens in 1989, he was sent to the Sherbrooke Canadiens in the American League. Along with teammate Jean-Claude Bergeron, he won the Harry Holmes Trophy, awarded to the goalies with the best goals-against average; he had maintained an average of 2.99 in 33 games. Called up to play for the Montreal Canadiens in 1990-1991, he went through a baptism of fire: in 13 minutes, he allowed three goals!

Over the next two seasons, he shuttled between Montreal and Fredericton, where the Canadiens' farm team had relocated in 1990. As Patrick Roy's backup in 1992-1993, he played 26 games, and only 11 the following season. With the arrival of Ron Tugnutt, who had been acquired on February 20, 1994, Racicot's career in Montreal came to an end. He joined the Portland Pirates in the American League in 1994-1995, playing 19 games and maintaining an average of 2.94. He also played three games with the Phoenix Roadrunners in the International League. Racicot has not played in the NHL since 1994. He spent the 1995-1996 season with the Peoria Rivermen in the International League.

# MANON RHÉAUME

The date was September 23, 1992. The Tampa Bay Lightning were playing the St. Louis Blues in an exhibition match. In the net for the Lightning stood a rather small goaltender, only 5 feet 6 inches tall, who was playing for the first time with the professionals. Another distinctive characteristic: the goalie was a woman and her name was Manon Rhéaume!

Manon Rhéaume wrote a new page in hockey history on November 26, 1991, by being the first woman goaltender to play in a major junior circuit, with the Trois-Rivières Draveurs in the Quebec Major Junior Hockey League. Then, invited to attend Tampa Bay's training camp by general manager Phil Esposito, Manon Rhéaume was in the media spotlight once again and played one period against the Blues. Finally, on December 13, 1994, she became the first woman to take part in a regular season game with a professional team, the Atlanta Knights in the International League. The following year, still with the Lightning, she played one period in an exhibition game against the Boston Bruins.

"My goal is to play in the 1998 Olympics, which will be the first Games to include women's hockey. By then, I'll only be 26," comments Manon.

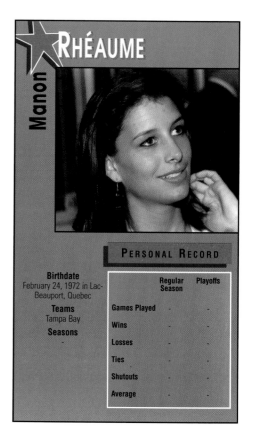

**Manon**
**RHÉAUME**

| PERSONAL RECORD | | |
| --- | --- | --- |

**Birthdate**
February 24, 1972 in Lac-Beauport, Quebec
**Teams**
Tampa Bay
**Seasons**

| | Regular Season | Playoffs |
| --- | --- | --- |
| Games Played | - | - |
| Wins | - | - |
| Losses | - | - |
| Ties | - | - |
| Shutouts | - | - |
| Average | - | - |

# MIKE RICHTER

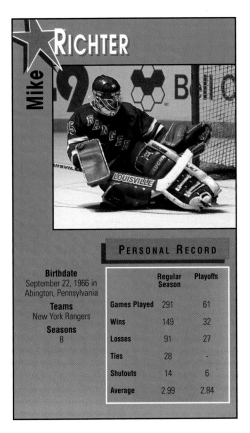

Mike RICHTER

## PERSONAL RECORD

**Birthdate**
September 22, 1966 in
Abington, Pennsylvania

**Teams**
New York Rangers

**Seasons**
8

| | Regular Season | Playoffs |
|---|---|---|
| Games Played | 291 | 61 |
| Wins | 149 | 32 |
| Losses | 91 | 27 |
| Ties | 28 | - |
| Shutouts | 14 | 6 |
| Average | 2.99 | 2.84 |

Ranford, Tom Barrasso and Patrick Roy. In addition, Richter managed a high of four shutouts and maintained an average of 2.07 as the Rangers won the Stanley Cup for the first time since 1940.

In the past two seasons, Richter has maintained averages of 2.92 and 2.68. However, the Rangers didn't last long in the playoffs, losing in the quarter finals each time.

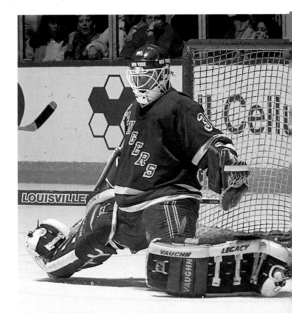

During the 1996 playoffs, Mike Richter played 11 games and maintained an average of 3.27. After eliminating the Canadiens, New York lost to Pittsburgh.

The Rangers' second pick in the 1985 draft, in 1994-1995 Mike Richter was in his seventh season with the team. In 1991-1992, he won 23 of his 41 games with the Rangers and maintained an average of 3.11. But Richter enjoyed his best season in 1993-1994, when he led the League's goalies for most wins in a season: 42 in 68 games. He maintained an average of 2.57 and the Rangers ended in first place overall with 112 points, compared to 79 points in the previous season. During the playoffs, Richter won 16 of his 23 games, becoming the fifth goalie to achieve such a record since 1988, after Grant Fuhr, Mike Vernon, Bill

Backed by star defenceman Brian Leach, Mike Richter makes a save against a Canadiens player.

# DOMINIC ROUSSEL

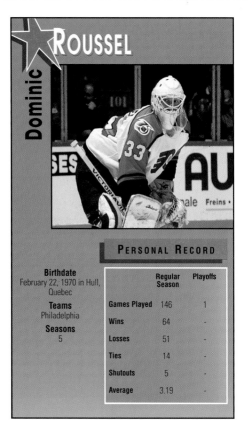

ROUSSEL

Dominic

33

### PERSONAL RECORD

**Birthdate**
February 22, 1970 in Hull, Quebec

**Teams**
Philadelphia

**Seasons**
5

|  | Regular Season | Playoffs |
|---|---|---|
| Games Played | 146 | 1 |
| Wins | 64 | - |
| Losses | 51 | - |
| Ties | 14 | - |
| Shutouts | 5 | - |
| Average | 3.19 | - |

Hershey, where he maintained an average of 3.56 in 35 games. When Ron Hextall left for Quebec as part of a major transaction that sent Eric Lindros to the Flyers, the situation changed considerably.

In 1992-1993 Roussel played 34 games with the Flyers, sharing goaltending duties with Tommy Soderstrom, who was in his first season with the NHL. He won 13 games and ended the year with an average of 3.76.

In 1993-1994, Roussel was considered to be the Flyers Number 1 goalie, and Soderstrom played as his backup. Roussel played 60 games, winning 29 and ending the season with an average of 3.34. For the fifth consecutive year, the Flyers were excluded from the playoffs, having won only 35 of 80 games.

For the 1994-1995 season, the Flyers got back veteran Ron Hextall, whom they were ready to bank on once again given his record the previous season (an average of 3.08 in 65 games with the Islanders, his best since joining Philadelphia in 1986-1987). With Hextall back as lead goalie, Roussel played only 19 games in 1994-1995. However, he had a good season, winning 11 games and maintaining an average of 2.34.

In 1995-1996, Roussel played only nine games with the Flyers, who decided to use Garth Snow as backup for Ron Hextall. Roussel went to the Winnipeg Jets, where he played only seven games. During the season, Roussel also played 12 games with the Hershey Bears in the American League.

A native of Hull, Quebec, Dominic Roussel was playing with the Trois-Rivières Draveurs in 1987-1988 when the Rangers made him their fourth draft pick. Roussel had won only 18 of his 51 games and had maintained an average of 5.18, but the Flyers' scouts believed he had potential. Roussel played two additional seasons in the Quebec Major Junior Hockey League, with Shawinigan, before joining the Hershey Bears in the American League in 1990-1991. In 45 games, he recorded 20 wins and maintained an average of 3.61. Roussel played his first games with the Flyers in the 1991-1992 season. He was asked to play in 17 games, won seven of them and maintained an average of 2.60. He spent most of the season with

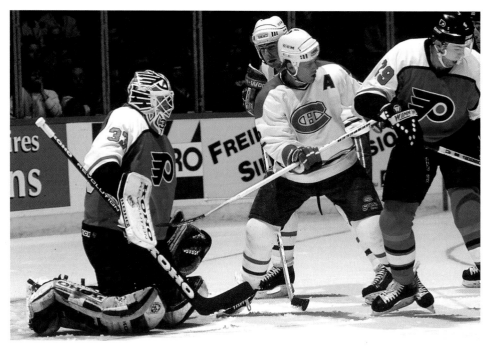

Dominic Roussel in a Flyers uniform, before he went to the Winnipeg Jets, a team that has become the Phoenix Coyotes for the 1996-1997 season.

# GARTH SNOW

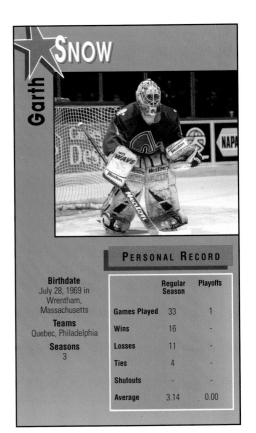

Garth SNOW

## PERSONAL RECORD

| Birthdate | | Regular Season | Playoffs |
|---|---|---|---|
| July 28, 1969 in Wrentham, Massachusetts | | | |
| **Teams** | Games Played | 33 | 1 |
| Quebec, Philadelphia | Wins | 16 | - |
| **Seasons** | Losses | 11 | - |
| 3 | Ties | 4 | - |
| | Shutouts | - | - |
| | Average | 3.14 | 0.00 |

Before being signed by the Quebec Nordiques in 1987, Garth Snow played junior hockey with the University of Maine from September 1988 to the spring of 1993. For three seasons (1990-1991, 1991-1992, 1992-1993), he was the team's biggest star and led the League with the most wins. In his last two seasons he took the lead once again, posting averages of 2.44 and 2.08.

Snow played with four teams in 1993-1994. He was on the United States's national team and on the American Olympic team; he played 16 games with the Cornwall Royals in the American League; and he played his first games with Quebec. He recorded three wins and maintained an average of 3.44 in five games with the Nordiques.

In 1994-1995, he maintained the second best average in the American League with Cornwall (2.73 in 62 games). He played only two games with the Nordiques.

In July 1995 the Quebec Nordiques (now the Colorado Avalanche) traded Snow to the Philadelphia Flyers for a draft choice. In 1995-1996, Snow played 26 games (for an average of 2.88), as backup to Ron Hextall.

# TOMMY SODERSTROM

Born in Stockholm, Tommy Soderstrom was picked by the Philadelphia Flyers in the 1990 draft. With Djurgarden in Sweden, a team that once starred Mats Sundin, Soderstrom had maintained averages of 2.67 and 2.79 for two consecutive seasons. When he arrived in America in 1992, he played seven games with the Hershey Bears in the American League, and later became the Flyers' Number 1 goalie after Ron Hextall left for Quebec. He played 44 games, winning 20 of them and maintaining an average of 3.42.

In 1993-1994, Dominic Roussel took over the lead goalie's job and Soderstrom played only 34 games. He recorded only six wins and his average increased to 4.01. He was traded to the New York Islanders, in a transaction that brought Hextall back to the Flyers. Soderstrom played 26 games with the Islanders, lowering his average to 3.11.

In 1995-1996, Soderstrom was the Number 1 goalie for the Islanders, playing 51 games for a cumulative average of 3.87. For the second consecutive season, the Islanders failed to make the playoffs.

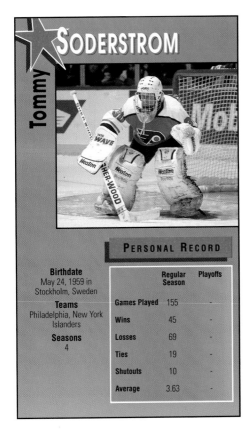

Tommy SODERSTROM

## PERSONAL RECORD

| Birthdate | | Regular Season | Playoffs |
|---|---|---|---|
| May 24, 1959 in Stockholm, Sweden | | | |
| **Teams** | Games Played | 155 | - |
| Philadelphia, New York Islanders | Wins | 45 | - |
| **Seasons** | Losses | 69 | - |
| 4 | Ties | 19 | - |
| | Shutouts | 10 | - |
| | Average | 3.63 | - |

# RICK TABARACCI

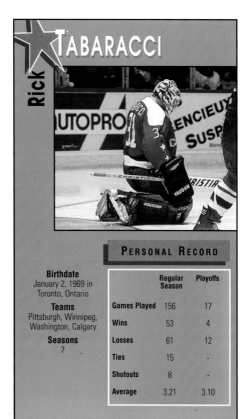

**PERSONAL RECORD**

**Birthdate**
January 2, 1969 in
Toronto, Ontario

**Teams**
Pittsburgh, Winnipeg,
Washington, Calgary

**Seasons**
7

| | Regular Season | Playoffs |
|---|---|---|
| Games Played | 156 | 17 |
| Wins | 53 | 4 |
| Losses | 61 | 12 |
| Ties | 15 | - |
| Shutouts | 8 | - |
| Average | 3.21 | 3.10 |

Rick Tabaracci has been playing in the National League since 1988-1989. A former goalie for the Cornwall Royals in the Ontario Hockey League—in 1987-1988 he won 33 of 59 games, a high—Tabaracci was the Pittsburgh Penguins' second choice in the 1987 draft. He made his debut in the National League with the Penguins in 1988-1989, where he played only one game before going to the Winnipeg Jets. In 1990-1991, during his first season with the team, Tabaracci played 24 games, winning only four and maintaining an average of 3.90. He played another season with the Jets, shuttling regularly between Moncton, in the American League, and Winnipeg before being traded to the Washington Capitals on March 22, 1993 in return for goalie Jim Hrivnak.

In 1993-1994 Tabaracci played 32 games with the Capitals, maintaining an average of 3.08. He wasn't as lucky in 1994-1995; despite Don Beaupre's departure for Ottawa, the arrival of rookie Jim Carey, with young Olaf Kolzig as a backup, limited Tabaracci's ice time to only eight games. He was traded to another team once again during the season, this time to the Calgary Flames, where he played only five games. In 1995-1996, Tabaracci played the most games of his career (43), maintaining an average of 2.94 with Calgary. Once again, the Flames failed to make it past the first round of the playoffs, losing to Chicago in a four-game series.

Rick Tabaracci when he was with the Washington Capitals, a team he stayed with only briefly. In this photo, he uses his stick to rob forward Oleg Petrov of a chance to score.

# JOSÉ THÉODORE

**José THÉODORE**

### PERSONAL RECORD

**Birthdate**
September 13, 1976 in
Laval, Quebec

**Teams**
Montreal

**Team in 1995-1996**
Hull Olympiques

**Seasons (NHL)**
1

| | Regular Season | Playoffs |
|---|---|---|
| Games Played | 1 | - |
| Wins | - | - |
| Losses | - | - |
| Ties | - | - |
| Shutouts | - | - |
| Average | 6.67 | - |

José Théodore, a young goaltender from Laval, Quebec, was the Montreal Canadiens' second draft pick in 1994. His solid performance in the net for the Saint-Jean Lynx in the Quebec Major Junior Hockey League had attracted the attention of Canadiens' scouts. In 1992-1993, he maintained an average of 3.78 in 34 games and in 1993-1994, he won 20 of his 57 games, for an average of 3.61.

In 1994-1995 he did better still. He won 32 games, managed five shutouts and maintained an average of 3.46 in 58 games. In 1995-1996, Théodore played 48 games with Hull and recorded an average of 3.38.

Before returning to Hull, José Théodore played only nine minutes with the Canadiens in 1995-1996. With Patrick Roy gone, he could well be called sometime soon to back up Jocelyn Thibault.

# JOCELYN THIBAULT

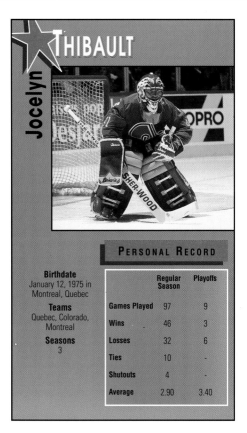

**THIBAULT**

Jocelyn

### PERSONAL RECORD

**Birthdate**
January 12, 1975 in
Montreal, Quebec

**Teams**
Quebec, Colorado,
Montreal

**Seasons**
3

|  | Regular Season | Playoffs |
|---|---|---|
| Games Played | 97 | 9 |
| Wins | 46 | 3 |
| Losses | 32 | 6 |
| Ties | 10 | - |
| Shutouts | 4 | - |
| Average | 2.90 | 3.40 |

Thanks to a June 1992 transaction that sent Eric Lindros from the Nordiques to the Philadelphia Flyers, the Quebec team acquired goaltender Jocelyn Thibault. In addition to players Ron Hextall, Peter Forsberg, Steve Duchesne, Mike Ricci, Kerry Huffman and Chris Simon, not to mention a significant sum of money, Philadelphia traded its first picks in the 1993 and 1994 drafts. As a result, Thibault was the Nordiques' first pick, the tenth overall, in the 1993 draft. He was the only goaltender chosen in the first round by the League's 26 teams, and the first goalie from the Quebec Major Junior Hockey League to be picked since 1990, when the Devils signed Martin Brodeur of the Saint-Hyacinthe Laser.

Thibault played junior hockey with Trois-Rivières in 1991-1992 and went to Sherbrooke the following season. With his new team, Thibault won 34 of 56 games and maintained an average of 2.99. He was selected to play on the league's first All Star team and was named best junior goaltender in the country. He was involved in his first games in the National League in 1993-1994, playing 29 games and maintaining an average of 3.31. He also played and won four games with the Cornwall Royals in the American League.

In 1994-1995, during a conflict between the National League's team owners and players, Thibault returned to Sherbrooke, where he played 13 games. When the shortened season finally began in the major circuit, he was ready; he returned as backup to Stéphane Fiset. That was the best season ever for the Nordiques, who finished second overall with 65 points, five less than Detroit. Thibault contributed to the team's success in 18 games, maintaining a very good average of 2.34 and recording 12 wins. He came in seventh among the League's goalies for the best goals-against average and third behind Dominik Hasek and Chris Osgood for best percentage, with .917.

In December 1995, Thibault was traded to Montreal in a deal that sent Patrick Roy and Mike Keane to Colorado. In 40 games with the Canadiens, he maintained an average of 2.83. However, he couldn't prevent the Rangers from eliminating his team in the first round of the playoffs.

The Montreal Canadiens are banking on their young goalie—aged only 21 before the 1996-1997 season—to be as successful in professional hockey as his predecessor.

# JIMMY WAITE

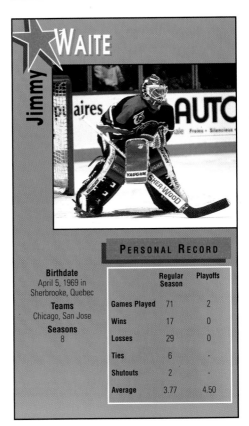

Jimmy WAITE

### PERSONAL RECORD

**Birthdate**
April 5, 1969 in
Sherbrooke, Quebec

**Teams**
Chicago, San Jose

**Seasons**
8

| | Regular Season | Playoffs |
|---|---|---|
| Games Played | 71 | 2 |
| Wins | 17 | 0 |
| Losses | 29 | 0 |
| Ties | 6 | - |
| Shutouts | 2 | - |
| Average | 3.77 | 4.50 |

Born in Sherbrooke, Quebec in 1969, Jimmy Waite caught the eye of National League scouts in the 80s when he was playing for Chicoutimi in the Quebec Major Junior Hockey League. In 1986-1987, he won 23 of 50 games and was selected to play on the league's second All Star team. He was signed in June 1987 by the Chicago Black Hawks and became the team's lead goalie. Waite played his first games with Chicago the very next season, but spent most of his time in the International League, first with Saginaw, then with Indianapolis in 1989-1990. He was chosen to play on the first All Star team and was named best goalie of the year for his record of 34 wins in 54 games and an average of 2.53, the best in the circuit. During the playoffs against Indianapolis, Waite won 9 of 10 games and maintained an average of 1.89. The next season, he was the goalie who won the most regular games (26 out of 49). In 1992-1993 Waite played 20 games with the Black Hawks, maintaining an average of 2.95. At the end of the season, however, he was traded to San Jose for defenceman Neil Wilkinson.

He played only 15 games in 1993-1994, while the Sharks' lead goalie, Arturs Irbe, played 74. On February 6, 1995, he still had not played a single game with San Jose when he was picked up by Chicago. He played only two games during the 1994-1995 season.

In 1995-1996, Waite played only one game with Chicago. He spent the season with the Indianapolis Ice in the American League (with an average of 3.40 in 56 games).

# Ken Dryden

A five-time winner of the Vézina Trophy and a six-time Stanley Cup winner in eight seasons in the National League, not to mention other distinctions and honours, Ken Dryden was unquestionably one of the dominant figures of hockey in the 70s. In 1970-1971, while tending goals with the Nova Scotia Voyageurs, the Canadiens' farm team in the American League, Dryden played 33 games and maintained an average of 2.68 before being called up to Montreal by the Habs. Until he hung up his skates at the end of the 1978-1979 season, he played 397 games and recorded 258 wins with the Canadiens.

At that time, already more than 20 years ago, most aspiring young goaltenders were wearing their idol's number 29 both on and off the ice. Wearing a mask that seemed to provide very little protection, Dryden quickly became a star, a role model for young goalies whose dream was to make it to the National League while also continuing their education, just as Dryden had made a point of finishing his law degree while also playing as a professional athlete. A phlegmatic man of few words, Ken Dryden was much more agile than he looked, as his opponents soon learned.

When he won the Vézina Trophy for the first time in 1973, Dryden's name was added to the list of goaltenders—Worsley, Vachon, Hodge, Plante, Durnan and Hainsworth—who shared the same award and who had defended the Canadiens nets with panache throughout the team's history.

Backed by defenceman Guy Lapointe, a member of the "Big Three" that contributed very significantly to their goalie's success, Ken Dryden stops a shot by a Vancouver Canucks player.

Ken Dryden is congratulated by fans during one of many Stanley Cup parades through the streets of Montreal in the 70s. In fact, during the 1970s the Habs won the coveted cup six times.

During his career, Dryden was selected five times to play on the first All Star team and once to play on the second team. In this photo, taken on January 21, 1975 at the Forum in Montreal, Dryden and defenceman Jerry Korab keep an opponent at bay.

(Opposite page) When Ken Dryden joined the Canadiens in 1971, leftwinger John Ferguson was in his eighth and last season with the team. Just over one year later, Dryden was chosen to play with Team Canada against the USSR, and Ferguson was named assistant to head coach Harry Sinden.

Barely four years after announcing his retirement, Ken Dryden was inducted into the Hockey Hall of Fame, becoming the sixth Canadiens goalie to receive the honour, after Lorne Worsley, Jacques Plante, Bill Durnan, George Hainsworth and Georges Vézina.

In 1972, in what became known as the Super Series, Dryden won two of his four games in the series that pitted Team Canada against the USSR. He finished the tournament with a goals-against average of 4.75.

Tall and sturdy, the Canadiens' Number 29 doesn't leave the North Stars forward with much room to manoeuvre the puck into the net.

A shot taken during a game between the Canadiens and the Chicago Black Hawks; Ken Dryden, Stan Mikita and Dennis Hull seem to be wondering where the puck has gone.

# Patrick Roy

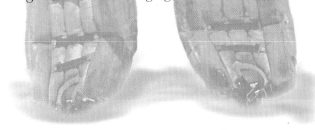

I n the mid 80s, a goaltender from Quebec City fired the imaginations of hockey fans everywhere, young and old alike. Patrick Roy made a thundering debut with the Canadiens in 1985-1986, winning the Stanley Cup in his first playoffs and earning the Conn-Smythe Trophy, as Ken Dryden had done 15 years earlier. Roy played only one regular season game with Sherbrooke in the American League in 1984-1985 and he performed brilliantly in the playoffs, winning 10 of 13 games.

At the start of his career, the Winnipeg Jets seemed to be lucky for Roy, since he won his first game in the National League at their expense (6-4, on February 23, 1985) and he managed the first shutout in his career against them (4-0) on January 15, 1986.

His dazzling debut with the Canadiens, his modesty and his friendliness quickly made him one of the most popular and identifiable players on the team. A three time winner of the Vézina and Jenning Trophies since his career began, Patrick Roy was a major factor in the Canadiens 1993 Stanley Cup victory, winning 16 of 20 games (including 10 in overtime, a new record in the National League). Roy's performance also earned him the Conn-Smythe Trophy for the second time in his career.

Fans quickly elevated him from the status of star player to that of an idol during Roy's very first season in the National League. Considered the best goaltender in the world for many years, Patrick Roy was a role model for countless young goaltenders, in his own country and abroad, who hoped to become as good in the net as the Canadiens' Number 33. After being traded to the Colorado Avalanche in December 1995, Roy showed his fans that he is still one of the best goaltenders in the League by leading his team to the Stanley Cup, the third of his career. During the playoffs, he dominated his counterparts by maintaining an average of 2.10 and managing three shutouts.

Patrick Roy stretches to stop a puck positioned on a Boston forward's stick.

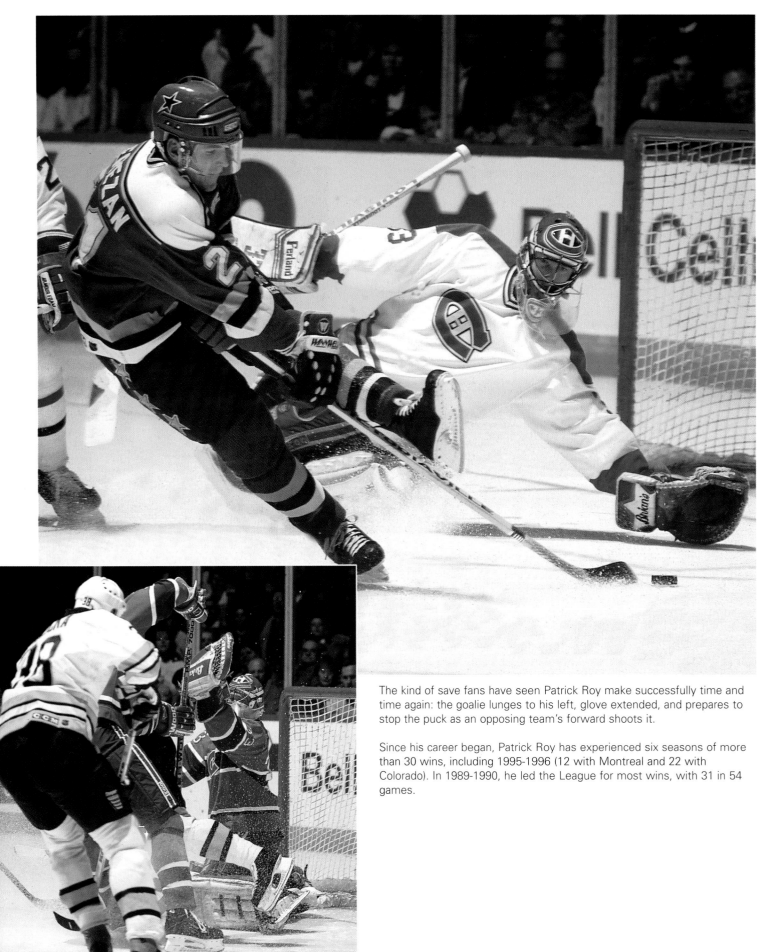

The kind of save fans have seen Patrick Roy make successfully time and time again: the goalie lunges to his left, glove extended, and prepares to stop the puck as an opposing team's forward shoots it.

Since his career began, Patrick Roy has experienced six seasons of more than 30 wins, including 1995-1996 (12 with Montreal and 22 with Colorado). In 1989-1990, he led the League for most wins, with 31 in 54 games.

Most hockey fans in Quebec believe that Patrick Roy was drummed out of Montreal by general manager Réjean Houle and head coach Mario Tremblay because of a 11-1 loss against Detroit on December 2, 1995. In Colorado, Patrick was reunited with Pierre Lacroix, his former agent, and saw his name engraved on the Stanley Cup for the third time in his career. (Photo: Bruce Bennett)

The Canadiens' fourth pick in the 1984 draft, Patrick Roy played another season in the junior leagues, with Granby, in 1984-1985; he joined the National League the following season.

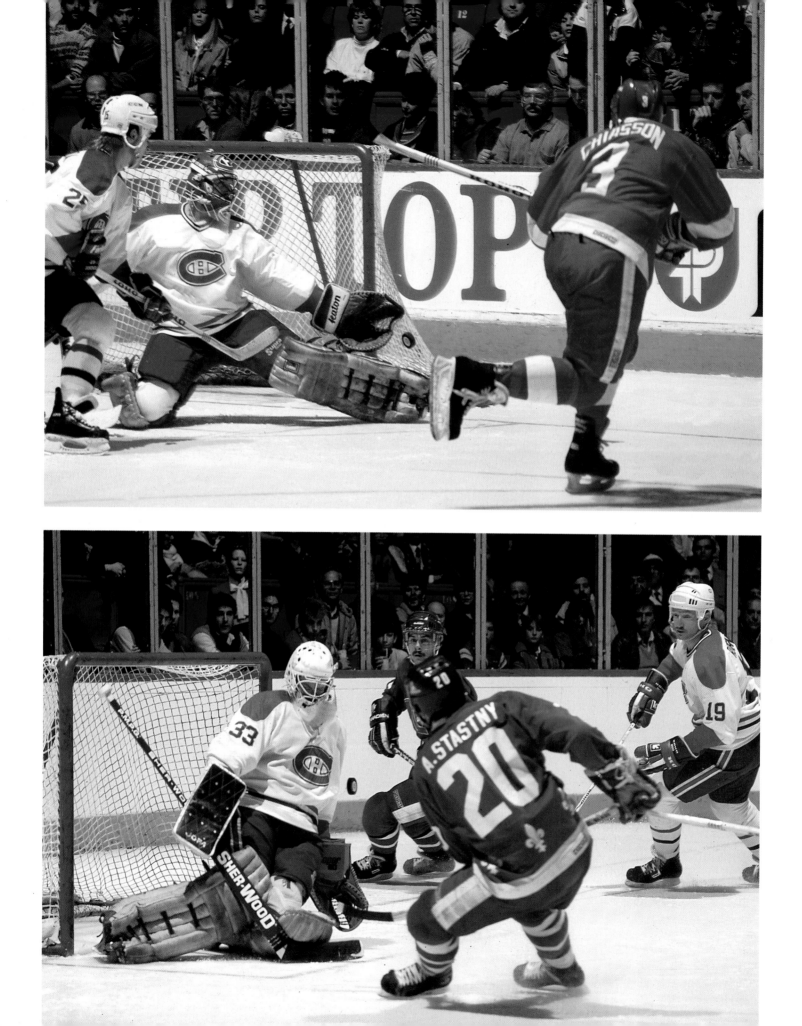

(Opposite page) Patrick Roy makes a nice save with his pads, at the expense of Steve Chiasson of the Detroit Red Wings, as defenceman Petr Svoboda keeps an eye on the action.

(Opposite page) Patrick Roy shortly after he joined the Canadiens, before he began wearing the more recognizable mask he is known for among hockey fans. On this play, forward Anton Stastny of the Quebec Nordiques misses a scoring opportunity while Michel Goulet and Larry Robinson get into position to retrieve the puck.

In 1995, for the first time in his career, Patrick Roy was not involved in the playoffs; the Canadiens failed to win a berth in the Stanley Cup series for the first time since 1970.

A duel between Steve Yzerman of the Detroit Red Wings and Patrick Roy; the goaltender stretches to stop the puck and emerges the winner.

# Martin Brodeur

**B**oth 1994 and 1995 were dream years for young goaltender Martin Brodeur. In 1993-1994, his first season in the National League, he was named rookie of the year and fell only one goal short of the Stanley Cup finals with the New Jersey Devils, who were eliminated in overtime during the seventh game of the Eastern Conference finals by the New York Rangers. In 17 playoff games, Brodeur maintained an excellent average of 1.95.

In 1995 came another moment of glory for photographer Denis Brodeur's son; the Devils made it all the way to the Stanley Cup finals, this time winning in four games against the Detroit Red Wings. Brodeur maintained an incredible average of 1.67 in 20 games and managed three shutouts. To add to the hockey player's excitement, on June 8th, during the Stanley Cup finals, Martin's companion Mélanie Dubois gave birth to the couple's first child, a boy named Anthony. Lastly, on August 19, 1995, Martin married Mélanie in Saint-Hyacinthe, Quebec, where he had played brilliantly in the junior league for three seasons. Wow! Two dream years for this young man.

In 1995-1996, Martin Brodeur enjoyed another good season, with an average of 2.34 in 77 games (34 wins) with the Devils. Brodeur and the other Devils goalies, Corey Schwab and Chris Terreri, ended the season with a cumulative average of 2.43, the second best in the League after the Detroit Red Wings goalies. In the spring of 1996, New Jersey failed to make the playoffs after winning the Stanley Cup the previous season, but the Devils know that they can continue to rely on their young goalie, already recognized as one of the best of his generation. After admiring Dryden and Roy as he dreamed of joining the National League, Martin is now a role model in his own right for young goaltenders who admire his style of play, his technique and his ability to stay cool under intense pressure.

Martin Brodeur stays in control of a tense situation as Pierre Sévigny of the Canadiens and defenceman Jaroslav Modry look on.

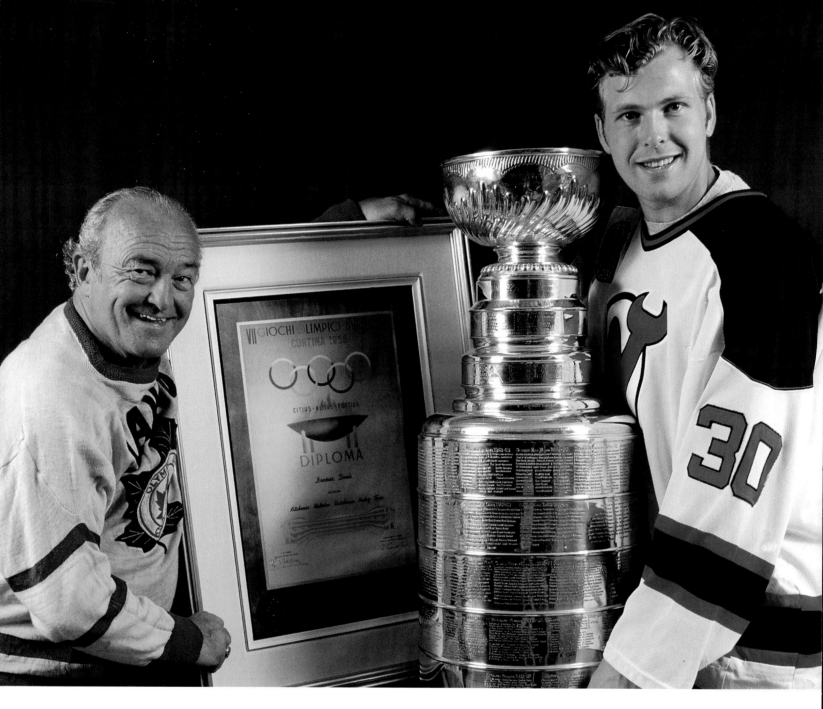

A first in hockey history: an Olympic champion and a Stanley Cup winner, father and son, pose for a picture. Denis Brodeur, a former goaltender, is wearing the sweater he wore during the 1956 Olympic Games, when he was playing with the Kitchener Waterloo Dutchmen. Brodeur and his teammates won the bronze medal, as shown in the certificate he is holding. At his side, his son Martin holds the Stanley Cup his team won in 1995.

On the ice at the Meadowlands Arena in New Jersey, the Devils celebrate their Stanley Cup victory.

Stéphane Richer and Martin Brodeur, teammates with the Devils and close friends, express their joy at winning the National League championship. This was Richer's second Stanley Cup; his first came with the Canadiens in 1986.

Martin Brodeur uses his stick to make an amazing save against Detroit Red Wings centre Kris Draper during the Stanley Cup finals.

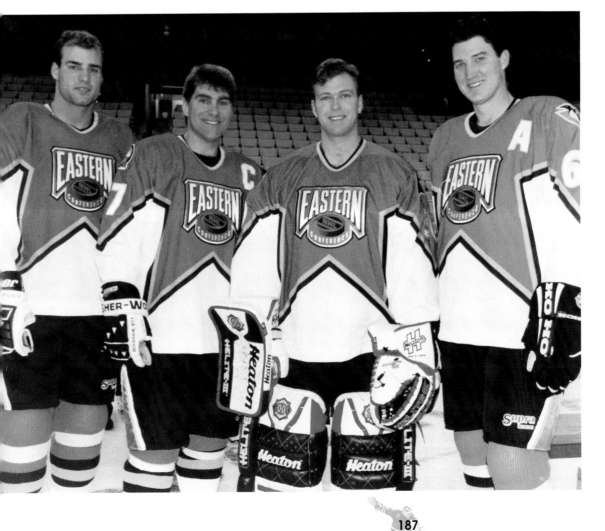

The 1996 All Star game, a first for Brodeur. Also pictured are Eric Lindros, Raymond Bourque and Mario Lemieux.

(Next two pages) Every hockey player's dream: drinking champagne from the Stanley Cup, a fantasy that came true for Martin Brodeur in his third season in the National League. (Photo: Denis Brodeur Jr.)

# The Most Spectacular Player on the Ice

The goaltender is undoubtedly the most spectacular player on the ice. Clad in a suit of armour designed to protect him from even the most lethal shots, he must be extraordinarily flexible and lightning quick to stop the pucks coming at him from all directions and taking the most unexpected trajectories. What could be more impressive than a miraculous catch, at the last second, when a puck travelling at 100 kph is hurtling straight for the net! How did he do it? How can he make it look so easy to snatch the puck into his glove? At times, the crowd roars at the sight of a dive into the heart of a tangle of players, without a second's thought for the blur of sticks and skate blades. At others, the goaltender suddenly becomes the hero of an agonizing duel that ends a breakaway, predicting the forward's every move as he lunges towards the net.

The goaltender knows that he is the ultimate guardian, he performs acrobatic skills, skates as far from his crease as he needs to, fiercely fends off all who venture into his territory. What reflexes! Denis Brodeur used reflexes every bit as remarkable to capture these truly spectacular athletes on film, in full action.

Rogatien Vachon, star goaltender of the Los Angeles Kings, tries to snare the puck before Canadiens forward Yvon Lambert does, as defenceman Barry Long rushes to the rescue.

Chris Terreri of the Devils keeps his eyes on the puck after deflecting it to the right of his net.

(Opposite page) Ken Dryden does everything he possibly can, but too late... Ed Westfall of the Bruins manages to get the puck past him.

(Opposite page) Richard Brodeur falls after making a save against Pierre Mondou of the Canadiens.

Patrick Roy confronts forward Kevin Stevens of the Pittsburgh Penguins.

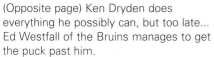

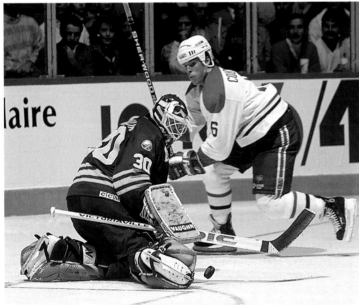

Although he is being dogged by defenceman Carol Vadnais, Réjean Houle does his best to rob the puck from Bruins goaltender Ross Brooks.

Clint Malarchuk of the Sabres watches the puck come dangerously close after a shot by Russ Courtnall.

(Opposite page) Daniel Bouchard keeps the puck in his glove, to rightwinger Mark Hunter's obvious frustration.

(Preceding two pages) Jim Montgomery of the Philadelphia Flyers would like to get control the puck, but Patrick Roy is on the verge of getting it out of harm's way.

Goaltender Réjean Lemelin has ventured too far from his crease on this play, but fortunately for him, Raymond Bourque can stop Guy Carbonneau.

As Yvon Lambert shadows him, Mario Lessard of the Los Angeles Kings succeeds in stopping the puck.

(Opposite page) The Hartford Whalers' goalie, Mike Liut, keeps the puck from going any further as Ryan Walter and Mike McPhee grapple for a second chance.

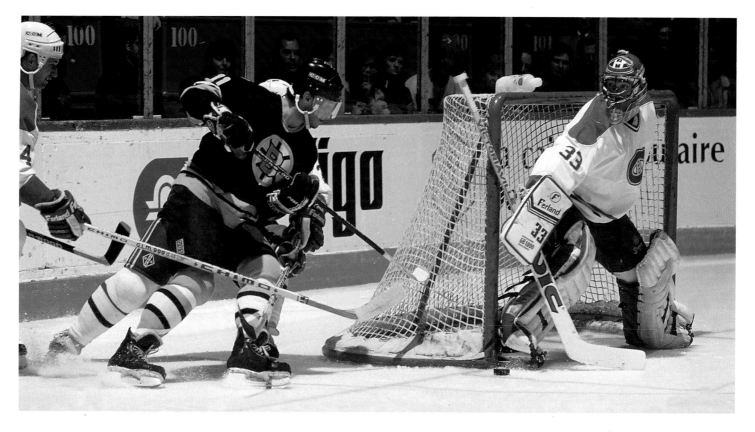

Patrick Roy sees the puck materialize on his right as a Bruins player skates around the net.

Mario Gosselin stops the puck on his pads while "the little Viking", Mats Natslund, slides into the crease.

Rick Tabaracci of the Winnipeg Jets wards off an attack by
John LeClair and Guy Carbonneau of the Canadiens.

Wayne Thomas goes down after failing to stop a shot.

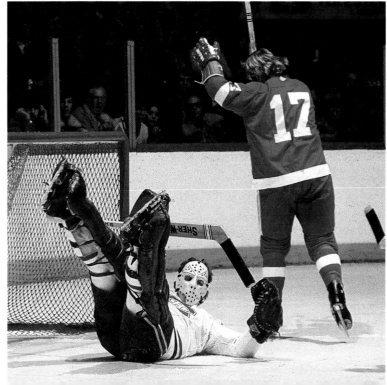

(Previous two pages) A fight to the finish between goaltender Glenn Healy of the Rangers and Brian Bellows of the Canadiens.

Chris Chelios, well positioned in front of the net, manages to slip the puck past Clint Malarchuk of the Nordiques.

Mats Natslund speeds toward Edmonton Oilers goalie Andy Moog, who wants to keep the puck at all costs.

Chris Chelios of the Canadiens is stopped by a nice move on the part of Pelle Lindbergh of the Flyers.

André Racicot manages to stop a shot by Steve Larmer of the Black Hawks in a one-on-one confrontation.

Mike Hough of the Nordiques makes an extra effort to dig the puck out from under Patrick Roy's knee pads.

During a two-on-one encounter, Bob Gainey of the Canadiens manages to outplay the Winnipeg Jets goalie, Steve Penney.

(Opposite page) Jacques Cloutier of the Nordiques watches helplessly as the puck slips away and slides right past his goalie.

Dimitri Khristich of the Washington Capitals tries to surprise Canadiens Roland Melanson as the goalie extends a leg to stop the puck.

Denis Herron wards off an attack led by Wayne Cashman of the Boston Bruins.

Goaltender Jeff Reese, who played in the NHL with Toronto, Calgary, Hartford and Tampa Bay before joining the Devils in June 1996, makes a save against Russ Courtnall of the Canadiens.

Mike Vernon of the Calgary Flames stops a shot by Canadiens player Bobby Smith.

(Next two pages) Goaltender Curtis Joseph of the St. Louis Blues, traded to the Edmonton Oilers in the summer of 1995, makes a spectacular save on Benoît Brunet of the Canadiens.

Keith Acton of the Canadiens pulls out all the stops to score a goal, but Robert Sauvé of the Sabres gives him very little room to manoeuvre as he moves out of his goal crease.

Mike Vernon of the Calgary Flames would love to get his gloves on the puck before forward Stéphane Richer of the Canadiens can get into position in front of the net.

Chris Terreri slides to stop a shot by Denis Savard as he hurtles toward the net.

Pat Jablonski of the Canadiens manages to stop the puck to put an end to an attack by the Canucks.

(Next two pages) In a desperate attempt to save the day, goalie Ron Hextall of the Philadelphia Flyers uses his pads to block access to the net; meanwhile, Canadiens Stéphan Lebeau struggles to get control of the puck.

Dominik Hasek, star goaltender for the Buffalo Sabres, makes a beautiful save against a Canadiens player.

Mark Fitzpatrick does what he can to cope with the sudden appearance of a forward from the rival team.

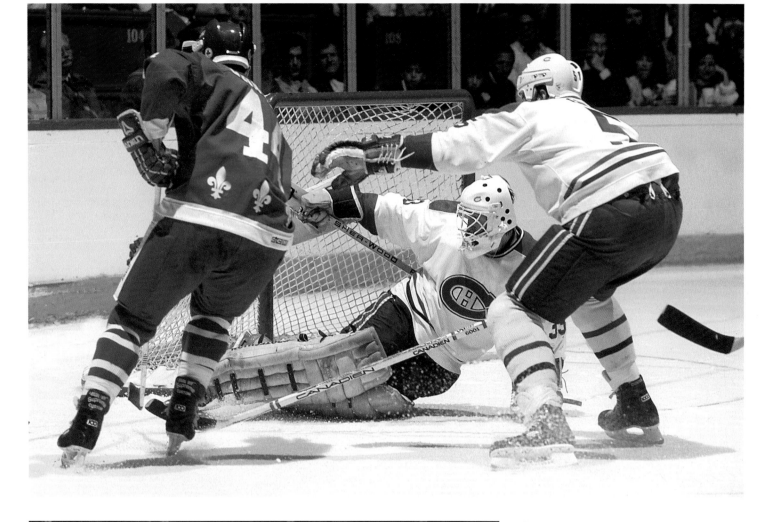

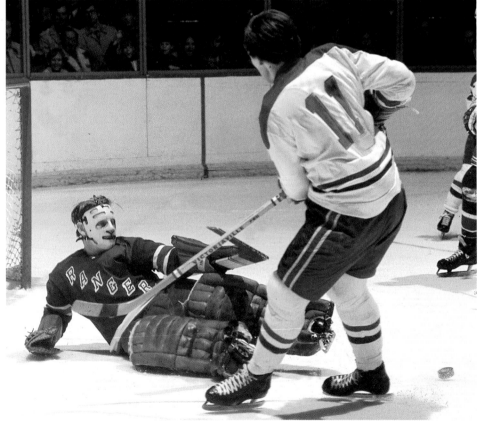

Patrick Roy makes a nice save against Mario Marois of the Nordiques as defenceman Rick Green watches and waits.

Gilles Villemure, who tended goal for eight seasons with the New York Rangers, deflects a shot by Marc Tardif of the Canadiens.

Swedish goaltender Pelle Lindbergh stops a shot by Serge Boisvert of the Canadiens, who goes all out to get the puck back.

Grant Fuhr, who led the Edmonton Oilers to five Stanley Cups, dives to the ice to stop a shot from Bob Gainey of the Canadiens.

Rick Wamsley withstands a Nordiques onslaught led by the formidable Dale Hunter.

Guy Carbonneau threatens the Los Angeles Kings' territory and its guardian, Glenn Healy.

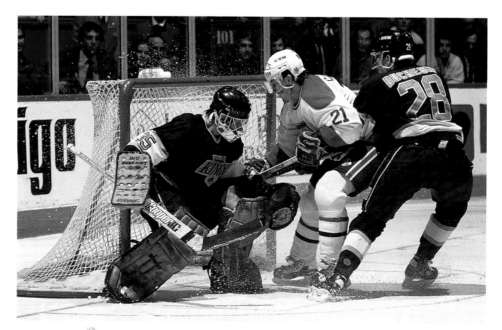

# Exploits and Memories

**T**his chapter features scenes captured by Denis Brodeur at various times and under special circumstances, notably during training sessions, in the dressing room, at All Star games, at international games and during special events. These specially selected photos are intended to highlight daring exploits as well as nostalgia-tinged moments in hockey history.

Claude Lemieux is swamped by teammates congratulating him on a goal against Bill Ranford of the Boston Bruins, who seems to need comfort from a linesman.

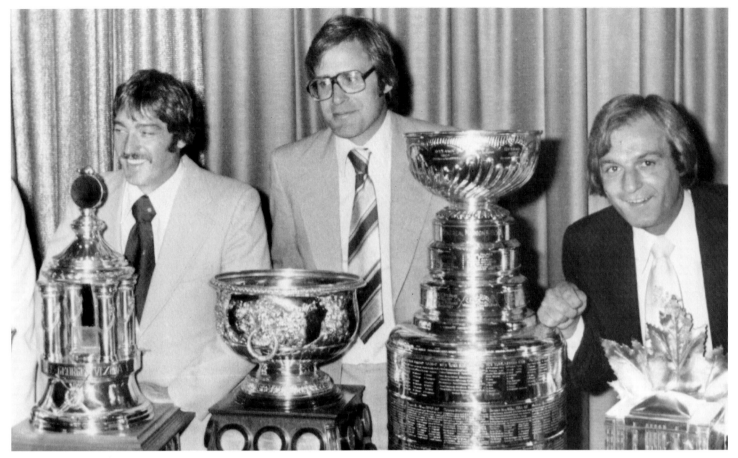

Michel Larocque, Ken Dryden and Guy Lafleur, seen here during a National League awards ceremony.

Ken Dryden, Guy Lafleur and Guy Lapointe, familiar faces during All Star games. Dryden was chosen to play on the first team five times and played on the second team once. Lafleur was on the first team six consecutive times, while Guy Lapointe played with the first team once and with the second team three times.

1978 was a glorious year for some Canadiens players. Dryden and Larocque took the Vézina Trophy, Larry Robinson was awarded the Conn-Smythe, Guy Lafleur won the Hart Trophy for the second year and Bob Gainey was the first player to win the Frank-Selke Trophy.

The Canadiens, led by Patrick Roy, exchange congratulations after yet another win.

Wayne Stephenson takes advantage of a brawl to rest in his net.

Wayne Thomas is given first aid after a facial injury.

(Previous two pages) Rogatien Vachon lifts his arms in victory at the end of a game in the finals involving Canada and Czechoslovakia, during the 1976 Canada Cup tournament. Vachon was a key factor in his team's success. When the tournament came to an end, the Team Canada goalie became friends with his rival, Dzurilla, who died in the summer of 1995.

During a Canadiens practice, Scotty Bowman gives a few tips to his star goalie.

Ken Dryden, in the Habs' dressing room after a game, as he shares his comments with reporters.

(Opposite page) Ken Dryden and Vladislav Tretiak exchange congratulatory comments at center ice, at the end of the famous match involving the Red Army team and the Canadiens, held on December 31, 1975. The game ended in a 3-3 tie.

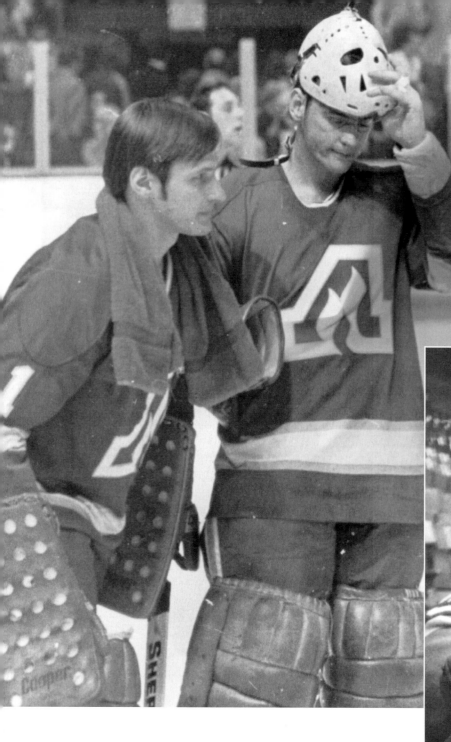

At the end of a game between the Canadiens and the Atlanta Flames at the Forum, Philippe Myre tries to comfort teammate Daniel Bouchard, who is disappointed by his team's loss.

Rogatien Vachon was 21 years old when he started playing with the Canadiens in 1966. In 1967-1968, his second season, he won the Vézina Trophy for the only time in his career, sharing the honour with Lorne Worsley.

Gilles Gilbert played seven seasons with the Bruins, from 1973 to 1980. During that time he took part in the Stanley Cup finals three times with Boston, without ever seeing his name engraved on the precious trophy.

During a series between the Soviets and the Canadiens in 1972, the Esposito brothers were reunited for the first time as National League professionals. However, both played with the Chicago Black Hawks at one time in their careers. Phil was Team Canada's uncontested leader and its best goal scorer, with seven goals and six assists in eight games. Tony played four games, maintaining an average of 3.25 and a 2-1-1 record.

Vladislav Tretiak and Mats Naslund shake hands before a game between the Red Army team and the Canadiens.

In 1972, Vladislav Tretiak's prowess in the net impressed fans and rivals alike. Consistently greeted like a hero by Montreal fans, Tretiak dreamed of playing in the National league with the Canadiens, but was unable to acquire the necessary authorization from his country's officials.

June 1972: Bernard Geoffrion, head coach of the Atlanta Flames, poses proudly with his two new goaltenders during the National League draft. Myre was acquired from the Canadiens and Bouchard from the Boston Bruins. The two men played six and eight seasons respectively with the Flames.

At the end of a game at the Forum, Ken Dryden and Jim Roberts pause before skating out onto the ice as the game's star players.

All very young at the time, Guy Lapointe and Pierre Bouchard take time out to sit with teammate Rogatien Vachon after a win.

During the All Star game held in Montreal in January 1975, players for the Prince of Wales Conference wait patiently for pre-game ceremonies to finish. From left to right are Carol Vadnais, Bobby Orr, Ken Dryden, Guy Lapointe and Guy Lafleur.

Ken Dryden and Jacques Lemaire, seen here as they wait it out on the bench during a game. Both ended their National League careers in 1979, after winning the Stanley Cup against the New York Rangers. Dryden's name was added to the trophy six times and Lemaire's appears eight times.

"In 1985, during a special ceremony at the Forum, there was no way I would have missed the chance to appear in a photo along with the greatest players who ever wore the Canadiens' colours," says Denis Brodeur. From left to right are Dickie Moore, Jacques Plante, Denis Brodeur, Maurice Richard, Aurèle Joliat, Jean Béliveau and Doug Harvey.

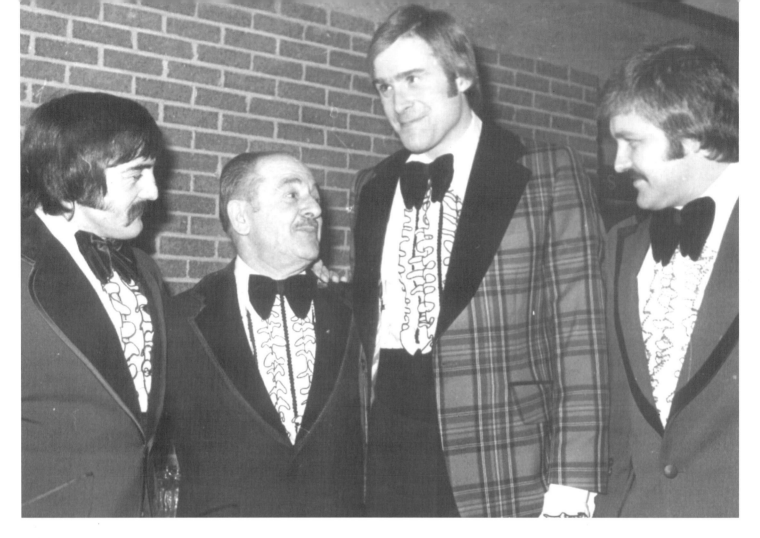

Camil DesRoches of the Canadiens along with three outstanding goaltenders, Rogatien Vachon, Ken Dryden and Bernard Parent, during a National League banquet in January 1975 to mark the NHL's 28th All Star game, played in Montreal.

Lorne Worsley has a bit of fun at the expense of goaltender Gary Smith of the Vancouver Canucks, who played as backup to Bernard Parent with the Campbell Conference team during the 1975 All Star game.

(Opposite page) A pensive Gerry Cheevers, shown here during a Bruins practice at the Montreal Forum. His mask was one of the most recognizable in the League because of the stitches he drew on it to show where he would have been injured by pucks without that protection.

Centre Peter Mahovlich congratulates teammate Ken Dryden after another Canadiens win.

Goaltender Richard Sévigny does a few warmup exercises before the game. Sévigny played five seasons with the Habs, followed by three seasons with the Nordiques.

(Opposite page) In 1975, during an All Star game, Rogatien Vachon and Ken Dryden kept the Clarence Campbell Conference team to only one goal and the Prince of Wales Conference won the game by 7-1.

Three Quebec players who are active in the National League today, pictured here during an All Star game in the junior league. Martin Brodeur, Stéphane Fiset and Félix Potvin line up beside Mario Baril, who coached the three players when they played AAA Midget hockey with the Montreal Bourassa.

Michel Bergeron, one of the National League team's coaches during Rendez-Vous 87, takes time out during a practice to have his picture taken with Clint Malarchuk, the Nordiques goaltender.

Daniel Bouchard of the Quebec Nordiques is ecstatic after his team eliminates the Canadiens in five games in 1982, in the division semifinals. In the background are Doug Jarvis and Pierre Mondou.

Photographer Denis Brodeur when he was playing with the North Bay team, in 1957. Here he uses his head to make a save on a Whitby forward, a certain Harry Sinden.

In 1957 as well, a Soviet team came to Canada to play a few exhibition games. After the first period, the team's coach asked that his players work at improving the ice surface using this odd looking machine, an ancestor of the monsters now seen on National League ice between periods. Things have changed a lot in 40 years!

During a National League Old Timers game in the 60s, Denis Brodeur was asked to play as Jacques Plante's backup. The photographer is in lofty company here, flanked by the Canadiens' former star goalie and Maurice Richard.

August 1972: Canada is training. Ken Dryden and Yvan Cournoyer, confident at the time that their team would coast to an easy win over the Soviets, chat leisurely with one of their coaches, John Ferguson.

Three goaltenders were selected to play with Team Canada in 1972: Ken Dryden, Tony Esposito and Ed Johnston. In this photo, Dryden and Esposito go through the paces during a practice.

Goalies Gerry Cheevers and Vladislav Tretiak fraternize during a practice at the Montreal Forum.

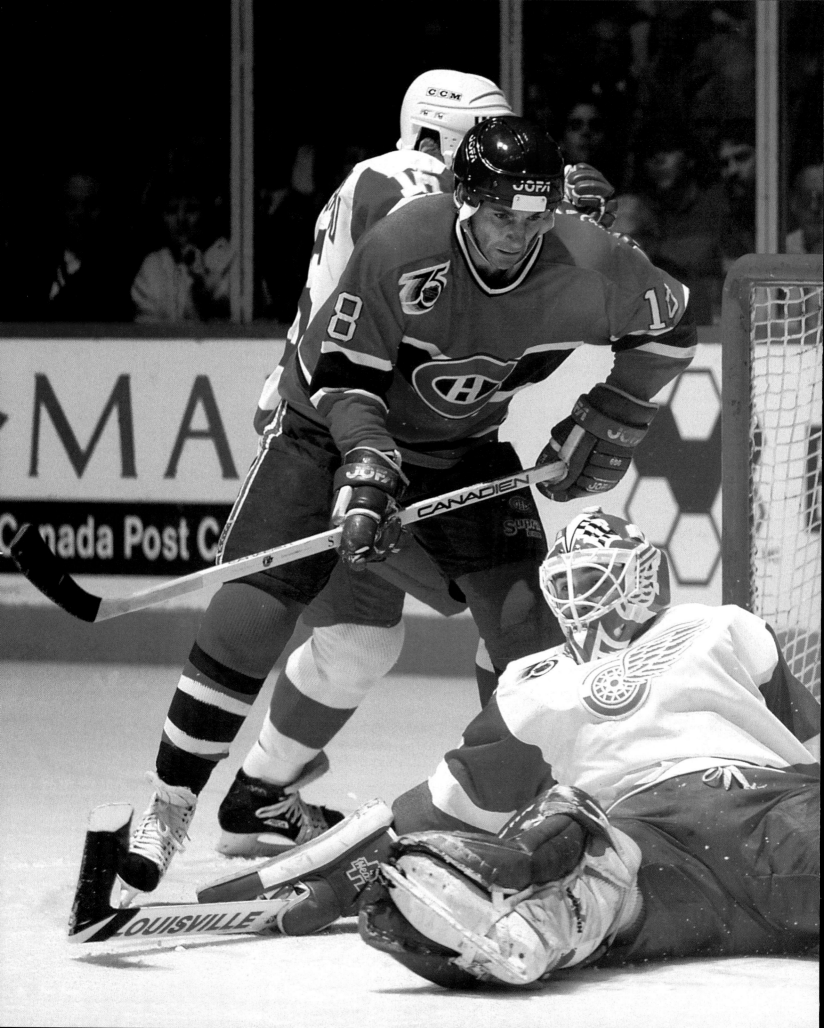

# Hockey's Acrobats

I t's perfectly natural for a photographer to focus on the goaltenders in a game. Confined to a small area, the goalie is a model of concentration, constantly alert, even when the puck is at the other end of the ice. Suddenly, he stretches out a pad or a glove, lifts an arm, moves his stick, hunches down, stands straight again, dives, gets back up. In one second, the goaltender becomes an acrobat to save the situation. Every bit as watchful, the photographer has followed every move in the sequence.

"Spectacular moves aren't uncommon," comments Denis Brodeur. "They include leaping into the air, checking, falling or diving. There's nothing more exciting than watching a puck sliding toward the goal line and suddenly seeing the tip of a skate, a pad or a stick stop it at the very last second. Or seeing a magic glove snatch the puck from sight when fans can already see it inside the net. I have always tried to capture these high-tension moments and the remarkable dexterity they inevitably involve."

Goaltender Tim Cheveldae uses his pad to make a save against centre Denis Savard of the Canadiens.

Arm stretched out, Chris Terreri tries to stop the puck with his stick before a Canadiens player gets it.

Richard Sévigny, photographed by Denis Brodeur as he leaves his net to pass the puck to a teammate.

(Opposite page) Well screened by his defencemen, Tim Cheveldae makes a save after a breakaway by Pierre Sévigny of the Canadiens.

Lying on the ice, Mike McPhee of the Canadiens still manages to shoot the puck toward Bruins goalie Réjean Lemelin, who makes the save. Meanwhile, defenceman Raymond Bourque charges to the rescue.

Michel Plasse

Rogatien Vachon
Acrobats, you say? How about jugglers!

Steve Penney

A spectacular play during a game between Montreal and Philadelphia.

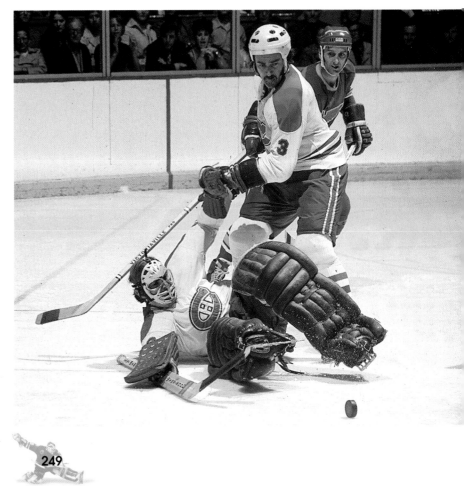

As defenceman Jean-Claude Tremblay keeps his eye on the puck, goaltender Ken Dryden makes a difficult save.

(Next two pages) Ron Hextall of the Philadelphia Flyers is forced to do the splits to prevent an opponent from scoring a goal.

Rick Wamsley, in the net for the St. Louis Blues, photographed in action.

A staggering save by Red Wings goaltender Jim Rutherford.

Claude Lemieux shakes up Mike Liut of the Hartford Whalers as the goaltender struggles to keep control of the puck.

(Opposite page) For Grant Fuhr, playing with the Buffalo Sabres in this photo, the end justifies the means when it comes to stopping pucks.

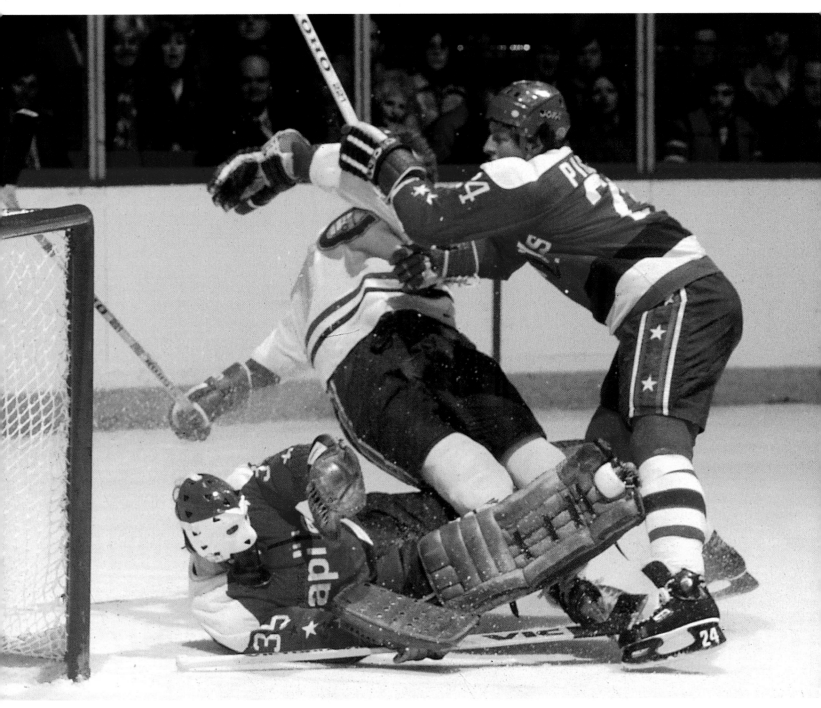

Defenceman Robert Picard roughs up a Canadiens forward as the Capitals goalie, Wayne Stephenson, pays the price.

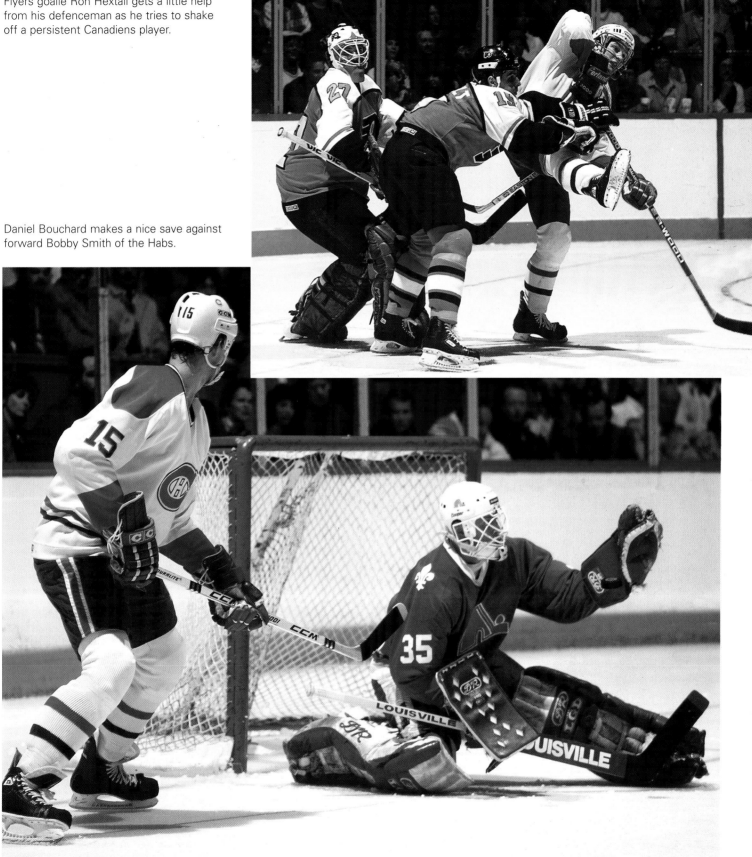

Flyers goalie Ron Hextall gets a little help from his defenceman as he tries to shake off a persistent Canadiens player.

Daniel Bouchard makes a nice save against forward Bobby Smith of the Habs.

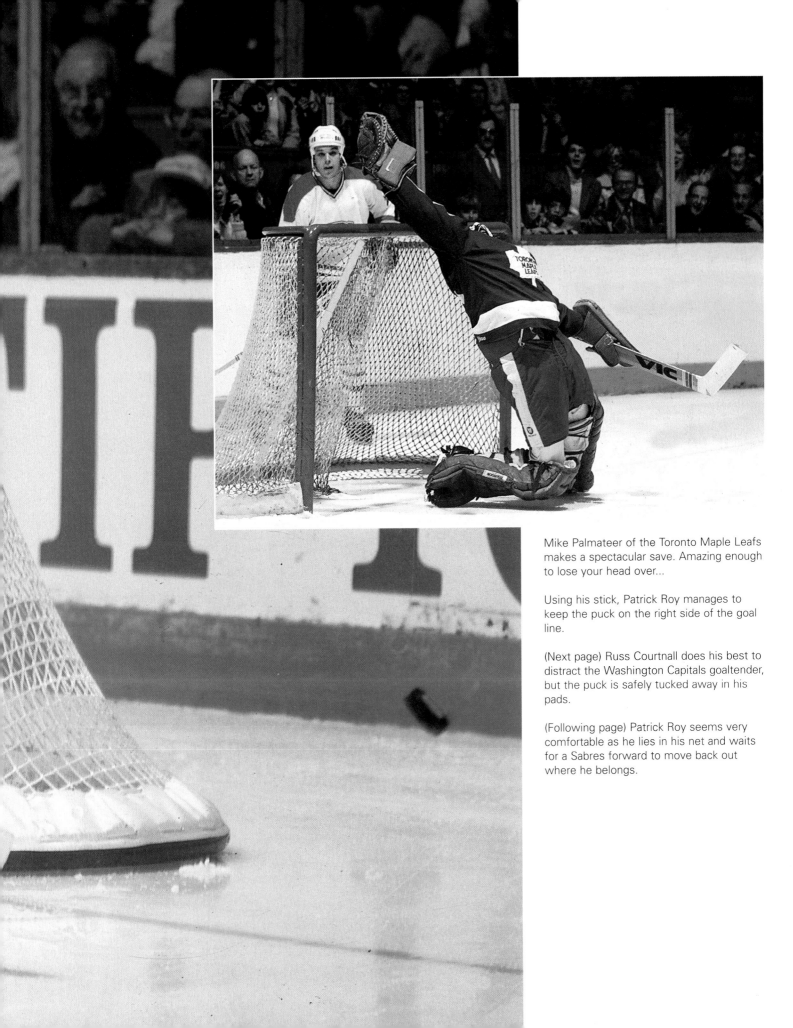

Mike Palmateer of the Toronto Maple Leafs makes a spectacular save. Amazing enough to lose your head over...

Using his stick, Patrick Roy manages to keep the puck on the right side of the goal line.

(Next page) Russ Courtnall does his best to distract the Washington Capitals goaltender, but the puck is safely tucked away in his pads.

(Following page) Patrick Roy seems very comfortable as he lies in his net and waits for a Sabres forward to move back out where he belongs.

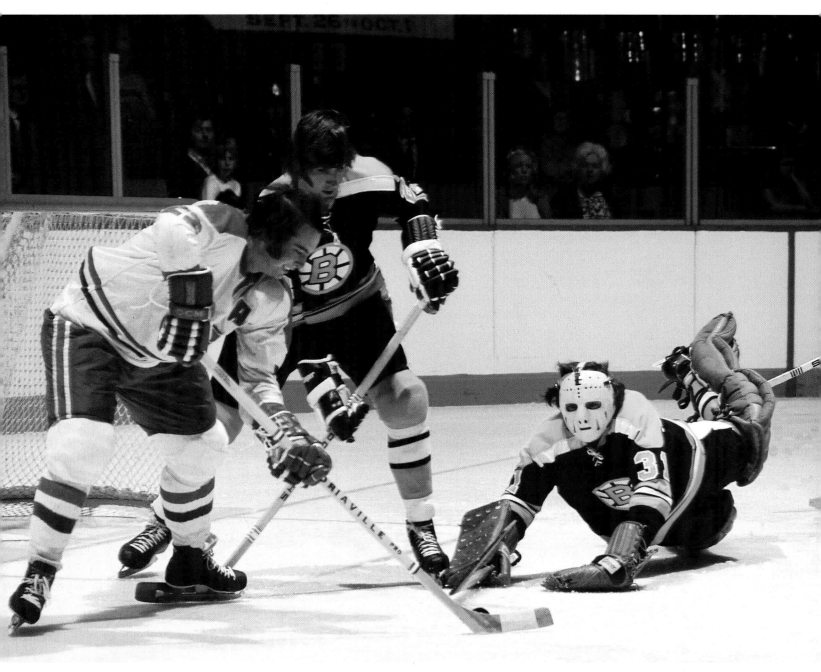

A clearly desperate attempt to prevent the other team from scoring.

"Stop, I've got it!" André Racicot seems to be saying as he catches the puck, to the surprise of forward Joe Murphy of the Edmonton Oilers.

Frédéric Chabot slows down Steve Larmer of the Chicago Black Hawks as his teammates set out for the opposite end of the ice.

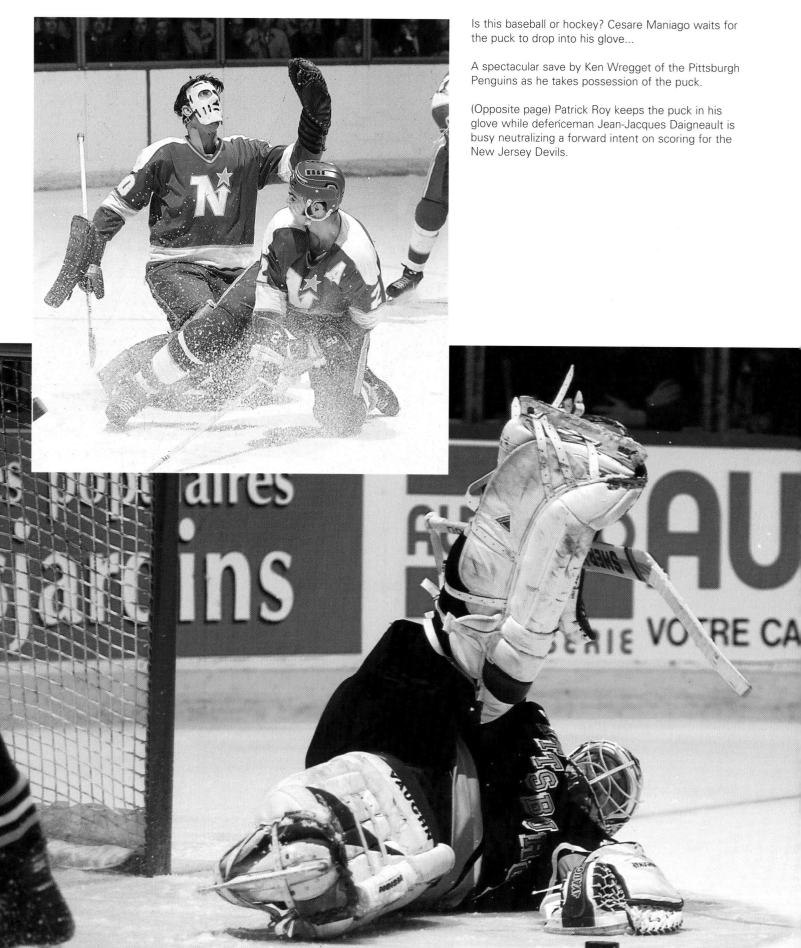

Is this baseball or hockey? Cesare Maniago waits for the puck to drop into his glove...

A spectacular save by Ken Wregget of the Pittsburgh Penguins as he takes possession of the puck.

(Opposite page) Patrick Roy keeps the puck in his glove while defenceman Jean-Jacques Daigneault is busy neutralizing a forward intent on scoring for the New Jersey Devils.

(Previous two pages) The Buffalo Sabres' goaltender, Tom Barrasso, is on the receiving end as a Canadiens player shows his frustration after being robbed of a goal.

Like a yo-yo, the puck bounces over the head of the Los Angeles Kings goalie Denis Dejordy as he tries to catch it with his glove.

Freeze frame!

(Opposite page) Michel Dion of the Pittsburgh Penguins tries to stop Mark Napier of the Canadiens as everybody else jostles for the puck.

Brian Hayward makes a nice save with his glove as he guards the Canadiens net.

Goaltender Kari Takko of the North Stars slides along the ice in hopes of making a save against Guy Carbonneau.

(Opposite page) An unwelcome visitor calls on Chris Terreri of the New Jersey Devils.

# When Goaltenders Leave Their Nets!

**J**acques Plante was the first goaltender to venture out of his own territory. A great goalie who played 18 years in the National League, 11 of those with the Canadiens, Plante was a bold and astonishing innovator. A fine skater, he believed that a goaltender could control the play by coming out of the net instead of waiting passively for his opponents' shots. He would move out to the front of the net to intercept a pass and would skate behind the net to take control of a puck along the bands, passing it to one of his teammates. In essence, Plante played virtually the same role as a quarterback, making the passes that led to counteroffensives. Of course, there was some degree of risk involved, and sometimes the puck failed to follow the expected trajectory, finding its way to a member of the opposing team alone in front of an abandoned net; but Plante was ready to take that gamble and he rarely regretted his initiatives.

This new approach to goaltending became popular and inspired each future generation of goalies. Today, no goaltender can afford to be a poor skater or stick handler, and must be able to make accurate passes. Some, such as Ron Hextall of the Philadelphia Flyers, have even made this style of play a specialty. Denis Brodeur has captured many goaltenders on film as they move away from their nets; at times the decision to forge into uncharted territory isn't always a very good one, but the photos are eloquent.

Patrice Brisebois and Éric Desjardins come to Patrick Roy's rescue as he grapples with a Quebec Nordiques forward.

A face-to-face encounter between Denis Herron and Bobby Clarke, eyeing each other a lot like boxers do.

(Opposite page) Doug Favell of the Flyers kills two birds with one stone as he gets rid of both Peter Mahovlich and the puck...

Richard Sévigny beats Rick Kehoe of the Pittsburgh Penguins to the puck, and successfully passes it.

Denis Herron of the Pittsburgh Penguins gets control of the puck as his defenceman prevents Yvon Lambert from getting any closer.

Ron Hextall, known for moving well out of his own territory, passes the puck to a teammate.

Playing for the New York Islanders, Hextall, who has already scored two goals in the National League, beats John LeClair of the Canadiens to the puck.

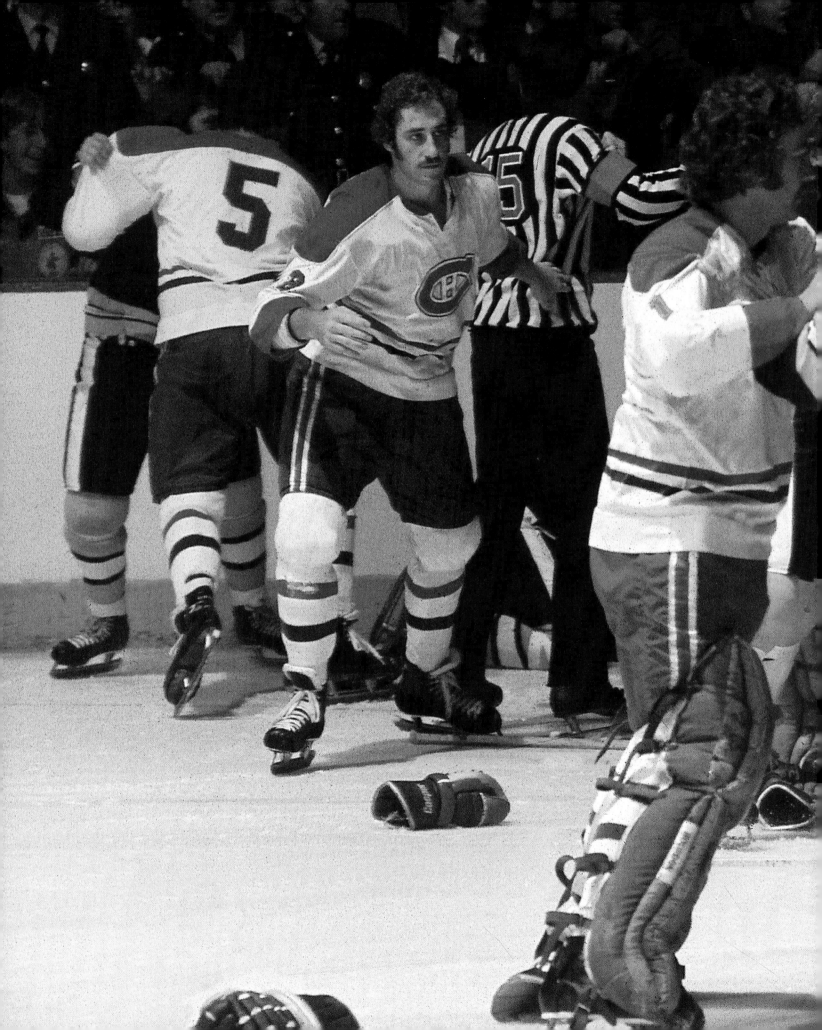

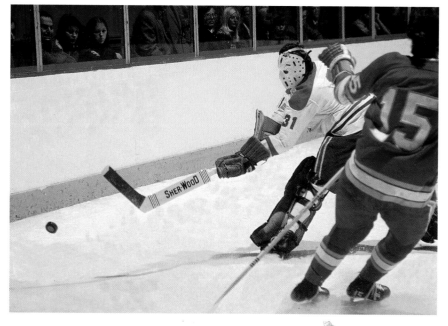

(Previous two pages) Things heat up as the Bruins and Canadiens take to the ice! Michel Larocque holds an opponent in place.

Defenceman Terry Harper is checked by Bob Gainey of the Canadiens while Red Wings goalie Jim Rutherford decides it's time to get back into the net.

Michel Larocque, in search of the elusive puck...

(Opposite page) Patrick Roy, behind his goal, makes a pass as a Flyers forward looks on.

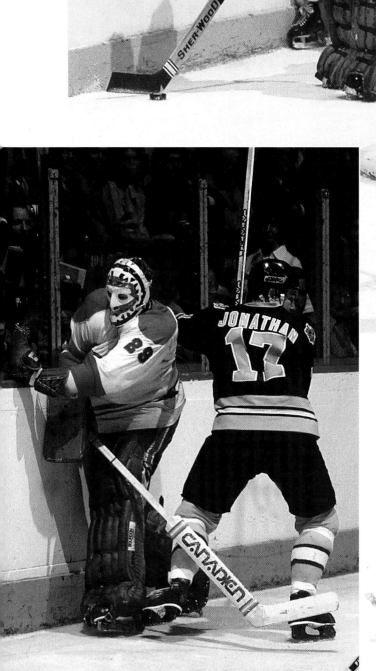

Ed Giacomin gets help from one of his defencemen as he calmly takes control of the puck.

Ken Dryden, 6' 4" checks Stan Jonathan, 5' 8"...

A Black Hawks player on his heels, Ken Dryden hurries back to his goal after passing the puck to a teammate.

Yvon Lambert fights to get the puck before goaltender Gary Smith of the Vancouver Canucks can beat him to it.

(Next two pages) Chris Nilan has defenceman Darren Veitch and Washington Capitals goalie Pat Riggin seeing stars as he tries to capture the puck.

The Canadiens' goaltender fights off Clark Gillies of the Islanders as Larry Robinson glances worriedly at the puck...

A goalie who moves out of his territory is always exciting for fans, but a good source of anxiety for coaches...

(Opposite page) Greg Millen manages to get ahead of a member of the opposing team and stretches to pass the puck to a teammate.

A good move on the part of Canucks goalie Gary Smith.

Gerry Cheevers is chased out of his goal by Mario Tremblay, who tries to make him lose control of the puck.

(Opposite page) Bon voyage! Doug Risebrough trips New York Islanders goaltender Billy Smith, caught where he doesn't belong.

## GOALIES, GUARDIANS OF THE NET

Ken Dryden, caught in the act as he moves into forbidden territory.

Gilles Villemure ventures out of the crease to try to ward off an attack by Murray Wilson.

(Opposite page) Réjean Houle harasses the Philadelphia Flyers' goalie.

288

# Award-Winning Goaltenders

The goaltenders whose names appear in the following pages have won at least one of the individual trophies awarded by the National League each year. George Hainsworth—who played 11 seasons with Montreal and Toronto, maintaining an amazing average of 1.91 in 465 games—was the first recipient of the Vézina Trophy, in 1927. He won the trophy again in the next two seasons; in the 1928-1929 season, he allowed only 43 goals in 44 games and recorded 22 shutouts, a record that still stands.

# Vézina Trophy
awarded to the best goaltender(s)

| Goaltender | Team | Year | Goaltender | Team | Year |
|---|---|---|---|---|---|
| Jim Carey | Washington | 1996 | Jacques Plante | Montreal | 1962 |
| Dominik Hasek | Buffalo | 1995 | Johnny Bower | Toronto | 1961 |
| Dominik Hasek | Buffalo | 1994 | Jacques Plante | Montreal | 1960 |
| Ed Belfour | Chicago | 1993 | Jacques Plante | Montreal | 1959 |
| Patrick Roy | Montreal | 1992 | Jacques Plante | Montreal | 1958 |
| Ed Belfour | Chicago | 1991 | Jacques Plante | Montreal | 1957 |
| Patrick Roy | Montreal | 1990 | Jacques Plante | Montreal | 1956 |
| Patrick Roy | Montreal | 1989 | Terry Sawchuk | Detroit | 1955 |
| Grant Fuhr | Edmonton | 1988 | Harry Lumley | Toronto | 1954 |
| Ron Hextall | Philadelphia | 1987 | Terry Sawchuk | Detroit | 1953 |
| John Vanbiesbrouck | Rangers (N. Y.) | 1986 | Terry Sawchuk | Detroit | 1952 |
| Pelle Lindbergh | Philadelphia | 1985 | Al Rollins | Toronto | 1951 |
| Tom Barrasso | Buffalo | 1984 | Bill Durnan | Montreal | 1950 |
| Pete Peeters | Boston | 1983 | Bill Durnan | Montreal | 1949 |
| Billy Smith | Islanders (N. Y.) | 1982 | Turk Broda | Toronto | 1948 |
| Denis Herron, Richard Sévigny, Michel Larocque | Montreal | 1981 | Bill Durnan | Montreal | 1947 |
| | | | Bill Durnan | Montreal | 1946 |
| Don Edwards, Robert Sauvé | Buffalo | 1980 | Bill Durnan | Montreal | 1945 |
| Ken Dryden, Michel Larocque | Montreal | 1979 | Bill Durnan | Montreal | 1944 |
| Ken Dryden, Michel Larocque | Montreal | 1978 | Johnny Mowers | Detroit | 1943 |
| Ken Dryden, Michel Larocque | Montreal | 1977 | Frank Brimsek | Boston | 1942 |
| Ken Dryden | Montreal | 1976 | Turk Broda | Toronto | 1941 |
| Bernard Parent | Philadelphia | 1975 | Dave Kerr | Rangers (N. Y.) | 1940 |
| Tony Esposito, Bernard Parent | Chicago, Philadelphia | 1974* | Frank Brimsek | Boston | 1939 |
| Ken Dryden | Montreal | 1973 | Tiny Thompson | Boston | 1938 |
| Tony Esposito, Gary Smith | Chicago | 1972 | Normie Smith | Detroit | 1937 |
| Ed Giacomin, Gilles Villemure | Rangers (N. Y.) | 1971 | Tiny Thompson | Boston | 1936 |
| Tony Esposito | Chicago | 1970 | Lorne Chabot | Chicago | 1935 |
| Glenn Hall, Jacques Plante | St. Louis | 1969 | Charlie Gardiner | Chicago | 1934 |
| Rogatien Vachon, Lorne Worsley | Montreal | 1968 | Tiny Thompson | Boston | 1933 |
| Denis Dejordy, Glenn Hall | Chicago | 1967 | Charlie Gardiner | Chicago | 1932 |
| Charlie Hodge, Lorne Worsley | Montreal | 1966 | Roy Worters | Americans (N. Y.) | 1931 |
| Johnny Bower, Terry Sawchuk | Toronto | 1965 | Tiny Thompson | Boston | 1930 |
| Charlie Hodge | Montreal | 1964 | George Hainsworth | Montreal | 1929 |
| Glenn Hall | Chicago | 1963 | George Hainsworth | Montreal | 1928 |
| | | | George Hainsworth | Montreal | 1927 |

* Goaltenders from different teams, with an equal number of votes.

# William M. Jennings Trophy
awarded to one or two goaltenders with the same team,
with the least goals-against in the season

| Goaltender | Team | Year | Goaltender | Team | Year |
|---|---|---|---|---|---|
| Chris Osgood, Mike Vernon | Detroit | 1996 | Brian Hayward, Patrick Roy | Montreal | 1988 |
| Ed Belfour | Chicago | 1995 | Brian Hayward, Patrick Roy | Montreal | 1987 |
| Grant Fuhr, Dominik Hasek | Buffalo | 1994 | Bob Froese, Darren Jensen | Philadelphia | 1986 |
| Ed Belfour | Chicago | 1993 | Tom Barrasso, Robert Sauvé | Buffalo | 1985 |
| Patrick Roy | Montreal | 1992 | Al Jensen, Pat Riggin | Washington | 1984 |
| Ed Belfour | Chicago | 1991 | Roland Melanson, Billy Smith | Islanders (N. Y.) | 1983 |
| Réjean Lemelin, Andy Moog | Boston | 1990 | Denis Herron, Rick Wamsley | Montreal | 1982 |
| Brian Hayward, Patrick Roy | Montreal | 1989 | | | |

# Hart Trophy
awarded to the most valuable player

| Goaltender | Team | Year | Goaltender | Team | Year |
|---|---|---|---|---|---|
| Jacques Plante | Montreal | 1962 | Charlie Rayner | Rangers (N. Y.) | 1950 |
| Al Rollins | Chicago | 1954 | Roy Worters | Americans (N. Y.) | 1929 |

# Calder Trophy
awarded to the best rookie

| Goaltender | Team | Year | Goaltender | Team | Year |
|---|---|---|---|---|---|
| Martin Brodeur | New Jersey | 1994 | Lorne Worsley | Rangers (N. Y.) | 1953 |
| Ed Belfour | Chicago | 1991 | Terry Sawchuk | Detroit | 1951 |
| Tom Barrasso | Buffalo | 1984 | Jack Gelineau | Boston | 1950 |
| Ken Dryden | Montreal | 1972 | Frank McCool | Toronto | 1945 |
| Tony Esposito | Chicago | 1970 | Frank Brimsek | Boston | 1939 |
| Roger Crozier | Detroit | 1965 | Mike Karakas | Chicago | 1936 |
| Glenn Hall | Detroit | 1956 | | | |

# Bill Masterton Trophy
awarded to the player who demonstrates perseverance, sportsmanship and dedication

| Goaltender | Team | Year | Goaltender | Team | Year |
|---|---|---|---|---|---|
| Mark Fitzpatrick | Islanders (N. Y.) | 1992 | Glenn Resch | Colorado | 1982 |

# Lester B. Pearson Trophy
awarded to the player of the year
(based on the NHL Players' Association selection)

| Goaltender | Team | Year |
|---|---|---|
| Mike Liut | St. Louis | 1981 |

# Conn Smythe Trophy
awarded to the most valuable player during the playoffs

| Goaltender | Team | Year | Goaltender | Team | Year |
|---|---|---|---|---|---|
| Patrick Roy | Montreal | 1993 | Bernard Parent | Philadelphia | 1975 |
| Bill Ranford | Edmonton | 1990 | Bernard Parent | Philadelphia | 1974 |
| Ron Hextall | Philadelphia | 1987 | Ken Dryden | Montreal | 1971 |
| Patrick Roy | Montreal | 1986 | Glenn Hall | St. Louis | 1968 |
| Billy Smith | Islanders (N. Y.) | 1983 | Roger Crozier | Detroit | 1966 |

# INDEX

**B**

Scott Bailey, 145

Murray Bannerman, 123

Tom Barrasso, 83, 95, 96, 98, 139, 141, 150, 165, 266

Don Beaupre, 77, 97, 135, 161, 168

Stéphane Beauregard, 144, 155

Ed Belfour, 96, 98, 121, 123, 131, 143, 154, 155, 162

Michel Belhumeur, 76

Clint Benedict, 12, 17

Jean-Claude Bergeron, 144, 164

Tim Bernhardt, 99

Daniel Berthiaume, 99

Craig Billington, 100, 135, 145, 161

John Blue, 145

Daniel Bouchard, 54, 133, 194, 228, 239, 255

Johnny Bower, 20, 21, 22, 28, 29, 31

Frank Brimsek, 15, 124

Martin Brochu, 146, 151

Turk Broda, 15, 17

Martin Brodeur, 59, 100, 135, 136, 143, 147, 148, 151, 158, 160, 170, 185, 187, 238

Richard Brodeur, 53, 56, 57, 66, 70, 193, 281

Andy Brown, 58

Sean Burke, 101, 127

**C**

Jim Carey, 149, 159, 168

Jacques Caron, 59

Jon Casey, 102, 122, 135, 160

Frédéric Chabot, 144

Lorne Chabot, 13

Gerry Cheevers, 31, 32, 33, 34, 35, 43, 53, 71, 234, 243, 286

Tim Cheveldae, 149, 150, 161, 245, 246

Jacques Cloutier, 96, 102, 206

Alex Connell, 12, 13

Roger Crozier, 31, 36, 37

Wilf Cude, 14

**D**

Byron Dafoe, 159

Joe Daley, 60

John Davidson, 60, 86

Denis Dejordy, 38, 59

Philippe Derouville, 150

Gerry Desjardins, 61

Michel Dion, 53, 61, 72, 266

Dave Dryden, 39, 71

Ken Dryden, 25, 28, 48, 50, 53, 62, 63, 64, 72, 73, 78, 80, 81, 88, 89, 133, 173, 174, 176, 177, 179, 193, 222, 226, 231, 232, 234, 236, 242, 249, 280, 281, 288

Bill Durnan, 16, 17, 19, 24, 64, 176

Vladimir Dzurilla, 226

**E**

Don Edwards, 61, 65, 83, 99

Tony Esposito, 15, 23, 38, 45, 47, 51, 53, 56, 66, 67, 68, 89, 93, 96, 242

Bob Essensa, 149, 150

**F**

Doug Favell, 45, 70, 272

Éric Fichaud, 143, 151

Stéphane Fiset, 152, 153, 167, 170, 238

Mark Fitzpatrick, 81, 113, 130, 138, 154, 216

Bob Froese, 103, 117, 138

Grant Fuhr, 76, 77, 95, 104, 105, 106, 114, 122, 128, 129, 136, 139, 140, 155, 162, 165, 218, 252

**G**

Bruce Gamble, 22
Chuck Gardiner, 12, 14
John Garrett, 53, 70
Jack Gélineau, 19
Ed Giacomin, 31, 34, 40, 41, 82, 93, 280
Gilles Gilbert, 71, 82, 194, 229
Mario Gosselin, 54, 107, 133
Ron Grahame, 75

**H**

Jeff Hackett, 154
George Hainsworth, 12, 13, 14, 64, 176
Glenn Hall, 19, 23, 26, 28, 31, 36, 38, 51
Glen Hanlon, 138
Dominik Hasek, 104, 131, 136, 143, 149, 155, 170, 216
Brian Hayward, 95, 108, 125, 140, 268
Glenn Healy, 109
Guy Hebert, 156
Jim Henry, 16, 22
Denis Herron, 72, 73, 80, 95, 133, 140, 208, 272, 274
Ron Hextall, 36, 95, 103, 110, 111, 112, 152, 166, 167, 170, 213, 249, 255, 271, 275
Charlie Hodge, 29, 42, 48
Mark Holden, 86
Jim Hrivnak, 156, 168
Kelly Hrudey, 113

**I**

Peter Ing, 104, 114, 129, 135
Gary Inness, 58
Arturs Irbe, 171

**J**

Al Jensen, 115
Darren Jensen, 103
Ed Johnston, 32, 43, 242
Curtis Joseph, 156, 157, 209

**K**

Mike Karakas, 15
Doug Keans, 82, 115, 221
Dave Kerr, 16
Trevor Kidd, 158, 168
Olaf Kolzig, 159, 168

**L**

Blaine Lacher, 145, 160
Michel Larocque, 72, 73, 74, 88, 133, 222, 278
Réjean Lemelin, 115, 116, 122, 145, 198, 200, 209, 248
Mario Lessard, 75, 82, 115, 198
Pelle Lindbergh, 95, 103, 117, 155, 204, 218
Mike Liut, 53, 75, 121, 198, 252
Ron Low, 76, 82
Harry Lumley, 17, 22, 28

**M**

Darrin Madeley, 161
Clint Malarchuk, 54, 118, 133, 194, 204, 238
Cesare Maniago, 40, 44, 262
Darrell May, 130
Frank McCool, 12, 17
Kirk McLean, 56, 119
Gerry McNeil, 17, 24, 25
Roland Melanson, 84, 120, 208
Gilles Meloche, 77, 97
Corrado Micalef, 120
Greg Millen, 121, 284
Ed Mio, 53, 76, 77
Andy Moog, 76, 102, 115, 116, 122, 129, 145
Philippe Myre, 50, 54, 78, 228

**O**

Chris Osgood, 139, 158, 161, 170

**P**

Marcel Paillé, 40
Mike Palmateer, 79, 87, 257
Darren Pang, 123
Bernard Parent, 31, 32, 45, 46, 53, 70, 87, 110, 117, 124, 131, 143, 155, 234
Pete Peeters, 87, 95, 117, 124, 213
Steve Penney, 108, 125, 126, 140
Jocelyn Perreault, 130
Robert Perreault, 43
Frank Pietrangelo, 127
Jacques Plante, 17, 19, 23, 24, 25, 26, 27, 28, 31, 40, 42, 51, 62, 64, 66, 176, 233, 241
Michel Plasse, 73, 80, 88
Félix Potvin, 128, 140, 146, 151, 158, 162, 163, 238
Daren Puppa, 96, 128, 144

**R**

André Racicot, 108, 144, 164, 205, 261
Bill Ranford, 122, 129, 137, 139, 165
Chuck Rayner, 16, 29
Eldon Reddick, 130
Jeff Reese, 140, 209
Glenn Resch, 81
Manon Rhéaume, 164
Damian Rhodes, 162, 163
Nick Ricci, 72
Mike Richter, 109, 139, 165, 204
Vincent Riendeau, 130, 145, 157
Pat Riggin, 115
John Roach, 12
Al Rollins, 17
Roberto Romano, 72
Dominic Roussel, 151, 166, 167
Patrick Roy, 86, 95, 98, 108, 125, 126, 128, 130, 131, 132, 134, 137, 139, 140, 143, 144, 146, 155, 164, 165, 169, 179, 180, 181, 183, 193, 198, 200, 206, 217, 223, 257, 262, 271, 278
Jim Rutherford, 82

**S**

Tommy Salo, 143
Robert Sauvé, 65, 83, 96, 212
Terry Sawchuk, 14, 16, 21, 23, 28, 36, 66
Richard Sévigny, 54, 72, 73, 125, 133, 134, 236, 246, 274
Peter Sidorkiewicz, 100, 114, 135
Don Simmons, 40
Billy Smith, 81, 84, 85, 95, 120
Gary Smith, 47, 234
Garth Snow, 167

Tommy Soderstrom, 166, 167
Doug Soetaert, 86, 125, 126
Rick St. Croix, 87
Wayne Stephenson, 70, 87, 223

**T**

Rick Tabaracci, 149, 156, 168, 201
Kari Takko, 97, 135, 268
Chris Terreri, 100, 101, 135, 136, 193, 213, 246, 268
José Théodore, 143, 169
Jocelyn Thibault, 151, 152, 153, 167, 170
Wayne Thomas, 73, 79, 86, 88, 201, 223
Cecil Tiny Thompson, 14
Andrei Trefilov, 143
Vladislav Tretiak, 28, 53, 89, 91, 92, 226, 230, 243
Ron Tugnutt, 137, 164, 261

**V**

Rogatien Vachon, 22, 29, 31, 38, 48, 49, 50, 53, 66, 75, 78, 191, 226, 228, 232, 234, 236
John Vanbiesbrouck, 103, 130, 138
Mike Veisor, 93
Mike Vernon, 139, 140, 150, 158, 161, 165, 212
Georges Vézina, 12, 64, 176
Gilles Villemure, 40, 93, 217, 288

**W**

Jimmy Waite, 171
Ernie Wakely, 51
Rick Wamsley, 72, 95, 125, 133, 140, 219, 252
Lorne Worsley, 19, 20, 21, 22, 29, 42, 48, 64, 66, 147, 176, 228, 234
Roy Worters, 13, 16
Ken Wregget, 99, 141, 150, 262

In this photo, taken by Denis Brodeur Jr., are the book's authors and Martin Brodeur.
The scene took place on August 1, 1995 in Saint-Léonard, Quebec, when the young goaltender was being celebrated for his success with the New Jersey Devils and the team's Stanley Cup victory.

# Table of Contents

Focusing on Goaltenders ........................................ 9

Goalies From Another Era .................................... 11

The 50s........................................................... 19

The 60s........................................................... 31

The 70s........................................................... 53

The 80s........................................................... 95

The 90s........................................................... 143

Ken Dryden ..................................................... 173

Patrick Roy...................................................... 179

Martin Brodeur ................................................ 185

The Most Spectacular Player on the Ice............ 191

Exploits and Memories ..................................... 221

Hockey's Acrobats............................................ 245

When Goaltenders Leave Their Nets! ............... 271

Award-Winning Goaltenders ............................. 291

Index ............................................................. 295

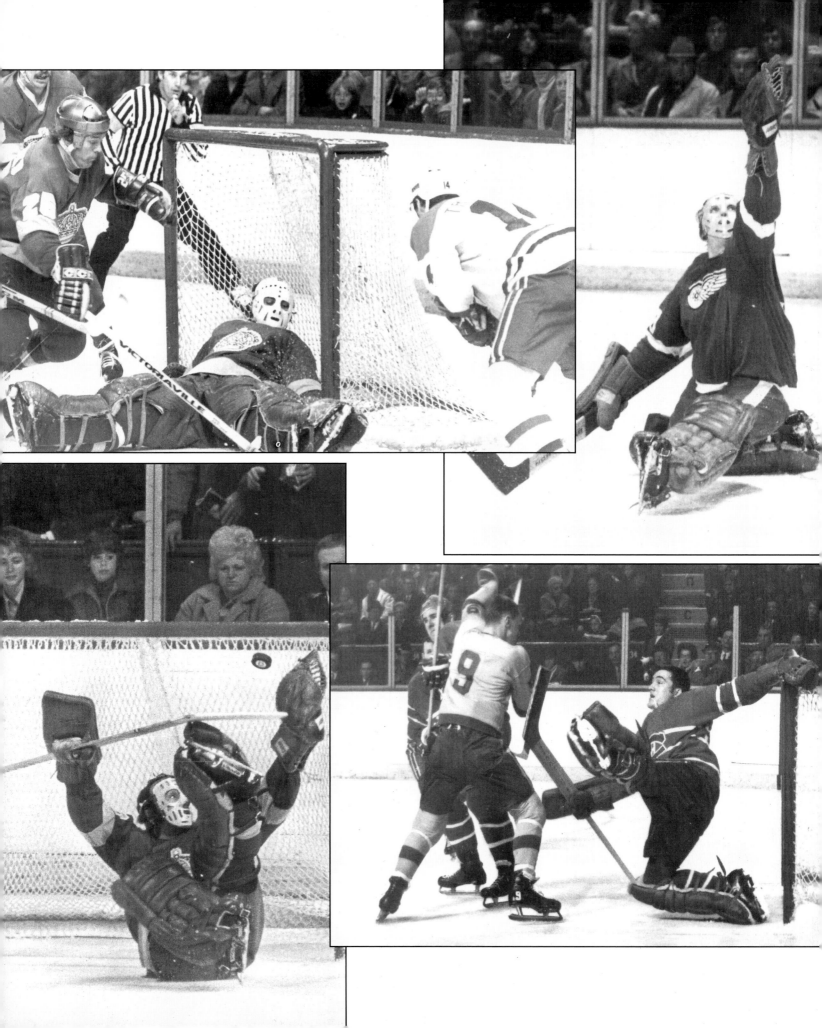

Printed in Canada
on presses operated by
the INTERGLOBE Inc. printing firm.